Environment Modeling-Based Requirements Engineering for Software Intensive Systems

Environment Modeling-Based Requirements Engineering for Software Intensive Systems

Zhi Jin

MORGAN KAUFMANN PUBLISHERS

AN IMPRINT OF ELSEVIER

Morgan Kaufmann is an imprint of Elsevier
50 Hampshire Street, 5th Floor, Cambridge, MA 02139, United States

Notices
Knowledge and best practice in this field are constantly changing. As new research and
experience broaden our understanding, changes in research methods, professional
practices, or medical treatment may become necessary.

Practitioners and researchers must always rely on their own experience and knowledge in
evaluating and using any information, methods, compounds, or experiments described
herein. In using such information or methods they should be mindful of their own safety
and the safety of others, including parties for whom they have a professional responsibility.

To the fullest extent of the law, neither the Publisher nor the authors, contributors, or
editors, assume any liability for any injury and/or damage to persons or property as a
matter of products liability, negligence or otherwise, or from any use or operation of any
methods, products, instructions, or ideas contained in the material herein.

Library of Congress Cataloging-in-Publication Data
A catalog record for this book is available from the Library of Congress

British Library Cataloguing in Publication Data
A catalogue record for this book is available from the British Library

ISBN: 978-0-12-801954-2

For information on all Morgan Kaufmann publications visit our website at
https://www.elsevier.com/books-and-journals

Working together
to grow libraries in
developing countries

www.elsevier.com • www.bookaid.org

Publisher: Glyn Jones
Acquisitions Editor: Glyn Jones
Editorial Project Manager: Naomi Robertson
Senior Production Project Manager: Priya Kumaraguruparan
Designer: Christian Bilbow

Typeset by TNQ Books and Journals

Contents

About the Author

Professor Zhi Jin graduated from the National University of Defense Technology with a PhD in computer science knowledge-based systems.

She is currently a full professor at Peking University. Her research interests include knowledge-based requirements engineering. She has published more than 100 papers in refereed journals and conferences in knowledge engineering and requirements engineering and related topics. She is the published author of two books: *Domain Modeling-Based Software Engineering: A Formal Approach* (ISBN: 0-7923-7889-X, Kluwer Academic Publishers) and a computer science textbook in Chinese published by Science Press. She has years of work experience in ontology engineering, knowledge-based requirements engineering, and service-oriented modeling.

Preface

Like knowledge engineers, requirements engineers play the role of midwife in bringing forth knowledge about the business logics of an application and making it explicit and representable. They convey implicit knowledge about an application in a form that system designers and developers can understand and can map onto system architecture and furthermore can encode into algorithms and data structures.

Requirements engineering, developed as a branch of system engineering, is a multidisciplinary subject that applies theories and techniques from three other fields:

1. Cognitive science inspires the processes and mechanisms by which we acquire and describe knowledge and information.
2. System science helps us observe and understand the real world as a system of systems, i.e., analyzes systems, the interactions within those systems, and/or interaction with its environment.
3. Software engineering provides the target of observation and cognition so that the results can serve as a specification through which a demanded application, i.e., the software-intensive system, can be developed in a systematic and engineering way.

With cognitive science, engineers can be equipped with a scientific method to focus on the nature of the targeted real-world problem and formulate the problem systematically. With system science, the complexity of the real-world problem can be treated holistically and by observing the interaction between a system and its embedded environment. With software engineering, the observed and collected knowledge and information can be implemented in software-intensive systems. Requirements engineering is a bridge across the application domain of the real world that needs to be observed in a systematic way and the software-intensive system in the computation domain that can be used to solve the real-world problem.

ORGANIZATION

Part One introduces requirements and requirements engineering and summarizes existing approaches and techniques for requirements engineering. It also contains some discussion about the challenges raised by software-intensive systems. Part One contains three chapters. Chapter 1 delivers general background knowledge about the requirements and discusses the main concerns in requirements engineering as well as its principles and processes. Chapter 2 introduces representative requirements engineering methodologies and discusses their metaphors as well as the main concerns. Chapter 3 talks about the importance of the interactive environment. It discusses the characteristics of the system environment, e.g., the openness, uncertainty and changeability, etc., and moves forward to explore the challenges to requirements engineering.

Part Two focuses on the ontologies. The principles of ontology and ontology-oriented domain modeling are introduced and the methodology of environment ontology construction is presented. The structures of the environment entity model and the environment goal model are described. Part Two consists of three chapters. Chapter 4 focuses on ontology-oriented interactive environment modeling. It discusses the conceptualization of system-interactive environments and tells how to develop the ontology of the system-interactive environment. Chapter 5 deals with domain environment ontology construction and is devoted to presenting techniques on building domain environment ontologies. Chapter 6 describes the feature model of the domain environment. The chapter aims to make the representation of the environment close to the system model, so that the environment model can be easily integrated into the system model.

Part Three presents the system capability model. The main idea is to ground the system capability onto environment models by using the key concept, i.e., the "effect" that the system brings to the environment for changing the environment. It consists of four chapters. Chapter 7 introduces the effect-based system capability, which bridges the desired actions the system should take and the desired effects imposed onto the environment. Chapter 8 talks about the capability comparison and composition. These are two basic capability reasoning mechanisms. Chapter 9 introduces the capability refinement that converts abstract capabilities into implementable capabilities by reducing nondeterminism and separating the concerns. The scenario-based capability refinement is defined. Chapter 10 presents capability aggregation. This is a kind of capability composition from an agent-based angle. This chapter includes modeling capability aggregation as a capability assignment problem and proposing a negotiation-based method.

Part Four introduces some topics about environment-related nonfunctionalities. Some of them include security, safety, dependability, and adaptivity, and they may need specific patterns for elicitation. This part talks about how to elicit, model, and specify these nonfunctionalities in terms of the environment model. It contains three chapters. Chapter 11 presents methods for identifying, eliciting, and modeling dependability requirements. A control-based architecture is introduced as the basic pattern. Chapter 12 shows how to model dynamic adaptation capability via conformance relationships among the three elements: environment, specification, and requirements. A view-based rule language is proposed to define adaptation logics. Chapter 13 discusses environment-related nonfunctionality patterns. They can be used to identify and specify the nonfunctionalities.

Acknowledgments

I appreciate the people from the community and my collaborators. The contributions and criticisms coming from the community were essential to the development of the idea of this book. Among them, I should mention my former doctoral students, Xiaohong Chen, Lishan Hou, Chun Liu, Jian Tang, Puwei Wang, Bo Wei, Budan Wu, Zhuoqun Yang, Bin Yin, Tianqi Zhao, Liwei Zheng, and Manlin Zhu. They have helped to shape this book by contributing their ideas, strategies, and efforts: Many thanks. Without their involvement, enthusiasm, and the coherent direction they provided, this book would not have been possible.

Great thanks are due to Prof. Lin Liu of Tsinghua University and Prof. Zhi Li of Guangxi Normal University, as well as Prof. Haiyan Zhao and Prof. Wei Zhang of Peking University. Their valuable insights and feedback, which were extended throughout the collaborative research, were concerned with many fundamental aspects of the proposed approach in this book.

Prof. Ruqian Lu of the Chinese Academy of Science, Prof. Hong Mei of Peking University, Prof. Jian Lv of Nanjing University, Prof. Wei-Tek Tsai of Arizona State University, Prof. Hong Zhu of Oxford Brooks University, and Prof. Didar Zowghi of the University of Technology, Sydney: To all of you, thank you for your constructive suggestions that led to the success of this book.

I am also indebted to the community of requirements engineering conferences. Each time I attended the conferences, listened to the talks, and discussed with other participants, I became inspired and my ideas widened. I gratefully thank the community.

Finally, I thank the editors and staff of Elsevier publishers for their patience and for waiting for this book to be finished much later than I would like to admit.

This work was supported financially by the National Basic Research and Development 973 Program (Grant Nos. 2015CB352200 and 2009CB320701), the National Natural Science Fund for Distinguished Young Scholars of China (Grant No. 60625204), the Key Projects of National Natural Science Foundation of China (Grant Nos. 90818026 and 61232015), and the International (regional) Cooperative Research Key Project of the National Natural Science Foundation of China (Grant No. 61620106007).

Background

The Internet has provided a global open infrastructure for the exchange various resources for people across the world. It has an increasingly essential role in connecting the cyber, physical, and social worlds. Computing devices, human society, and physical objects will soon be integrated together seamlessly, and software systems will orchestrate information, processes, decisions, and interactions in this Internet environment. With such developments, software-intensive information and embedded systems will realize increasingly innovative functionality and become more and more important in our daily lives. Many innovative applications are expected, such as smart houses, mobile online education, Internet of vehicles, etc.

Internetware (Mei and Lü, 2016) is a term coined to describe the emerging software paradigm for the Internet computing environment. It can be defined as a software system that consists of self-contained, autonomous entities situated in distributed nodes of the Internet and coordinators connecting these entities statically and dynamically in various kinds of interactive styles (passively and actively). Such a system is expected to be able to perceive the changes of an open and dynamic environment, respond to changes through architectural transformations, and exhibit context-aware, adaptive, and trustworthy behaviors in such an environment. These feature exactly the characteristics of those innovative applications.

How to establish and use sound engineering principles systematically in the development of such systems, to obtain systems economically that are reliable and efficient in a real application environment, is currently challenging the software engineering field.

As usual, the first challenge, among others, is in the requirements engineering stage. From the viewpoint of requirements engineering, some difficulties exist:

- Many such systems are software-based innovations in different domains. This means that they are normally personalized and can only be designed fully targeted.
- Many such systems are safety relevant or even safety critical and more pervasive. Thus they come with very high reliability or dependability demands.
- Many such systems interact closely with reality. Thus the complexity of the systems greatly increases along with the complexity of the reality with which the systems need to interact.

How to deliver the system specification systematically and effectively is an important issue in the current software-enabling innovation era.

This book entitled *Environment Modeling Requirements Engineering for Software-Intensive Systems* aims to deliver a systematic methodology for engineering the requirements of innovative software-intensive systems. This methodology is intended to identify the different aspects of such systems clearly when developing requirements. That will help requirements analysts to understand such innovation applications and produce the specification more systematically. Also, as indicated in the book's subtitle, *Towards Internetware-Oriented Software Eco-systems,* it is also expected that this methodology can enable the establishment of Internetware-based software ecosystems.

Part 1 will be devoted to an introduction of background knowledge about requirements and requirements engineering. It will discuss requirements engineering principles and its main concerns. It will also present some of the representative methodologies in requirements engineering that are related to the modeling and analysis of the software-intensive systems. Finally, the challenges we are facing are also discussed.

Requirements and Requirements Engineering*

1

1.1 REQUIREMENTS

Generally, the development of any artificial product relies on some physical and functional needs that a particular design of the product must be able to perform. These physical and functional needs contribute to the "requirements" of the artificial product. Software and software-intensive systems are kinds of artificial products. The development of software and software-intensive systems is triggered by some needs and desires.

What are requirements? According to Institute of Electrical and Electronics Engineers standard 610.12-1990 (IEEE-Std-610.12-1990), the term "requirements" for software refers to:

1. a condition or capability needed by a user to solve a problem or achieve an objective
2. a condition or capability that must be met or possessed by a system or system component to satisfy a contract, standard, specification, or other formally imposed documents
3. a documented representation of a condition or capability, as in 1 or 2

---

*This chapter serves to deliver general background knowledge about requirements and requirements engineering.

Environment Modeling-Based Requirements Engineering for Software Intensive Systems
http://dx.doi.org/10.1016/B978-0-12-801954-2.00001-7

From these statements, the explanation of the term "requirements" has two aspects: the first is that requirements refer to the need to solve an application problem with some constraints; the second is that requirements refer to the capabilities that the software has to provide and the constraints that need to be met in software development. The following two requirements statements illustrate these two aspects in the context of software development:

- [R1.1] The system should be reliable and trustworthy. Even when running on an open network environment, it should be able to protect itself from potentially malicious attacks.
- [R1.2] The system should be able to detect and prevent various viruses from invading and launch the emergency process when key components have been infected.

The two statements clearly demonstrate the difference between the two aspects of the term "requirements." The first regards the commitment, promise, or purpose of the system to the outside world. It states the problem that needs to be solved and how well to solve it. The second identifies the functions that the system should possess. It specifies what the system will do.

Of course, these two aspects are not separate but rather are related to each other. Fig. 1.1 illustrates the relationship between them and how the relationship can be understood in different ways.

1.1.1 SYSTEM LEVEL VERSUS FUNCTION LEVEL

One way to clarify the terminology is to distinguish the system-level requirements and the function point—level requirements. For these two example statements, the

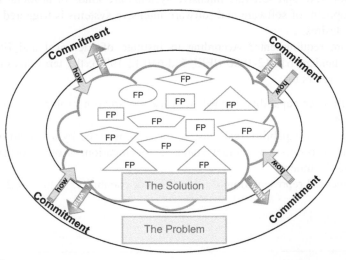

FIGURE 1.1

Relationship between requirements of different levels. *FP*, Function point.

first can be categorized as the "system-level requirements" whereas the second is the "function point—level requirements." The following are other examples that can be used to differentiate the two kinds of requirements statements:

- [R1.3] The system should offer a user-friendly interface (system level requirements).
- [R1.4] The system should open the door if the personal identification number that the user enters into the keypad is correct (function point level requirements).
- [R1.5] The system should record each granted access through the door (i.e., the date, the time, and the person's ID) (function point level requirements).

The to-be system is an artificial product. The commitment of the product relies on the function points that the to-be system will possess. This is because the commitment can be made only when the to-be system has these implemented function points that can realize to what it commits, i.e., what it can deliver depends on the function points with which the designer or developer equips it. The commitment or capability of the system depends on the function points with which the system is equipped.

On the other hand, the to-be system needs to be equipped with or possess certain function points because it has been asked to make the commitment or to have the capability. In other words, what function points need to be possessed and what constraints need to be met by the to-be system are the needs that have to be implemented or realized in the system; i.e., the reason for the system to possess the function points is because of the commitment or capability. The system-level requirements ask for the function points and the function points make the commitments or enable the capabilities. Both the system-level requirements statements and the function point—level requirements statements are what we need to describe and specify the to-be system.

1.1.2 "WHAT" VERSUS "HOW"

The relationship between requirements of different levels can also be explained by "what—how" pair (Buseibeh, 2001), which has been discussed in the requirements engineering community for decades, by recognizing that the requirements specify "what should be developed" whereas the system designs specify "how the system should be developed."

However, from Fig. 1.1, another explanation for the "what—how" pair can be sorted out: i.e., what the system should commit and how these commitments can be achieved. Requirements engineering works on both of them and tries to build a bridge between them. In this sense, requirements could include all of the statements and assertions about them, and the phenomena in between.

1.1.3 PROBLEM VERSUS SOLUTION

The "what—how" pair can also be characterized as the relationship between problem and solution in the sense of requirements refinement. Fig. 1.2 gives an example (Pohl, 2010) illustrating the corresponding relationship. A system requirement

Problem Definition: What
R1.6 The navigation system shall allow the driver to enter the destination of the trip conveniently.

Solution Definition: How
R1.7 When the driver starts a new trip, the navigation system shall display a roadmap of the area centered on the current position.
R1.8 The navigation system shall allow the driver to scroll and zoom into the roadmap.
R1.9 After the driver has selected a destination on the roadmap, the system shall allow the driver to edit the destination details, e.g. city, street, etc.

Excerpted from (Pohl, 2010)

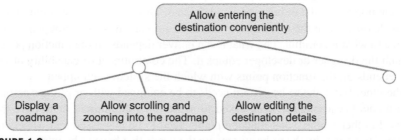

FIGURE 1.2

Relationship between problem and solution definition.

(R1.6) is refined by the three function point requirements (R1.7, R1.8, and R1.9). R1.6 describes the "what" and R1.7–9 describe the "how" that is a candidate way to realize R1.6.

1.1.4 SUMMARY

Correct system development depends on precise, correct, and complete system description or specification. How to obtain the requirements statements and produce a correct and complete system specification is the main task of requirements engineering. Textbooks of requirements engineering declare that the requirements statements come from the stakeholders, the domain knowledge and regulation, and/or the as-is systems, etc., and claim that these statements should talk about the facts or phenomena of the application domains and the outside world with which the to-be system will interact. However, where to start and how to conduct the requirements engineering process to obtain a clearly represented, accurate, and complete set of requirements statements are still in question.

1.2 REQUIREMENTS ENGINEERING

Requirements engineering refers to the process of defining, documenting, and maintaining requirements statements. In early software development methods, e.g., the waterfall model, requirements engineering is presented as the first phase of the development process. However, later software development methods (e.g., Rational Unified Process, extreme programming, Agile, etc.) assume that requirements engineering continues through the whole life cycle of a system.

Concretely, the term "requirements engineering" means a set of activities concerned with identifying, communicating, and documenting the **purpose** (which normally means there is a problem or challenge in reality that is intended to be solved), the **capability** (which describes the ability to do something to achieve the purpose), and the **constraint** (which indicates the conditions under which the to-be system can be developed and the developed system with the desired capability can solve the problem).

The requirements engineering process is initiated when there is an innovative application demand in reality or when the as-is system is disappointed. That means that requirements engineering is intended to produce a new system specification that, if being implemented, can be used to meet the demand or replace an old system. In this sense, requirements engineering acts as the bridge between the real-world needs of users, customers, and other constituencies affected by a system (i.e., the purpose and the constraint) and the capabilities and opportunities that can be afforded by information technologies (i.e., the capability).

Therefore, the tasks of requirements engineering can be roughly divided into two subtasks, as shown in Fig. 1.3. The first is referred to as "requirements modeling and analysis," which is for eliciting and determining needs or conditions to meet for a new or altered product, and for gathering requirements by requirements models so that the correctness of the requirements can be guaranteed. The second is referred to as "requirements evolvement and management," which is for managing all of

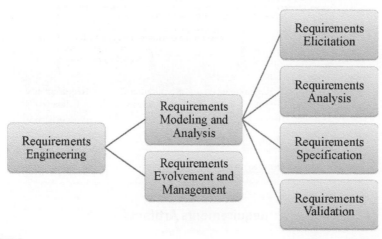

FIGURE 1.3

Components of requirements engineering.

the artifacts that have been produced during requirements modeling and analysis, and for managing the changes to these artifacts.

This book mainly focuses on the part of requirements modeling and analysis. We explore it in more detail as:

- identifying and collecting the requirements-related statements from stakeholders or other sources (**requirements elicitation**)
- processing this information to understand it, classify it into various categories, and relating the stakeholder needs to possible system requirements (**requirements analysis**)
- structuring this information and derived requirements as written documents and model diagrams (**requirements specification**)
- validating the documents and/or models to confirm that the specified requirements are accurate, complete, and correct (**requirements validation**)

These activities are normally not in a linear and one-pass sequence process, but in an interleaved, incremental, and iterative process. Like the requirements engineering framework presented in (Pohl, 2010), this process needs to be embedded explicitly in the system development context and to be annotated with the produced requirements artifacts, as shown in Fig. 1.4.

Among the three main parts (the system development context, the requirements activities, and the requirements artifacts) the system development context identifies the boundary of the problem. The requirements activities part contains four core

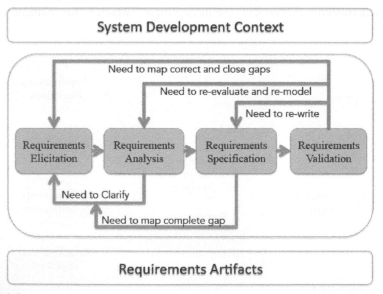

FIGURE 1.4

Incremental and iterative requirements engineering process.

activities: elicitation, analysis/refinement, specification/documentation, and valida-tion/negotiation. These activities are obviously interrelated throughout the require-ments engineering process. The requirements artifacts part is about the types of artifacts produced during the requirements engineering process.

Traditionally, requirements modeling and analysis conducted by requirements analysts focuses on reading documentation about the domain, asking questions (via brainstorming, interviews, questionnaires, joint requirements development sessions, etc.), listening to what stakeholders say, watching what they do, and so on. However, it has been argued that it is not enough or efficient for requirements analysts just to collect and write down what stakeholders say about their needs or desires.

As mentioned, requirements analysts need to identify, locate, state the problem coherently first. However, normally people in the outside world are not familiar with the problem. When the problem is not trivial, it is not easy for requirements analysts to capture the key points about it if they do not have guidelines. Even for the stakeholders, it is not easy to observe the reality and think about the actual prob-lem systematically, even though it is within their domain.

There have been many efforts to develop requirements engineering approaches aimed at helping stakeholders think about their needs on a higher level and in a sys-tematic way, and to provide requirements analysts with some clues to describe their process. Many simple and intuitive hints for identifying the problem and for under-standing underlying motivations and real needs have been proposed. They can also be used to predict needs for the near future. For example, Goal-Oriented Require-ments Engineering (van Lamsweerde, 2009), the Actor and Intension-Based Approach (I*) (Yu, 2010), the Problem Frame Approach (Jackson, 2001), and Scenario-Based Requirements Engineering (Sutcliffe, 2003) are well-known re-quirements engineering approaches among others. Chapter 2 will discuss them on a methodological level.

1.3 THREE DIMENSIONS OF REQUIREMENTS ENGINEERING

Requirements engineering is all about the description. It normally starts from scratch and ends with a detailed documentation of the system specification. During this pro-cess, what is the goal or target?

The three dimensions of the requirements engineering are identified in (Pohl, 1994), namely, the specification, the representation, and the agreement:

- **content:** all requirements are known and understood in detail
- **agreement:** sufficient stakeholder agreement is established
- **documentation:** requirements specification is compliant with the defined for-mats and rules

The **content** dimension deals with an understanding of the system requirements attained. At the very beginning of requirements engineering, only a few high-level and vague system requirements are known, whereas at the end of the process, all requirements are known and understood at the required level of detail.

The **agreement** dimension deals with the level of agreement achieved among relevant stakeholders about the known requirements. At the very beginning, the requirements might represent only individual views. There might be conflicts between those individual views. However, at the end of the process, sufficient stakeholder agreement should be established about system requirements.

The **documentation** dimension deals with documenting and specifying the system requirements using different documentation or specification formats.

The content dimension is always the core concern in requirements engineering methodologies and their processes. All of the requirements engineering activities work on the content and all the requirements artifacts are for describing the content. However, different requirements engineering methodologies distinguish themselves by focusing on different kinds of content, which represent their viewpoints and metaphors of observing the reality and recognizing the problem.

These three dimensions form a requirements engineering cube, as shown in Fig. 1.5. This cube can be used to represent the goal or target of the requirements engineering process. Any particular requirements engineering process undertakes a curved path from the original point. Here, there are no requirements statements at all. The ideal point denotes that the analysts have obtained the complete and precise description about the to-be system in formal statements that have been agreed upon by all of the stakeholders.

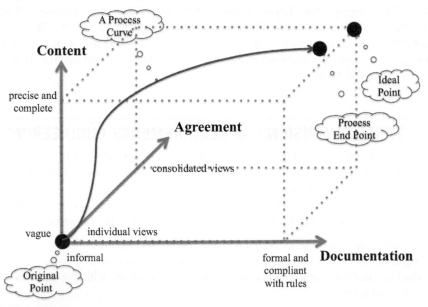

FIGURE 1.5

Three dimensions of requirements engineering and a requirements engineering process curve (based on (Pohl, 1994)).

A particular requirements engineering process undertakes a particular process curve. It starts from scratch at the original point with no description of the to-be system in the very beginning. Then it increases and improves the description on each of the three dimensions. Ideally, it needs to end at the ideal point. However, usually a requirements engineering process ends at a point within the cube that is not ideal but good enough. That means that enough requirements have been identified (the content dimension), have been documented in a suitable form (the documentation dimension), and have obtained enough agreement (the agreement dimension).

This is the phenomenon of "just enough requirements elicitation" (Davis, 2005). The reason is obvious: if too little requirements elicitation is performed, it is likely you will run the risk of building the wrong system, whereas if too much requirements elicitation is performed, you may spend too much time identifying the problem, so that you risk not having enough time to solve it.

Requirements Engineering Methodologies

2

CHAPTER OUTLINE

Requirements engineering is the process of eliciting stakeholder needs and desires and developing them into an agreed-upon set of detailed requirements that can serve as a basis for all subsequent development activities.

People agree to focus directly on the problem at the beginning of the requirements engineering; that is, amidst all of the information about the reality, we should first locate and identify the problem. This is reasonable, because only after locating the problem and identifying the commitments should the to-be-built system advance toward solving the problem and can we invent proper strategies to achieve commitments via some functionalities.

Many requirements engineering methodologies focus on how to locate and identify the problem and how to derive the implementable functionalities with state-of-the-art techniques. The purpose of requirements engineering methodologies is to make the problem that is being stated clear and complete, and to ensure that the solution is correct, reasonable, and effective.

As we will see later, each methodology has a special metaphor for locating and identifying the problem. This chapter is devoted to exploring state-of-the-art of requirements engineering methodologies by emphasizing their metaphors.

Environment Modeling-Based Requirements Engineering for Software Intensive Systems
https://doi.org/10.1016/B978-0-12-801954-2.00002-9

2.1 METAPHOR: "TO-BE SYSTEM IS FOR AUTOMATICALLY MEASURING AND CONTROLLING THE REALITY"

Four-variable models (FVM), which were proposed by David Parnas in 1995, takes the viewpoint (Parnas and Madey, 1995) in which it is assumed that reality can be measured by some measurable parameters and can be controlled by some controllable parameters, and that the measurements and controls are implementable by input devices and output devices. Fig. 2.1 shows a framework that depict the main idea in which four kinds of variables are explicitly identified:

- monitored variables (M) of the environment that need to be observed and responded to
- controlled variables (C) in the environment that need to control
- input variables (I) through which the system senses the monitored variables
- output variables (O) through which the system changes the controlled variable

From the viewpoint of requirements engineering, the FVM expresses that the requirements of the to-be system can be captured by two sets of variables: monitored and controlled. The former is for declaring what of the context can be sensed and the latter is for declaring what of the context can be affected. Based on these two sets of variables, the requirements are represented as the relationships that should be enabled and maintained between them by the to-be system. The other two sets of

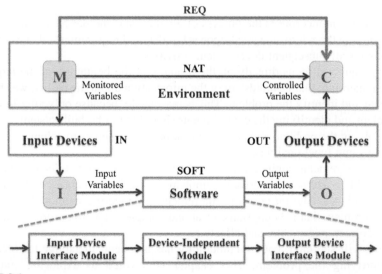

FIGURE 2.1

Parnas' four variable models. *C*, controlled variables; *I*, input variables; *IN*, input devices; *M*, monitored variables; *NAT*, natural constraints; *O*, output variables; *OUT*, output devices; *REQ*, system requirements; *SOFT*, software.

variables are for modeling the interactions between the system and the environment via the input–output devices, and then for distinguishing the allowable system behaviors and the ideal system behaviors.

The following three groups of mappings capture the functionalities implied by the FVM:

- environment-related mappings
    - NAT: (M, C) models the environmentally natural constraints on system behavior: that is, the constraints imposed by the physical laws of the system environment. It provides the possible values corresponding to the monitored and controlled variables.
    - REQ: (M, C) defines the system requirements as relationships between the monitored and the controlled quantities that must be enabled and maintained by the system.
- interaction-related mappings
    - IN: (M, I) models the input devices (e.g., sensors or analog-to-digital converters). They relate values of monitored variables of the environment to values of input variables of the software.
    - OUT: (O, C) models the output devices (e.g., digital-to-analog converters or actuators). They relate values of the output variables of the software to values of the controlled variables.
- system-related mappings
    - SOF: (I, O) models the software, which transforms values of input variables to values of output variables.
    - SYS: (M, C) models a system as a composition of the input devices, the software, and the output devices, to relate physical quantities measured (M) by the system, to physical quantities (C) controlled by the system.

Thus, FVM-based requirements engineering can be conducted by a process for specifying requirements. This process consists of the following four steps:

- system requirements specification
  This step has two activities: (1) environmental quantities (including controlled quantities and monitored quantities) relevant to the system behavior are identified and represented by a mathematical variable; (2) the desired system behavior is documented by describing two relations, i.e., NAT and REQ. This step assumes that the system can obtain perfect values of the monitored quantities and compute perfect values of the controlled quantities.
- system design specification
  This step mainly has two activities: (1) to identify and document the characteristics of the resources that are available, estimate values of the monitored variables, and set values of the controlled variables. These values are usually read from or written to sensors and actuators; and (2) to describe the input variables and output variables as well as the relationship between the input and output variables and the monitored and controlled variables.

- software requirements specification
  This step breaks down the relationship between the input and output variables into three parts: two device-dependent parts, i.e., the input device interface module and the output device interface module, and a single device-independent module, i.e., the function driver module. The input device module specifies how estimates of the monitored variables are computed in terms of the input variables. The output device module specifies how estimates of the controlled variables are used to compute the values of the output variables. Then the function driver module uses these estimates of monitored variables to compute estimates of the controlled variables.
- dealing with hardware malfunctions
  This step extends the system requirements specification by adding additional function points to handle sensor or actuator failures. The specification of the function driver module has been identified by REQ. However, it needs to extend the required behavior identified by REQ, by describing how to deal with the system malfunction.

2.2 METAPHOR: "TO-BE SYSTEM IS FOR FULFILLING REAL-WORLD GOALS THAT STAKEHOLDERS WANT TO ACHIEVE"

Goal-Oriented Requirements Engineering (van Lamsweerde, 2009) originated from the observation that any system is built to achieve certain business goals. For example,

- [R2.1] The goal of developing a meeting scheduling system is to make sure that a "meeting is scheduled so as to maximize the attendance of invited participants."
- [R2.2] The goal of building a train control system is for the "guaranteed safe transportation of all passengers."

In goal-oriented requirements engineering, a goal is a perspective statement of intent that the to-be-built system should satisfy through the cooperation of its agents. From this angle, requirements engineering can be solidified into the following questions:

- **Why** is a to-be-built system needed?
- **What** needs must be addressed by the to-be-built system?
- **Who** in the system will take part in fulfilling such needs?

Fig. 2.2 shows the metamodel of the goal-oriented approach and the relationship between the why—what—who. Here, the key concern is "goal." Other concerns are derived from the goal via the following strategies:

- System requirements are goals that want to be achieved.
- Higher-level goals need to be refined or be broken down into lower-level goals.
- When a goal is operational, other system components, e.g., constraint, action, object, agent, event, entity, can be included to achieve this goal by realizing some function points.

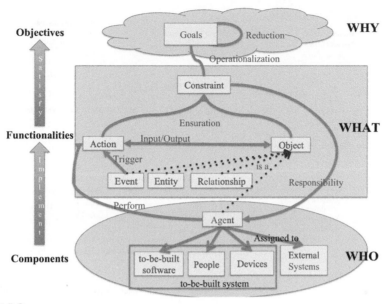

FIGURE 2.2

Metamodel of goal-oriented requirements engineering.

- System components with their realizable function points constitute the system specification.

Guided by this metamodel, goal-oriented requirements engineering suggests using "business goals" as the main concern in different requirements activities, in which such business goals are somehow subjective intentions of the stakeholders. For example:

- [R2.3] The system shall guarantee safe transportation of all passengers.
  is a high-level goal in a train control system, i.e., "Maintain safe train transportation." Such business goals are among the first categories of information that need to be captured and described.

Then the requirements analysis is conducted by a goal refinement mechanism that elaborates finer-grained goals or constraints (for expressing technical objectives related to system design options) into a higher level, and coarser-grained goals (for expressing strategic objectives related to the business) into a lower level. A set of goal refinement heuristics and patterns are provided to conduct the refinement (e.g., the and-refinement pattern, the or-refinement pattern, as well as the milestone-driven refinement pattern and its variants, the case-driven pattern, the guard-introduction pattern, the divide-and-conquer pattern, etc.).

For example, Fig. 2.3 shows the refinement of higher-level goals into their subgoals. After obtaining the goals of suitable granularity, the goals can be assigned to

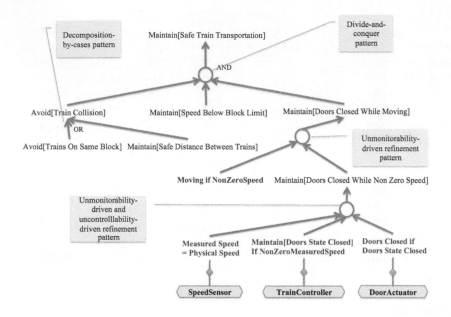

FIGURE 2.3

An example for goal refinement.

particular system components on one side. When a system component is assigned a goal, it will restrict its behavior by adequately controlling system items. For example:

- [R2.4] Doors-State shall always have the value "closed" when Measured Speed has a nonnull value; requires the train controller to enforce it. On the other hand, the goal or the constraint can occur as the action on some entity and relationship as input—output are triggered by some event. This action is conducted by the assigned agent.

  In this way, requirements engineering is for eliciting the goals (and related concerns), developing the goal decomposition trees, negotiating the alternative choices, and producing the agreed-upon system function points.

2.3 METAPHOR: "TO-BE SYSTEM IS FOR IMPROVING THE DEPENDENCIES AMONG INTENTIONAL ACTORS"

The intentionally oriented perspective is proposed by the I* approach (Yu, 2010). Following this perspective, the requirements engineering process is for answering the question, "How do we model and analyze the social world to lead to better system requirements?" The I* approach sees the world as having intentionality, which consists of a set of intentional actors. Each actor has its own intents, reasons, and motivations behind its behaviors. Actors are autonomous and can choose what actions to take to fulfil their own wants and desires. Modeling in the I* approach has two layers.

The first layer is the actor dependency layer. I* assumes that a system consists of a set of intentional actors. Each actor has its own goals and the actors relate to each other at an intentional level. They are coordinated through their respective wants, desires, and commitments. This coordination is captured by a network of directed dependency relationships, *depender, dependum, dependee* between actors, indicating that one actor (the *depender*) depends on another (the *dependee*) for something (the *dependum*). All dependency relationships between actors constitute a system model, which is called the Strategic Dependence model. There are four types of the requirements elements in I*, i.e., four types of dependencies are captured. Fig. 2.4 mimics the four types of dependencies among four actors involved in a Car Insurance System, i.e., the "Car Owner," the "Body Shop," the "Insurance Company," and the "Appraiser."

The meanings of these dependencies are as follows:

- Goal dependency: the depender relies on the dependee to bring about a certain state of affairs in the world. The dependum is expressed as an assertion

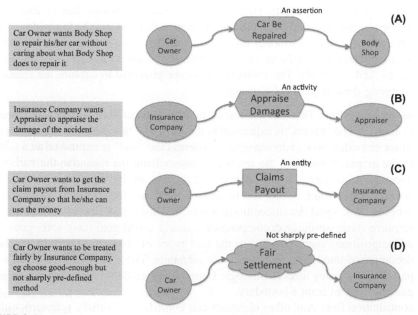

FIGURE 2.4

Four types of dependencies among intentional actors.

statement. The dependee is free and is expected to make whatever decisions are necessary to achieve the goal (namely, the dependum). The depender does not care how the dependee goes about achieving the goal. Fig. 2.4A shows an example.

- Task dependency: the depender relies on the dependee to carry out an activity. The dependum names a task that specifies what task is to be performed, but not why. The depender has already made decisions about why the task needs to be performed. The dependee still has freedom of action within these constraints. Fig. 2.4B shows an example. It just stipulates what needs to be done.
- Resource dependency: The depender relies on the dependee for the availability of an entity (physical or informational). By establishing this dependency, the depender gains the ability to use this entity as a resource. A resource is the finished product of some deliberation-of-action process. In a resource dependency, it is assumed that there are no open issues to be addressed or decisions to be made. Fig. 2.4C shows an example.
- Soft-goal dependency: The depender relies on the dependee to perform some task that meets a soft goal. A soft goal is similar to a goal except that the criteria of success are not sharply defined as priorities. The meaning of the soft goal is elaborated in terms of the methods that are chosen in the course of pursuing the goal. The depender decides what constitutes satisfactory attainment of the goal, but does so with the benefit of the dependee's know-how. Fig. 2.4D shows an example.

At the second layer, for exhibiting autonomy, actors are modeling with their own knowledge, strategy, capability, etc., and have freedom to choose their actions. This is modeled by the so-called Strategic Rationale model. I* adopts the same idea of the goal-oriented approach to model the actor's individual knowledge. The Strategic Rationale model captures the intentional elements of each actor, such as goals, tasks, resources, and soft goals. The following links are provided to capture the relationships among these intentional elements:

- means−ends link: This link indicates a relationship between an end and a means to attain it. The "means" is expressed in the form of a task, because the notion of a task embodies how to do something, whereas the "end" is expressed as a goal. In the graphical notation, the arrowhead points from the means to the end.
- decomposition link: A task element is linked to its component nodes by decomposition links. A task can be decomposed into four types of elements: a subgoal (task−goal decomposition), a subtask (task−task decomposition), a resource (task−resource decomposition), and/or a soft goal (task soft−goal decomposition), corresponding to the four types of elements. The task can be decomposed into one or many of these elements. These elements can also be part of dependency links in Strategic Dependency model(s) when the reasoning goes beyond an actor's boundary.
- contribution link: Any other elements can contribute to satisfy software, either supporting/helping or breaking/hurting.

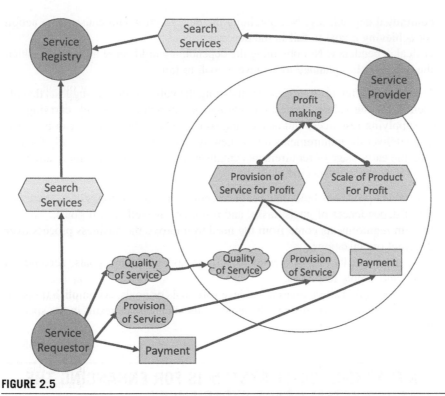

FIGURE 2.5

Strategy Rationale Model (*inside the circle*) and Strategy Dependency Model.

Fig. 2.5 gives an example of the service-oriented computing model. Inside the dashed circle is the strategy rationale model of the actor "Service Provider." It is obvious that with both the strategy dependency model and the strategic rationale model, the representation has been obtained for describing the current situation of the community for the actors involved. The aims of inventing a new system are to improve the community and optimize the satisfactory degrees of the actors.

The I* approach focuses on analyzing the dependency links. The dependency link represents that the depender, by depending on the actor who is the dependee, is able to achieve goals that it was not able to achieve before, or not as well, or not as quickly. It proposes that the vulnerability of the community is implied by the dependency link(s). However, this results in the depender becoming vulnerable to the intentions of the dependee. This vulnerability is implied because the dependee may fail to accomplish the specified element. The model distinguishes three degrees of strength for the dependency according to the level of vulnerability:

- open dependency (uncommitted): Not obtaining the dependum would affect the depender to some extent, but not seriously.

- committed dependency: Not obtaining the dependum would cause some action for achieving a goal to fail in the depender.
- critical dependency: Not obtaining the dependum would cause all actions, which the depender has planned to achieve a goal, to fail.

I* provides different strategies for analyzing the vulnerability. It suggests that after identifying the vulnerabilities, the alternatives for achieving goals, carrying out tasks, supplying resources, and/or meeting soft goals in a better way, can be introduced to deliver the requirements for the new system. However, I* currently focuses only on the early stage of requirements engineering; it does not give more attention to deriving the system specification.

- Any social process is built on a set of intentional actors. Among them, there is a set of dependences of goals, tasks, and resources as well as soft goals.
- System requirements come from the need to improve the business process over different organizations.
- Each actor has its own strategies to achieve soft goals and goals, accomplish tasks, and supply resources.
- When actors find alternatives to achieve soft goals or goals, accomplish tasks, or supply resources normally in a better way, the alternatives result in the specification of a new system.

2.4 METAPHOR: "TO-BE SYSTEM IS FOR ENHANCING THE AS-IS SYSTEM USAGE EXPERIENCE"

In general, a scenario is defined as the outline or script of a film, with details of scenes or an imagined sequence of future events. The most common form is examples or stories grounded in real-world experience. Scenarios have been advocated as an effective means in areas of business system analysis as well as requirements engineering, which has led to scenario-based requirements engineering (Sutcliffe, 2003).

Several interpretations of scenarios have been proposed:

- A scenario can be a story or example of events as a grounded narrative taken from real-world experience.
- A scenario can be a future vision of a designed system with sequences of behavior and possibly contextual description.
- A scenario can be a single thread or pathway through a model, which is just like an animated display of an event sequence.
- A scenario can be seen as a continuum from real-world descriptions and stories to models and specifications.

Discovering requirements from scenarios and anchoring requirements analysis in real-world experience are the main purpose of scenario-based requirements engineering, among others. Hence, scenarios serve different roles and vary in their formality of expression in terms of language and media.

- In the early stages of requirements engineering, **the scenarios are real-world descriptions,** like observed system usage experience, expressed in nature, pictures, or other media, for capturing the behaviors of an existing real-world system. These scenarios can be used as an aid to understanding an existing system.
- By identifying important scenarios involved in using an existing system, some real-world examples can be structured and the strengths and weaknesses of the existing system can be mapped out. In this way, **these scenarios become tools for eliciting requirements**, because they result in identifying new requirements and lead to envisioned scenarios in some informal representations, such as storyboards, demonstrations of concepts, and prototypes.
- In later stages, **a complete and consistent set of scenarios can effectively model the intended behaviors of a system.** Generalized models of system behavior can be invented by system analysts from those informal representations to describe the to-be system concisely.

Fig. 2.6 shows the roles of scenarios and the relationships among them:

- When scenarios come from the as-is system, the real-world scenes are captured from the existing real-world system by recording observations of the system usage. Otherwise, a set of authored scenarios can be derived by some newly emerged goals for capturing the new expectation of stakeholders.

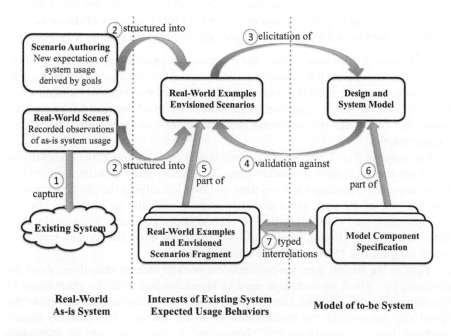

FIGURE 2.6

Roles of scenarios.

- These real-world scenes are structured into real-world examples.
- Real-world examples are generalized during requirements analysis to produce models by a process of abstraction and to prototypes by a process of design.
- Models and requirements specifications become transformed into designs and eventually implemented. During that process, scenarios, which represent the behavior of designed artifacts, have a role in validation.

2.5 METAPHOR: "TO-BE SYSTEM IS FOR ESTABLISHING RELATIONSHIPS AMONG PHENOMENA OF REALITY"

The problem frames approach was invented by Michael Jackson (2001). The rationale behind the problem frames approach is that a system, i.e., the machine, is needed to establish new relationships of the phenomena of reality. It follows the requirements engineering assumptions, i.e., the problem is located in the world outside the system to be built. Concretely:

- There is a reality problem located within a set of physical entities in the outside world asking for a new system to enable some new relationships within these entities.
- These external physical entities have their own inherent phenomena that can be shared with the new system.
- System requirements, i.e., the commitments of the system, are those desired relationships among these phenomena, and the functionalities of the system indicate how to enable the shared phenomena to make the desired relationships.

By following these assumptions, the requirements analysis and structuring of the problem frames approach is primarily an analysis and structuring of the world, not of the system. The system development is considered to be the action of building a system (machine) to solve a problem in an identified part of the world (physical domains that constitutes the real-world problem context) to meet a customer's need (requirements).

For example, Fig. 2.7 presents an example of a system development problem for the cruise control system in modern cars. The starting point of using the problem frame approach is placing a to-be system, and then identifying the physical domains that are part of the real world and will connect with the to-be system. In this example, they are "engine," "wheel," "vehicle under control," "increase/decrease buttons," "driver," "display," and "cruise speed." These form the context, which answers the question, "Where is the problem located?"

Then as the second step, the requirements need to include something about the domains, i.e., which relationships need to be established with the phenomena of the domain. In this example, there are two pieces of requirements, i.e., setting the speed and maintaining the cruise speed in a safe manner. The problem frames approach proposes using concept "phenomena" as representations of interaction that domains communicate or interact only at the direct interface. Three kinds of

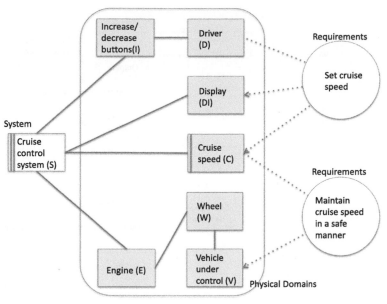

FIGURE 2.7

Context diagram and problem diagram.

phenomena, i.e., events, states and values, have been differentiated. These phenomena are further recognized as two categories in terms of their features: (1) causal phenomena (phenomena that can cause other phenomena and can be controlled); and (2) symbolic phenomena (phenomena that are used to symbolize other phenomena and the relationships among them).

The problem frames approach treats the domains in a deeper way compared with FVM, in which the environment is represented only as quantitative variables. One kind of problem is distinguished from another by different domain types. First, on the basis of phenomena, the problem frames approach classifies the domains into three main types: (1) causal domains (a domain whose properties include a predictable causal relationship among its causal phenomena); (2) biddable domains (a domain that usually consists of people; it is physical but lacks positive predictable internal causality); and (3) lexical domains (a domain that is a physical representation of data, that is, of symbolic phenomena).

By differentiating the phenomena and the domain, the problem frames approach proposes several problem frames for capturing the types of requirements that can be treated as the specification patterns. Fig. 2.8 shows the problem structures of some frames.

These basic problem frames have their own intuitive, inherent semantics:

- required behavior frame (Fig. 2.8C): There is some part of the physical world whose behavior is to be controlled so that it satisfies certain conditions. The problem is to build a machine that will impose that control.

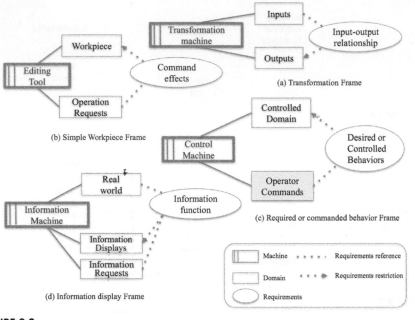

FIGURE 2.8

Problem structure in problem frames approach.

- commanded behavior frame (Fig. 2.8C): There is some part of the physical world whose behavior is to be controlled in accordance with commands issued by an operator. The problem is to build a machine that will accept the operator's commands and impose the control accordingly.
- information display frame (Fig. 2.8D): There is some part of the physical world about whose states and behavior certain information is continually needed. The problem is to build a machine that will obtain this information from the world and present it at the required place in the required form.
- simple work pieces frame (Fig. 2.8B): A tool is needed to allow a user to create and edit a certain class of computer-processable text or graphic objects, or a simple structure, so that it can be subsequently copied, printed, analyzed, or used in other ways. The problem is to build a machine that can act as this tool.
- transformation frame (Fig. 2.8A): There are some given computer-readable input files whose data must be transformed to give certain required output files. The output data must be in a particular format and it must be derived from the input data according to certain rules. The problem is to build a machine that will produce the required outputs from the inputs.

Problem frames offer a way to classify software development problems. They emphasize physical domains, physical phenomena, and interfaces, because the point of software development is to build machines that interact with the world and change it. The satisfaction of the requirements comes down to observable effects in the world.

2.6 SUMMARY

This chapter summarizes available representative requirements engineering methodologies, mainly focusing on the principles. Requirements engineering approaches are processes to bridge real-world problems into digital world solutions. Each approach has its own particular thinking about the real-world problem and follows a particular process to build the system specification as the solution.

However, there are some common grounds for these methodologies. First, any of the approaches holds the view that the requirements engineering problem comes from the reality or the disagreements about the current solution. Second, they assume that the real-world problem can be determined, defined, or decided before or during the requirements engineering process, or can be identified from the current available system. With this thinking, the relationship between the three elements, i.e., *Env* (Environment), *Spec* (Specification), and *Req* (Requirements), is understood as: Given *Env* when *Req* is required, find *Spec* as the solution to allow the relationship to hold. Thus the process of requirements engineering is normally identifying and deciding the real-world problem based on the requirements and then deriving the specification.

Importance of Interactive Environment

3

CHAPTER OUTLINE

Requirements engineering is used to define problems so that a software system can serve some useful purpose in solving. These problems are found in many different contexts and forms. Currently, software systems serve increasingly more functions and have a more central role in solving many different kinds of problems. Some new generations of software systems, such as cyber-physical systems or software-intensive systems in general, bear witness to this.

3.1 SOFTWARE-INTENSIVE SYSTEMS

Software-intensive systems have an important role in almost every part of human society, e.g., transportation systems, energy networks, and communication systems. For example, software-intensive systems in modern vehicles provide comfort to occupants and ensure their safety, such as in electronic stability, engine management, precrash detection, and adaptive cruise control systems.

The term "software-intensive system" (IEEE Std-1471-2000) refers to systems that incorporate software, hardware, physical devices, and human activities, as well as the natural environments (via a wide variety of sensors) to achieve a specified purpose with certain constraints. In such a system, "software" is a key component because software enables others to be linked together for the same purpose (i.e., the capability). That is, software is the core that is responsible for planning, decision making, and coordination, and others are the environments that demonstrate the physical effects into the real world by the instructions of the software.

The main features of software-intensive systems are:

1. Software contributes essential influences the design, implementation, and evolution as well as the usage of the system as a whole;
2. Software is embedded in physical or technical processes through its direct interactions with other systems, devices, sensors and people.

From these features, we can conclude that software-intensive systems refer mainly to systems that incorporate software, hardware, physical devices, and human activities, as well as the natural environments (via a wide variety of sensors) to achieve the specified purpose with certain constraints. Such systems are built with a reliance on the incorporation and surrounding of software. They are typically distributed and decentralized, assembled as a dynamically changing orchestration of autonomous entities.

This viewpoint can be further demonstrated intuitively by examining examples of existing software-intensive systems:

- [S1.1] A banking system's purpose comes from the desire of customers for more convenient ways to make transactions and the desire of banks to provide competitive and profitable services. The desired capability is decided by the business activities of banks and the day-to-day needs of their customers. The intended context is bound by the interactions between the desired banking system, the external systems, and the system users (including the customers and the banks' staff). Banking software is part of the banking system. Its purpose consists of subgoals of the banking system's goal. Its capability is decided by supporting the banking system to achieve its purpose but it is limited by current available information technology and constraint from the context.
- [S1.2] The purpose of an aircraft flight control system lies in the need to reduce pilot error and workload at key times such as landing and takeoff, or to make flying more stable. The capability and context of the system are determined by the purpose, such as by how much the workload needs to be reduced. Flight control systems consist of flight control surfaces, the respective cockpit controls, connecting linkages, the necessary operating mechanisms, and so on. The software in a flight control system is designed to automate some parts of the functionalities and coordinating the mechanical devices to provide increased

safety for the crew and passengers, as well as optimize the aircraft's performance.

- [S1.3] The purpose of a mobile online electronic learning system is based on the need to transcend the conventional boundaries of school-based education, by providing unprecedented access to educational resources, mentors, experts, and online educational activities. It is physically based on the Internet infrastructure and various mobile devices and logically based on information processing techniques for transforming and processing educational resources. It cannot be established without the mobile computing technology that must be used to realize it.

Software-intensive systems exist. However, they are difficult to construct because such systems are becoming increasingly distributed and decentralized, assembled as dynamically changing orchestrations of autonomous services, and are expected to adapt to continuously changing requirements and environments (Broy, 2006). Any software-intensive system relies on the incorporation of software and its surrounding devices. The required functionality and commitment are performed and guaranteed by software but will be imposed on the outside world by devices. How to corporate or coordinate the surrounding devices to make the commitment is the duty of the software. The openness, uncertainty, and complexity of the system's surroundings bring huge challenges to the field of requirements engineering.

3.2 CHALLENGES TO REQUIREMENTS ENGINEERING

Software-intensive systems are widespread in our daily lives. The engineering processes for software-intensive systems encounter many challenges.

3.2.1 INCREASING SIZE AND COMPLEXITY

Over the past years, there has been a significant increase in the size and complexity of software-intensive systems. For example, Braun et al. (2014) shares observations about the continuously increasing number of software-based functions in modern vehicles. The study reported that a typical upper-class vehicle in 2007 contained about 270 implemented functions to interact with the driver, whereas the most recent generation of upper-class vehicles contained more than 500 such functions. The size of the software in vehicles also grew significantly. The amount of binary code in an upper-class vehicle in 2007 was about 66 megabytes, whereas the current generation of such vehicles requires more than 1 gigabyte of binary code.

The increasing number and size of software-based functions come with a growth in complexity. These software-based functions require more fine-grained functions than individual component subsystems, e.g., the braking system, engine management, driving assistance system, etc., and intensive interactions within these subsystems. In this way, the complexity of the system is tremendously increased.

Another example that demonstrates complexity is software in an airborne system, i.e., avionics.[1] Avionics is the electronic systems used on aircraft. Avionics systems include communications, navigation, the display and management of multiple systems, and the hundreds of systems that are fitted to aircraft to perform individual functions. Each of these subsystems has its own functions but they are closely related to each other.

A communication system connects the flight deck to the ground and the flight deck to the passengers. A navigation system determines the position and the direction on or above the surface of the earth. It calculates position automatically and displays it to the flight crew on a moving map display. A monitoring system is the glass cockpit that refers to the use of computer monitors instead of gauges and other analog displays.

With the increase in such functions, aircraft progressively acquired more displays, dials, and information dashboards that eventually competed for space and pilot attention. In the 1970s, the average aircraft had more than 100 cockpit instruments and controls. The challenge in glass cockpits is to balance how much control is automated and how much the pilot should perform manually.

Generally, more and more flight operations are automated, while ensuring that the pilot is constantly informed. This also affords more evidence of continuously increasing numbers of software-based functions.

Some other important software-based systems in aircraft include collision-avoidance systems, black boxes, and weather systems. Collision-avoidance systems can detect the location of nearby aircraft and provide instructions to avoid a midair collision. Black boxes are cockpit data recorders that store flight information and audio from the cockpit. They need to be secure because they will be used to determine control settings and other parameters after an aircraft crash or during such an incident.

Weather systems such as weather radar and lighting detectors are important for aircraft flying at night or in meteorological conditions in which it is impossible for the pilot to see the weather ahead.

On the other hand, as indicated in Holzl et al. (2008), the development of software-intensive systems is driven in large part by improvements to available advanced hardware technologies, e.g., the dramatic decrease in cost, size, and energy consumption of integrated circuits and the availability of computational elements based on new principles. This enables the control of devices with software and makes it economically feasible.

Conversely, the widespread integration of software in devices thus enables novel features for many classes of device, such as network connectivity for household appliances. The development of multicore processors with tens to thousands of cores integrated on a single chip implies that even single-chip systems will have to be treated as consisting of large numbers of individual nodes.

---

[1]http://en.wikipedia.org/wiki/Avionics.

These trends and challenges demand systematical methodologies of engineering large, networked, software-intensive systems along with massive numbers of computational nodes.

3.2.2 OPEN AND NONDETERMINISTIC ENVIRONMENT

Different from traditional software, which was assumed to work in an environment that was current during the time of design, software-intensive systems will operate in an open and nondeterministic environment. For example, in future megascale ubiquitous systems for urban computing (Zheng et al., 2014), a large amount of heterogeneous data generated by a diversity of sources in urban spaces, such as sensors, devices, vehicles, buildings, and humans, will be acquired, integrated, and analyzed in software-intensive systems. Many interesting applications can be built upon the collected data (Murty et al., 2008). The systems are expected to cope with island heat phenomena after collecting information about temperature, humidity, wind direction, and so on through meteorological sensors. They are also expected to help maintain old highways or roads and detect the deterioration of old construction through deployed sensors. Also, help in delivering emergency medical services and the monitoring of chronic diseases is becoming significant in the sensing of vital signs in humans. In all of these situations, it can be seen that the environment is dynamic and nondeterministic.

Yet, the environment is open. Much evidence can be witnessed. For example, many mobile phones, personal digital assistants (PDAs), personal computers, and even radio-frequency identification—equipped goods are networked via different scales of network. In turn, the increase in available devices entices service providers to offer new services or to remove service offers that are no longer profitable or that have been superseded by newer offers. They must replace services that are no longer available with others that offer similar functionality; they should also be able to take advantage of new services provided by the network environment that were not foreseen when the system was designed. Therefore, the environment of software-intensive systems, which are built on the changing space of services, is never closed.

3.2.3 SITUATION AWARENESS AND ADAPTATION

Apart from the challenges raised by complexity and uncertainty, software-intensive systems that were once fitted with only the basics are now being targeted for the introduction of new information technologies. For example, cell phones, electronic navigation systems coupled with global positioning system locational devices, and the automation to perform tasks ranging from traffic conflict detection to automated spacing and lane following are being incorporated into automobiles. This enables the system to be more embedded in the changeable and open environment.

These new technologies also create the possibility that the system can be aware of the whole picture surrounding the system and then enabled to make better online decisions.

In fact, future software-intensive systems will often have to operate under conditions that differ significantly from those for which they were designed. Even on the execution platform layer, they should not only be able to adapt to changes in their network environment, they should also be able to work reliably in the face of changes to their execution platform; even today reinstalling all necessary programs is a major burden when we switch to a new computer. Because future software-intensive systems will be more ubiquitous and more widely distributed, and will assimilate a larger number of adaptations during their operation (Mei et al., 2012; Tsai et al., 2009), the prospect of reinstalling them from scratch when switching to a new platform becomes unfeasible.

The dynamics of the situation (how much and how rapidly things are changing in an environment) is an important feature. This asks for online decision making. In these complex domains, decision making must do more than simply perceive the state of the environment to have good situation awareness that incorporates an understanding of the situation as a whole. In fact, it highly depends on a constantly evolving picture of the state of the environment (Endsley and Jones, 2012).

3.2.4 INNOVATION-ENABLED REQUIREMENTS

Requirements engineering for a large and complex system is difficult. Difficulties arise when the referred stakeholders (i.e., the domain experts, end users, and customers) cannot provide the complete and correct requirements statements. Even worse, many innovative applications, e.g., some of the most popular applications such as WeChat, On-line Shopping, etc., are driven by technology development and the innovative thinking of product designers but are not required by the stakeholders. The domain experts and end users cannot realize technology development, which is outside the scope of their imagination when information technology is advancing as quickly as it is in this era. They are unaware of what is possible or have misconceptions about what is feasible by state-of-the-art information technology. There is another challenge when developing such Internet-enabled, innovative software-intensive applications.

3.3 ENVIRONMENT, REQUIREMENTS, AND SPECIFICATION

From an analysis of the previous section, "environment" becomes a core issue for these challenges. Let us go back to the relationship between the basic elements in requirements engineering. Besides the system commitments and software function points, requirements statements may contain another kind of information, i.e., the properties of the interactive environment or the problem context, such as the monitor/control variables in four-variable models and the physical domains in the problem frame approach. It is important to understand these interactive environments or the problem context and capture their properties. The reason is that the system commitments may be made only within some problem context or situation and the software functionalities can be realized by collaboration with the interactive entities in the environment.

In fact, the recognition that understanding and modeling the environment should be an integral part of requirements modeling and analysis has been a milestone and has become the most important principle in the requirements engineering field.

People in the requirements engineering community have acknowledged that environment is a key factor in identifying needs and desires and that system requirements should be defined in relation to its future environment.

3.3.1 RELATIONSHIPS AMONG THE THREE

The three sets of statements and the relationship among them are illustrated by (Jackson, 1997):

- *Env, Spec* $\models$ *Req*

where *Env* is the set of indicative properties about the phenomena of the interactive environments, i.e., mainly regulated by the relevant domain knowledge; *Req* is the set of optative descriptions about the phenomena of the environments that are desirable to be achieved, i.e., the commitments that the system is required to make; and *Spec* is the set of optative properties about the shared phenomena at the interface between the machine, (i.e., the system) and the environment. They are about the implementable function points.

This entailment relationship indicates that if a system whose behavior satisfies *Spec* is installed in the interactive environment that has the properties described in *Env*, the environment will exhibit the properties described in *Req*. Fig. 3.1 vividly presents the relationship among the three sets of phenomenon statements.

Most available requirements engineering methodologies pay less attention to the environment properties but assume they can be determined and fixed at the design time. From the fixed environment properties, the system specification is derived and the implemented system can be deployed to satisfy the requirements.

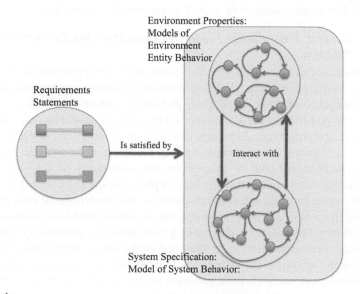

FIGURE 3.1

Three sets of statements and relationship among them.

However, as we know from previous sections, many software-intensive systems will run within a complex, open, and dynamically changeable environment. The environment properties cannot be ignored at run-time.

3.3.2 ENVIRONMENT PROPERTIES IS THE FIRST CITIZEN

We propose that the environment properties must be the first citizen in requirements engineering (Jin, 2006; Wang et al., 2008) and will become run-time models. Why is this the case?

3.3.2.1 First, Requirements Are the Problem That Is Expected to Be Solved

To identify the environment of the to-be system, we have to put ourselves into the reality that can be characterized by a set of observable phenomena, e.g., the facts about and the events that occurred upon real-world entities, and so on. That is, we should first identify the portion of reality in which there may be some problem (i.e., the **requirements**).

The problem is the motivation of developing a system that might be an innovative solution to this problem, e.g., the stakeholders want to change some real-world phenomena and/or their relationships. For example, some phenomena do not hold or cannot occur at the moment, but they expect them to hold or happen after the to-be-built software is put in reality. In other words, whenever a software-intensive system is needed, there is a portion of the real world in which some changes are needed and these changes are required to be enabled by the software-intensive system. For example,

- [R3.1] The home should have comfortable conditions; e.g., thermal comfort, air quality, and so on can be improved.
- [R3.2] The tourists need to be guided to explore the resort sites.

3.3.2.2 Second, Environment Properties Constitute the Context of the Problem

Some portion of the environment possesses some real-world phenomena that are relevant to the desired phenomena. These environment phenomena are captured and identified as the context of the problem. These phenomena can be explained as "in which situations the problem occurs or the expected phenomena should be observable," "if that happens, the problem could be regarded as having been solved or the needs have been met," and so on. These phenomena may constitute the candidate situation to make the problem solvable or to establish the constraints of problem solving. Then, the relationships among the environment phenomena can be built. The environment phenomena and their relationships constitute the **environment properties**.

Among those environment phenomena that could be candidate situations, some phenomena might be able to be affected by a to-be software-intensive system. These environment phenomena need to be identified as the shared phenomena. The to-be software-intensive system can be useful only when the environment and the system can be linked together. With these connections, the system can impose its effects onto the environment phenomena to enable them and then to meet the requirements.

The connection is achieved by the shared phenomena between the environment and the system in that facts or events are observable to both the environment and the system. Only because of these shared phenomena can the system affect the environment and be affected by the environment. For example:

- [E3.1] If the rooms have air-conditioning systems, the condition (temperature, humidity, etc.) of the air in the rooms can be modified or altered, e.g., by distributing the conditioned air to improve thermal comfort and indoor air quality.
- [E3.2] If the tourists can obtain introductory material or visitor guides to read about the scenery, when they enter the sites, they can be guided.

3.3.2.3 Third, the System Is a Candidate Solution for Solving the Problem Within the Context

The to-be system has its own private phenomena (i.e., the software specifications) after being developed and installed within its environment. The shared phenomena request for the private system phenomena can enable those shared phenomena in a collaborative way. These private system phenomena will result in the **system specifications**.

The following are examples that can result in the private system phenomena being candidates of the solution to meet the requirements:

- [S3.1] If the room temperature is too cold (the system may know this by temperature sensors), send a message to turn on the heating air conditioner (the system can do this by sending a message to the air conditioner actuator); if the temperature in the room is too warm, turn on the cooling air conditioner.
- [S3.2] When detecting the tourist in a certain sightseeing area (the system can do this by sensing the tourist's position through the PDA that the tourist keeps), the system transmits exploration guidance for this area onto this PDA.

As shown in the examples, sometimes some environment phenomena (normally shared phenomena) may be included in the process of defining the private system phenomena, e.g., including some physical devices such as temperature sensors and air-conditioner actuators. In this way, the process may be iterative until the information is complete to some extent.

3.3.3 INTERFACES ARE ANOTHER CONCERN

Interfaces offer a bridge between the environment and the system, and vice versa. Notice that *Spec* of the software-intensive system contains statements about the system phenomena whereas the system consists of software and some physical devices such as sensors or actuators. These physical devices serve as interfaces between the physical world (i.e., the environment) and the digital world (i.e., the software). They realize the transformation from the real-world property quantities to the information that the software needs, and vice versa.

For traditional information systems, mostly users take care of the transformation. All necessary data or information is input by the users and all outputs are interpreted by the users. We normally assume that users can input the right information at the right time and understand and interpret the output of the software in the right way. That is, the users take full responsibility for the input data and use of the output data. The software accepts the data with only some limited validity checking. In this case, the transformation between the physical world and the digital world can be ignored and it is assumed that information exchanges between the software and the environment can be enabled as correctly, precisely, and instantly as expected.

However, this is not the case for software-intensive systems. In software-intensive systems, physical devices such as sensors, probably through wire or wireless networks, collect much input data. These devices or networks may fail to collect data at the right time or may collect wrong data because of external interference, device limitation, etc. The information transformation between the two worlds needs to be taken into account when building the system model and designing the system.

There are two kinds of interfaces for sharing phenomena between the environment and the system. What the interface between the environment and the software is transforming is the real-world phenomena into the software phenomena. There is another interface between the physical devices and the software that goes further and then transforms into the software phenomena.

The phenomena of these interfaces can no longer be ignored. Moreover, these devices are included in the reality only because of the environment and the requirements. In this sense, they are part of the to-be-built system. Referring to the equation mentioned earlier, the phenomena of these devices are part of *Spec*. However, if we tighten the scope to include only the software, they are outside this scope but are newly introduced into the real world by becoming the new environmental entities of the software. When we think of software development, their properties can be seen as another kind of domain.

To clarify the conceptual model, we would do better to refine the system specifications statements into two sets. That is, after conducting the requirements engineering process, two sets of statements need to be constructed. Statements about the phenomena that will be shared by the environment and the to-be system describe interactions of the environment and the to-be software. These statements are about the phenomena of the "interface" between the software and its environment. Statements about the properties of to-be software are those that will be realized by the software development. These are "software specifications."

3.3.4 SUMMARY

The environment, the system, and the requirements for the system are three independent and yet tightly integrated concerns in requirements engineering. The description of the environment and the requirements are the first concerns. One is for indicatively defining the given existence within the bounded scope; the other is for indicating the existing problem within the bounded scope and optatively expressing the desires for a new system aimed at solving the problem. The third concern of the system specifications delivers a candidate solution plan that may be able to solve the problem within the scope when it is implemented and installed within the environment. The third concern appears to be derived but it is also independent because its correctness, feasibility, and so on are based on its ability to be realized, subject to the constraints of the techniques, staff, cost, etc.

More precisely, the initiative requirements describe the intentions of solving the problems about the environment, i.e., the application problem, whereas the tasks of requirements engineering are recognizing and expressing the requirements and developing the software specifications with which and how to solve the application problem. With these assumptions, the task can be entailed to develop or derive the software specification *Spec*, based on the given properties of the environment *Env* and the interface *Int* after obtaining the desired or optative description *Req*. In other words, requirements engineering contains three main tasks:

- *Env*, *Req* <u>require</u> *Sys*
- *Int*, *Soft* <u>realize</u> *Sys*
- *Sys*, *Int*, *Env* <u>satisfy</u> *Req*

Yet, Klaus Pohl in his book (Pohl, 2010) depicted the relationship among these four sets of statements in another way. Fig. 3.2 illustrates the adjusted picture to highlight the location of the software. This shows that:

- A software-intensive system is always located in an environment.
- The stakeholders' needs for a system are about the desired environment.
- Requirements for the system come from the intention of solving the problem about the environment.
- They are influenced directly by the context environment of the system.

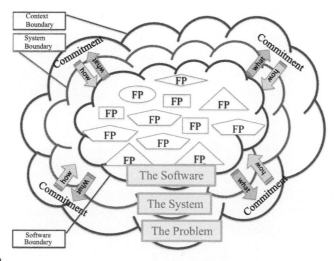

FIGURE 3.2

Context boundary, system boundary, interface, and software. *FP,* Function point.

Part One References

P. Braun, M. Broy, F. Houdek, M. Kirchmayr, M. Muller, B. Penzenstadler, K. Pohl, T. Weyer, Guiding requirements engineering for software-intensive embedded systems in the automotive industry, Computer Science Programming 29 (2014) 21–34.

M. Broy, The "Grand Challenge" in informatics: engineering software-intensive systems, IEEE Computer 39 (10) (2006) 72–80.

B. Buseibeh, Weaving together requirements and architectures, Computer 34 (3) (2001) 115–117.

A.M. Davis, Just Enough Requirements Management: Where Software Development Meets Marketing, Dorset House, 2005.

M.R. Endsley, D.G. Jones, Designing for Situation Awareness: An Approach to User-Centered Design, CRC Press, Taylor & Francis Group, 2012.

M. Holzl, A. Rauschmayer, M. Wirsing, Engineering of software-intensive systems: state of the art and research challenges, in: Software-Intensive Systems and New Computing Paradigms: Challenges and Visions, Lecture Notes on Computer Science, vol. 5380, Springer-Verlag, 2008.

Institute of Electric and Electronic Engineers, IEEE Standard Glossary of Software Engineering Terminology (IEEE Std 610.12–1990), 1990.

Institute of Electric and Electronic Engineers, IEEE Recommended Practice for Architectural Description for Software-Intensive Systems, (ANSI/IEEE Std 1471–2000), 2000.

M. Jackson, The meaning of requirements, Annals of Software Engineering 3 (1997) 5–21.

M. Jackson, Problem Frames: Analysing and Structuring Software Development Problems, Addison-Wesley, 2001.

Z. Jin, Revisiting the meaning of requirements, Journal of Computer Science and Technology 21 (1) (2006) 32–40.

A. van Lamsweerde, Requirements Engineering: From System Goals to {UML} Models to Software Specification, John Wiley, 2009.

H. Mei, G. Huang, T. Xie, Internetware: a software paradigm for internet computing, IEEE Computer 45 (6) (2012) 26–31.

H. Mei, J. Lü, Internetware — A New Software Paradigm for Internet Computing, Springer, 2016, pp. 3–442. ISBN: 978-981-10-2545-7.

R.N. Murty, G. Mainland, I. Rose, A.R. Chowdhury, A. Gosain, J. Bers, M. Welsh, CitySense: an urban-scale wireless sensor network and testbed, in: IEEE Conference on Technologies for Homeland Security (HST2008), 2008, pp. 583–588.

D. Parnas, J. Madey, Functional documents for computer systems, Science of Computer Programming 25 (1995) 41–61.

K. Pohl, The three dimensions of requirements engineering: a framework and its applications, Information Systems 19 (3) (1994) 243–258.

K. Pohl, Requirements Engineering: Fundamentals, Principles and Techniques, Springer-Verlag, 2010.

A.G. Sutcliffe, Scenario-based requirements engineering, in: Proceedings of IEEE International Requirements Engineering Conference (RE2003), 2003, pp. 320–329.

W. Tsai, Z. Jin, X. Bai, Internetware computing: issues and perspectives, International Journal of Software and Informatics 3 (4) (2009) 415−438.

Wang, et al., Building towards capability specifications of web services based on an environment ontology, IEEE Transactions on Knowledge and Data Engineering 20 (4) (2008) 547−561.

E. Yu, Social Modeling for Requirements Engineering, MIT Press, 2010.

Y. Zheng, L. Capra, O. Wolfson, H. Yang, Urban computing: concepts, methodologies, and applications, ACM Transactions on Intelligent Systems and Technology 5 (3) (2014). Article 38.

Ontology and System-Interactive Environment Ontology

2

Part 1 showed that the interactive environment, the software-intensive system, and the requirements for it are independent but have three tightly integrated concerns regarding requirements engineering. Part 2 focuses on modeling the interactive environment.

Originally, ontology was a concept in philosophical terms. It describes the essence and composition of the world as philosophers see it. In computer science, ontology is mainly used for knowledge representation and provides a means for sharing knowledge.

Domain analysis refers to the activity of identifying the objects and operations of a class of similar systems in a particular problem domain. It is the process of identifying, collecting, organizing, and representing the relevant information in a domain, based on the study of existing systems and their histories of development, knowledge captured from domain experts, underlying theory, and emerging technology within the domain. The product of domain analysis is the domain model. It is the necessary foundation of the model-based approach.

System-interactive environment modeling involves building the domain model according to the following two aspects. First, as explained in Part 1, a system environment consists of the real-world interactive objects of to-be systems. Their behaviors indicate the requirements of to-be systems and will exhibit the satisfactory nature of the requirements. The interactive environment is the real problem domain of to-be systems. The more general the environment is, the bigger the coverage is of the problem domain. The general environment model can be specialized into different environment instances from different angles or by dealing with different concerns.

Second, a model-based approach can also be used in environment modeling. At the highest abstract level, the environment model should answer questions such as which kinds of interactive objects the software-intensive systems will face and which kinds of problems the systems can solve via interactions with these objects. At the middle level, the environment model should contain particular types of interactive objects in a certain application domain. It will highlight common problems and their characteristics in this application domain. At the lowest level is the environment model of the particular application.

Of course, interactive environment ontology will be different from general ontology because it is developed to allow it to be able to exhibit the capability of to-be systems. Therefore new ontological structure is needed. Traditional domain ontology represents only the static characteristics of the domain whereas the interactive environment ontology should be able to capture the dynamic or behavioral characteristics of the domain.

Part 2 focuses on the development of the interactive environment ontology, permitting it to be able to capture the capability of to-be systems. It first introduces the essence and principles of ontology and ontology-oriented domain modeling. It will detail the process of developing an interactive environment ontology. This part also proposes an extended ontological structure to represent the behavioral characteristics of the interactive environment in accordance with the need to capture the capability of to-be systems. In addition, it discusses the approach to building an interactive environment ontology from the general domain ontology on the Web. Finally, a feature model-based domain environment ontology representation is defined.

Ontology-Oriented Interactive Environment Modeling

CHAPTER OUTLINE

This chapter first introduces what ontology is in the computer sciences domain and what ontology-based modeling is. Then it discusses the conceptualization of system-interactive environments and how to develop the ontology of software interactive environment.

4.1 ONTOLOGY AND ONTOLOGIES

4.1.1 BACKGROUND

Historically, ontology is listed as part of the major branch of philosophy known as metaphysics. It is the philosophical study of the nature of being, becoming, existence, or reality, as well as the basic categories of being and their relationships. Generally speaking, ontology deals with questions concerning what entities exist or may be said to exist, and how such entities may be grouped, related within a hierarchy, and subdivided according to similarities and differences.

Environment Modeling-Based Requirements Engineering for Software Intensive Systems
http://dx.doi.org/10.1016/B978-0-12-801954-2.00004-2

Since the mid-1970s, researchers in the field of knowledge engineering recognized that capturing knowledge is the key to building large and powerful knowledge-based systems. They argued that they could create ontologies as computational models that would enable certain kinds of automated reasoning. Thus, in many cases, ontologies would present their own methodological and structural aspects.

Since then, different ontologies have been created and have been widely used in the fields of artificial intelligence, the Semantic Web, the systems engineering, the software engineering, etc., to limit complexity and organize information. Ontology can then be applied to problem solving.

We consider ontology from different angles. On the methodological side, ontology refers to a particular system of categories accounting for a certain vision of the world. On the structural side, ontology refers to an engineering artifact constituted by a specific vocabulary that can be used to describe a certain reality. In the simplest case, ontology describes a hierarchy of concept categories related by subsumption relationships. In more sophisticated cases, suitable axioms are added to express other relationships between concept categories and constrain their intended interpretation.

More practically, ontology supplies a unifying framework for communication and establishes the basis of knowledge about a specific domain. It provides formal specifications and harmonized definitions of concept categories used to represent knowledge of a specific domain. It is a formal naming and definition of the types, properties, and interrelationships of the entities that really or fundamentally exist for a particular domain of discourse. It is thus a practical application of philosophical ontology, with taxonomy.

The widely cited paper in this domain, "A translation approach to portable ontology specifications," (Gruber, 1993), is credited with a deliberate definition of ontology as an "explicit specification of a conceptualization." Since then, several other small adaptations have been made to this definition. Thus, a common definition is:

> An ontology is an explicit specification of a **shared conceptualization** that holds in a particular **context**.

This definition highlights three concerns about ontology. First, the adjective "shared" is important. The primary goal of ontologies in knowledge engineering was to enable knowledge sharing, owing to the enormous need for shared concept categories in the distributed world of the Web. That was endorsed by the particular popularity of ontologies in the context of Semantic Web efforts.

Second, this definition stands on the engineering side (i.e., it is an explicit specification) but uses "conceptualization" to refer to the philosophical side. Conceptualization ensures that two ontologies can be different in the vocabulary used while sharing the same conceptualization.

Third, in practice, we are confronted with many different conceptualizations, i.e., ways of viewing the world. It is often noted that even in a single domain there can be multiple viewpoints. "Context" is therefore an important notion when reusing ontology. If the context of the ontology has not been explicated, the conceptualization might not be understandable to others.

4.1.2 DIFFERENT VIEWPOINTS ON ONTOLOGY

What does ontology look like and how is ontology developed? There are different viewpoints and principles from various groups of people.

The Philosopher's Generic Ontologies (Sowa, 1999): Philosophers usually build their ontologies from the top down. They start with grand conceptions about everything, from the universal type of the entity, i.e., the neutral representation, by using "Thing," which is a synthesis of the philosophical insights about existence or beings. For example, Fig. 4.1 shows that everything that exists must be an instance of "Thing." Beneath "Thing" is a two-way split between the category Physical and the category Abstract. The former is for representing anything consisting of matter or energy, and the latter for pure information structures. Then, beneath Physical and Abstract is the three-way division according to Peirce's distinction, i.e., Firstness, Secondness, and Thirdness. This results in six categories of existence: Actuality (Form), the Physical (Abstract) entity of Firstness, Prehension (Proposition), the Physical (Abstract) entity of Secondness, and Nexus (Intention), the Physical (Abstract) entity of Thirdness.

Different distinctions can be combined. Another view (Peirce's trichotomy) to split "Thing" can be applied that may generate three categories: Independent, Relative, and Mediating, which correspond to Firstness, Secondness, and Thirdness, respectively. The result is that the category hierarchy includes multiple inheritances. A third view to split "Thing" is Continuant and Occurrent. The continuant—occurrent distinction applies to the entities about which information is recorded and to the physical media on which information is stored. With this binary

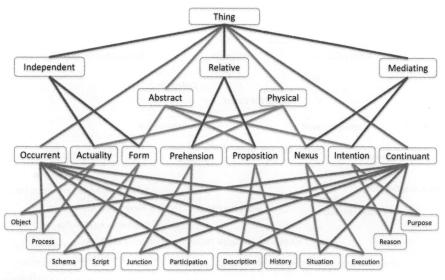

FIGURE 4.1

Top-level distinction for categories (Sowa, 1999).

distinction between continuants and occurrents, the six categories beneath Physical and Abstract are split into 12 categories (as shown in Fig. 4.1). They are derived by combinations of the three basic distinctions for subdividing the universal type. Each of the other categories is a synonym for the combination of categories from which it was derived. For example, Object features Independent Physical Continuant.

The Knowledge Engineer's Knowledge Encyclopedia: Many knowledge engineers focus on how to accommodate all of human knowledge to support the computational questions that need human-level reasoning. Cyc ontology in Fig. 4.2 is a typical example from the knowledge engineer's viewpoint. This figure shows the most general categories at the top of one of the early versions of Cyc hierarchy. Beneath the top levels are all of the concept types used in the rules and facts of the Cyc knowledge base.

Using the same way, the most general category "Thing" is a concept whose extension contains all of the concepts in the focusing application domain. Under "Thing" are the differentiae that distinguish the next level of categories. These are Individual Object, Intangible, and Represented Thing. In this sense, particular ontologies are specific to application domains. Concerning the ontology building, how to identify the concepts, and the subsumption relation between concepts, or which concepts and subsumption relations, are also specific to the application domains.

The Application Developer's Viewpoint: Application developers tend to work from the bottom up. They start with limited ontologies or microworlds, which have a small number of concepts that are tailored to a single application. Moreover, from the practitioner's point of view, ontologies are often equated with taxonomic hierarchies of concept categories, including concepts and their subsumption relations. Fig. 4.3 illustrates the geographical categories excerpted from the Chat-80

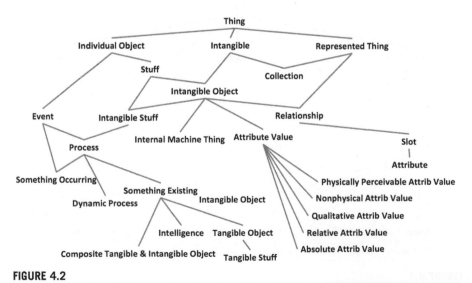

FIGURE 4.2

Top-level categories in Cyc ontology (Sowa, 1999). *Atrib*, attribute.

FIGURE 4.3

Term categories of geographical features (Sowa, 1999).

question-answering system.[1] It represents a typical microworld designed for a single application by containing just enough categories and at the proper abstract level.

Limited ontologies are always useful for single applications in highly specialized domains. However, to share knowledge with other applications, ontology must be embedded within a more general framework provided by philosophy, i.e., its guidelines and top-level categories form the superstructure that can relate to the details of the low-level projects.

4.1.3 COMMON STRUCTURE OF ONTOLOGY

Currently, common ontology components are concept categories, instances, attributes, and associations. Concept categories are types of objects or kinds of things. They can be defined as an extension or an intension. According to an extensional definition, they are abstract groups or collections of objects. According to an intentional definition, they are abstract objects that are defined by values of aspects, which are constraints for being members of the concept category. Instances are individuals or objects. They normally include concrete objects such as particular people, devices, plants, animals, etc., as well as abstract individuals such as particular numbers and words. A particular ontology needs not include individuals, but it should provide a means of classifying individuals.

Fig. 4.4 is an ontological example about animals:

- Animal, the classification for all animals, or the abstract object that can be described by the criteria for being an animal
- Fish, the classification for all fish, or the abstract object that can be described by the criteria for being a fish

---

[1]http://www.nltk.org/howto/chat80.html.

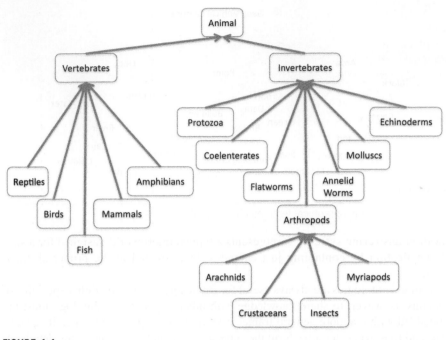

FIGURE 4.4

A concept category hierarchy of a sample animal ontology.

- Insects, the classification for all insects, or the abstract object that can be described by the criteria for being an insect

A concept category can subsume or be subsumed by other concept categories. A concept category subsumed by another is called a subclass (or subtype) of the subsuming concept category (or supertype). For example, *Animal* subsumes *Vertebrates* because necessarily, anything that is a member of the latter concept category is a member of the former. The subsumption relation is used to create a hierarchy of concept categories, typically with a maximally general concept category such as *Animal* at the top and a very specific concept category, e.g., *any particular cow number 123 in some farm in a particular time*, at the bottom.

A critically important consequence of the subsumption relation is the inheritance of properties from the parent (subsuming) concept category to the child (subsumed) concept category. Thus, anything that is necessarily true of a parent concept category is also necessarily true of all of its subsumed child concept categories. In some ontologies, a concept category is allowed to have only one parent (single inheritance), but in some others, concept categories are allowed to have any number of parents (multiple inheritance), and in the latter case all necessary properties of each parent are inherited by the subsumed child concept category.

A partition is a set of related concept categories and associated rules that allow objects to be classified by the appropriate subsumption. The rules correspond with the aspect values that distinguish the subclasses from the superclasses. For example, Fig. 4.4 contains the partial diagram of an ontology that has a partition of the *Animal* concept into the subconcepts *Vertebrates* and *Invertebrates*. The partition rule (or subsumption rule) determines whether a particular animal is classified to be *Vertebrates* or *Invertebrates*. If the partition rule(s) guarantees that a single *Animal* cannot be in both concept categories, the partition is called a disjoint partition. If the partition rules ensure that every concrete object in the parent concept category is an instance of at least one of the partition concept categories, the partition is called an exhaustive partition.

Any concept category in ontology can be described by relating it to other things, i.e., aspects, properties, features, characteristics, or parameters that the concept category can have. These related things are often called attributes. The kind of concept categories and the kind of attributes determine the kind of relationship among them. A relationship between a concept category and an attribute expresses a fact that is specific to the concept to which it is related. For example, concept "*Cow*" has attributes such as:

- **namedAs**: Cow
- **hasParts**: leg (with number: 4)
- **hasMother**: cow
- **hasColor**: {black, brown, black-white}
- **hasBirthDayOf**: Date {XX-XX-XXXX}.

The value of an attribute can be an instance of other concepts. In this example, Cow's birth date can only be one instance of the concept category: Date. Cow's mother can only be one instance of Cow.

Apart from the relations built by concept category/attribute/value pairs, there are also associations of some types between concept categories in ontology, which also specify how concept categories are related to each other. For example, "everyone has a mother" can be expressed as:

Person has a mother *Female Person*

"Carnivores depend on the nutrients found in animal flesh for their survival" and "an herbivore is an animal adapted to eating plant material" can be expressed as:

Carnivores eat *Animals*
Herbivores eat *Plants*

Such a relationship is slightly different from the one built by concept category/attribute/value pairs. The latter is private and localized to the concept category but the association is public and global to the ontology.

Normally speaking, ontologies are true ontologies if concept categories are related to each other by associations or concept categories/attributes/value pairs. If that were not the case, you would have either a taxonomy (if hyponym relationships exist between concepts) or a controlled vocabulary. These are useful but are not considered true ontologies.

4.2 TYPES OF ONTOLOGIES

Philosophers can classify ontologies in various ways using criteria such as the degree of abstraction and field of application. Based on the criteria, ontologies exist in many forms. In fact, the application of a philosophical perspective to domains at different levels of generality yields knowledge systems that are called, according to the concerns or the level of abstraction, e.g., top-level ontologies or foundational ontologies, core domain or domain ontologies, task-specific ontologies, interface ontologies, process ontologies, and application ontologies. That is, there could be different kinds of ontologies according to their level of generality, as shown in Fig. 4.5.

Top-level or foundational ontologies stay closest to the original philosophical idea of ontology. This type of ontology aims to provide conceptualizations of general notions in the domain of discourse. Some notable foundational ontologies include the Suggested Upper Merged Ontology[2] and the Descriptive Ontology for Linguistic and Cognitive Engineering,[3] as well as lexical resources such as WordNet.[4] It contains concepts supporting the development of ontology, that is, a metaontology.

Core domain or domain ontologies are associated with more restricted fields of interest. A foundational ontology can serve as a unifying framework for representing and integrating knowledge and may support the communication and harmonization

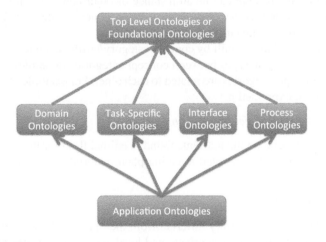

FIGURE 4.5

Kinds of ontologies.

---

[2]http://ontology.teknowledge.com/.
[3]http://www/loa-cnr.it/dolce.html.
[4]http://wordnet.princeton.ude/.

of conceptual systems in the domain of discourse, whereas a domain-specific ontology is intended for sharing concepts and relations in a particular area of interest. It contains concepts relevant to a particular topic or area of interest: for example, information technology or computer languages, or particular branches of science.

A third type of ontology is task-specific ontologies. They specify conceptualizations that are needed to carry out a particular task. For each task type, one can specify domain conceptualizations needed to accomplish it. In general, conceptualizations of domain information needed for reasoning algorithms typically take the form of a task-specific ontology.

Other types of ontologies include the interface ontology that consists of concepts relevant to the juncture of two disciplines and the process ontology including inputs, outputs, constraints, sequencing information, etc., involved in business or engineering processes.

Finally, application ontology describes concepts depending on a particular domain application, which are often specifications of both related ontologies.

4.3 ONTOLOGY-ORIENTED DOMAIN MODELING

For ontology oriented domain modeling, we will take the application developer's viewpoint by using the techniques of domain engineering. Domain engineering is a process for creating reusable system abstractions for the development of a family of systems in a domain. The process consists of the phases of analysis, design, and implementation. Domain analysis identifies reuse opportunities and specifies the common ingredients of a family of applications. The product of this phase is a domain model.

4.3.1 THE PROCESS FOR ONTOLOGY-ORIENTED DOMAIN MODELING

As mentioned in previous sections, ontologies are knowledge representation structures especially useful for the specification of high-level reusable ingredients. They provide an unambiguous terminology that can be shared by all stakeholders involved in the system development process. Thus, ontologies can be good candidates to represent the products of domain engineering. Use of ontologies representing the domain models is called ontology-oriented domain modeling.

As shown in Fig. 4.6, ontology-oriented domain modeling is an iterative process consisting of a set of activities:

1. determining the domain of interest and scope and naming the top concept category of the targeted domain. This concept is treated as the "top" of the ontological hierarchy. In many cases, people use "T," denoting "Thing," the top concept category that is covering anything in this domain.
2. determining the concept classes

$$CatS = \{Cat_1, \ldots\ldots, Cat_n\}$$

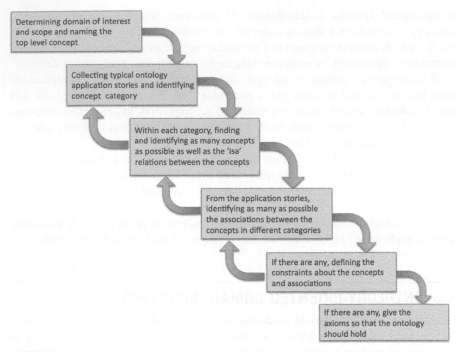

FIGURE 4.6

Process of ontology-oriented domain modeling.

in the targeted domain. To help with class identification, some motivating scenarios can be collected to express the purpose of using this ontology. The scenarios can be represented in a narrative way, e.g., via the usage stories. From these usage stories, a set of domain terms can be extracted. By abstraction, the concept classes are refined and the terms for the concept classes become the second-level concept categories in the ontological hierarchy.

3. from the set of domain terms, identifying the more specific terms $\{con_1,\ldots\ldots con_m\}$ as the concept categories/individuals[5] under each concept class $Cat \in CatS$ to form the vocabulary of the concept class:

$$Cat: ClassS = \{Cat\} \cup \{con_1, \ldots\ldots, con_m\}$$

and within each concept class, identifying the subsumption relations between the concept categories in its vocabulary. All subsumption relations in all the concept classes in this domain will produce the concept hierarchy of the domain.

---

[5]We treat individuals as a class with only itself as its instance or member.

4. in terms of the domain usage scenarios, identifying the attributes of each concept category:

$$attr: con \rightarrow value$$

Here, *value* might indicate some instance of another concept category. It is also necessary to the associations between concept categories:

$$asso: c_1 \rightarrow c_2 \text{ given that } c_1 \in Cat_i \cdot ClassS, c_2 \in Cat_j \cdot ClassS \wedge i \neq j$$

Generally, each concept is featured by a set of relations and associations representing one of the ontological principles: any concept category's semantic is captured by its related concept categories.

5. if there are any, capturing and defining constraints about the concept categories and/or associations. Any constraint is stating a condition that confines the instance legality of the concept category or association. The mandatory concept categories and/or associations can be refined by constraints.

6. if there are any, capturing and defining the axioms that need to hold for this ontology. Any axiom is stating a condition that confines the legality of its instance ontology. Currently, only a few ontologies contain axioms, mainly because of the difficulties and the lack of the accurate recognition of the domain.

4.3.2 **THE STRUCTURE FOR DOMAIN ONTOLOGY**

Let *Dom* be a domain and *n* the number of its concept categories. The formal structure of the conceptualization of the domain is thus:

$$\langle Con, Isa, Asso, Cont, Axi \rangle$$

where

- $Con = \{T\} \cup \cup_1^n Cat_i \cdot ClassS$: the set of the concept categories as the vocabulary of the domain. For each concept category $cat \in \cup_1^n Cat_i$, there is a set of $Attr = \left\{ attr \rightarrow val : val \text{ is a } constant \text{ or } cat' \in \cup_1^n Cat_i, \ cat' \neq cat \right\}$, whereas the latter case means the value could be an instance of the concept category cat'.
- *Isa*: the set of subsumption relations on *Con*. $\langle Con, Isa \rangle$ forms the concept hierarchy, where the concept categories in *Con* are the nodes and the subsumption relations in *Isa* are the branches.
- $Asso = \{r : c_1 \rightarrow c_2 \mid c_1 \in Cat_i \cdot ClassS, c_2 \in Cat_j \cdot ClassS \wedge i \neq j, \ 1 \leq i,j \leq n\}$: the set of associations between the concept categories in *Dom*. $\langle Con, Isa, Asso \rangle$ forms a hierarchical concept association graph, in which $\langle Con, Isa \rangle$ is the concept category hierarchy and the associations in *Asso* define the links between concept categories.
- *Cont*: the set of constraints on *Con* and/or *Ass*.
- *Axi*: the set of axioms about the ontology.

4.4 TOP-LEVEL ENVIRONMENT ONTOLOGY

System environment ontology is the shared conceptualization of the system environment as well as the interactions between the systems and their interactive environment. The development of the system environment ontology should follow the ontology development process.

4.4.1 SOFTWARE SYSTEM PROBLEM AND ITS LOCATION

First, we choose three widely used problem analysis methods as the background knowledge for the environment modeling. They are the use cases, the four-variable model, and the problem frames. The following statements express the respective concerns of these methods when conducting the problem analysis.

[E1] The first step in employing use cases to present a business problem is drawing the use case diagrams. The use case notation in such a diagram is composed of **actors**, **use cases**, and **associations**. An actor reflects a role that is normally played by a human (it could be nonhuman in a broader sense) with respect to a system. Actors execute use cases. The link between actors and use cases is shown by an association, which indicates that there is **communication** between the actor and the use case, such as the **sending and receiving of messages** (Fig. 4.7A shows a use case example).

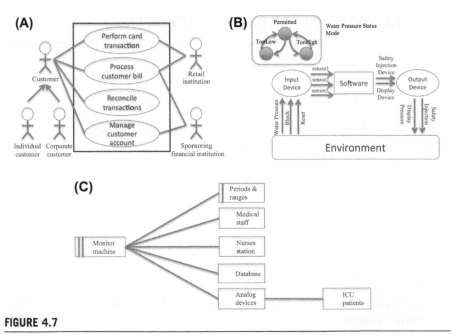

FIGURE 4.7

Samples of the problem location according to different methods. (A) The use case diagram for credit and validation system. (B) Four variable model for safety injection (Heitmeyer, 1996). (C) Context diagram for monitor machine in ICU (Jackson, 2001). *ICU*, intensive care unit.

[E2] The four-variable model describes the required system behavior as a set of mathematical relations on four sets of variables; monitored and controlled variables, and input and output data items (Parnas and Madey, 1995). **A monitored variable represents an environmental quantity that influences system behavior; a controlled variable represents an environmental quantity that the system controls**. Input devices measure the monitored quantities and output devices set the controlled quantities. The variables that the devices read and write are called input and output data items (Fig. 4.7B shows an example of the four-variable model).

[E3] The problem is located in **the world outside the machine** you must build (Jackson, 2001). You fix the location by drawing a problem context diagram. A context diagram structures the world into **the machine domain** and **the problem domain**, and shows **how they are connected**. The machine domain in one context may be a problem domain in another. The context bounds the problem: **the domains are the parts of the world that are relevant** (Fig. 4.7C shows an example of the context diagram in problem frames).

The three samples each analyze locating the problem in the physical world, not in a conceptual space, but by explicitly identifying the actors, the problem domains, and the environmental quantities, as shown in Fig. 4.7. All emphasize grounding the problem analysis in observable physical phenomena. This is helpful to check whether there is a real problem. They also highlight ways to identify the environmental context in which the to-be system will be located and to identify the explicit connections between the environmental entities and the to-be system.

Fig. 4.8 gives a concrete example from a cruise control system to show how to identify the real-world environmental entities as well as the interactions between the to-be system and the environmental entities. It shows that the cruise controller (the system) has four direct interactors and three indirect interactors as its environmental entities. The reason for including the indirect interactors is that the shared phenomena between the to-be system and the direct interactors are caused by the shared phenomena between the direct interactors and the indirect interactors. The causality cannot be ignored.

From these problem context identification heuristics, the following concerns can be inspired by problem analysis:

- the real-world entity: Any of the environmental entities are real-world entities. They are neither concepts nor notations but are physical, concrete, observable/sensible entities.
- the phenomena shared between an environmental entity and the to-be system: These real-world entities will interact with the to-be system. Because they are physical and concrete, the interfaces between them and the to-be system are physical and concrete. The interactions imply that there are physical phenomena shared between the real-world entities and the to-be system.
- the interaction in which an environmental entity is involved with the to-be system: Any interaction is a sharing of some physical phenomena. Any environmental entity is physical, so interactions between the environmental entity and the to-be system are physical.

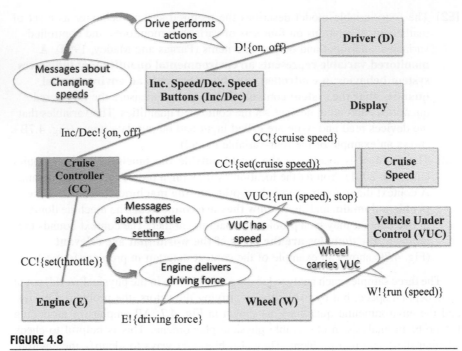

FIGURE 4.8

An example of the environmental entity and interaction identification (diagram notations come from the problem frames).

4.4.2 CONCEPT CATEGORIES AND ASSOCIATIONS OF SYSTEM ENVIRONMENT

These concerns constitute the categories of the concepts for conceptualizing the system environment. Thus, the top-level environment ontology contains mainly the three concept classes: entity, phenomenon, and interaction.

Fig 4.9 shows the backbone of the concept hierarchy of the top-level environment ontology. For the first two concept categories, the assumptions are followed in the problem frame approach (Jackson, 2001) about the system context. We summarize three kinds of "environmental entities": **autonomous**, **symbolic**, and **causal**. They are the abstractions of any kinds of the interactors in software-intensive systems. The phenomena represent the potential interactions of environment entities with the outside. To conceptualize the phenomena further, three categories about the "entity phenomena" are included. The three categories of the phenomena are **value, state**, and **event**.

Another concept category is "interaction": that is, for conceptualizing the interaction or communication between the environment entities and the to-be systems. Inclusion of the concept category is based on the assumption that interactions through the interfaces are a critical bridge to cross the environment and the to-be

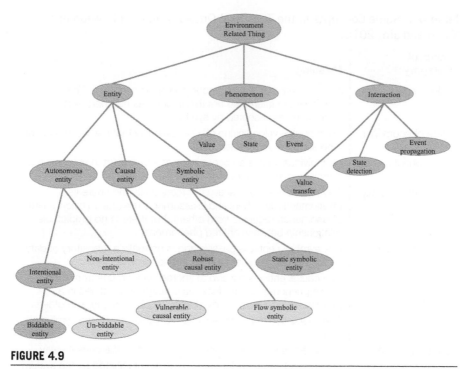

FIGURE 4.9

Backbone of concept hierarchy of top-level environment ontology.

systems, and vice versa. The properties of the interactions become an important concern in modeling system function points.

The meanings of some lower-level concept categories, as well as the associations between these concept categories in top-level environment ontology, are given in Tables 4.1 and 4.2, respectively. Generally, each entity/phenomenon/interaction may have attributes, is formed as:

$$Entity|Phenomenon|Interaction \rightarrow (Attr \rightarrow Value)$$

As shown in Fig. 4.9, top-level environment ontology covers almost all aspects that will be taken into account in environment modeling—based requirements engineering. For example, taking care of the nonintentional entity, the unbiddable entity, the undetermined causal entity, the streaming symbolic entity, etc., may imply the need for some nonfunctionalities such as self-adaptation, security, fault tolerance, and real-timeliness, etc. In Part 4, we will discuss some of these nonfunctional issues in detail. In Part 3, we focus only on function point modeling. Thus, only the three-leaf concepts, i.e., the biddable entity, the robust causal entity, and the static symbolic entity, will be considered.

Finally, a set of axioms can be included with top-level environment ontology to express the top-level ontology developer's will about the consistency and

Table 4.1 Some Concepts in the Top-Level Ontology and Their Meanings (Chen and Jin, 2016)

Concept Category	Meaning
Value phenomenon	An individual that cannot undergo change over time. The values in which we are interested are things such as numbers and characters, represented by symbols.
State phenomenon	An attribute–value pairing of a causal entity that can be true at one time and false at another.
Event phenomenon	An individual that is an occurrence at some point in time, such as atomic and instantaneous.
Autonomous entity	Any biddable entity is active to create itself and share its phenomena with others and is assumed to be able to follow shared phenomenon requests from others, but there is no predictable relationship between shared phenomena.
Symbolic entity	Any symbolic entity is passive and is normally a repository of data. Other entities can share the value phenomena with it.
Causal entity	Any causal entity is passive to shared phenomena from others. Some phenomena can trigger its change on its states in a predictable way followed by sharing its phenomena with others.
Value transfer	The interaction that is for sharing the value of/with the symbolic entity.
State detection	The interaction that is for sharing the state of the causal entity.
Event propagation	The interaction that is for sharing the event initiated by the system or the autonomous entity.

Table 4.2 Associations Among Concept Categories in Top-Level Environment Ontology (Chen and Jin, 2016)

Association	Formation	Meaning
raiseEvent	Autonomous entity → event	An autonomous entity can initiate an event
stateIn	Causal entity → state	A causal entity situates in a state
changeFrom	Causal entity → (state → (event → state))	A causal entity can change from one state to another triggered by an event
raiseEvent	Causal entity → (state → (state → event))	A causal entity can trigger an event when it changes from one state to another
Initiate	Interaction → environment entity	An interaction is initiated by an environment entity
Receive	Interaction → environment entity	An interaction is initiated to an environment entity
Contain	Interaction → phenomenon	An interaction is about a phenomenon

completeness of domain environment ontology as well as application environment ontology. These axioms will be used as constraints to develop domain environment ontology as well as application environment ontology. As examples, we list some axioms. In addition, other axioms can be included to guarantee the completeness and consistency of domain/application environment ontologies:

1. $\forall ent_1, ent_2 : ent_1$ isA $ent_2 \rightarrow \neg(ent_2$ isA $ent_1)$
2. $\forall ent_1, ent_2 : ent_1$ partOf $ent_2 \rightarrow \neg(ent_2$ partOf $ent_1)$
3. $\forall ent \in EntS : symbolic(ent) \rightarrow \exists_1^n attribute(ent, (Attr_i, Value_i))$
4. $\forall ent \in EntS : autonomous(ent) \rightarrow \exists_1^n raiseEvent(ent, Event_i)$
5. $\forall ent \in EntS : causal(ent) \rightarrow \exists stateDiagram(ent, StateDiagram)$
6. $\forall D \in StateDiagramSet : \exists_1 s \in State(D) \wedge startState(s)$
7. $\forall D \in StateDiagramSet : \exists_1^n s \in State(D) \wedge endState(s)$
8. $\forall D \in StateDiagramSet, startStarte(s_1) : \exists_1 endState(s_n) \wedge path(s_1, s_n)$

Among these, the first two guarantee the directed cyclicity of the entity hierarchy. Axioms 3—5 express typical features of the three types of environment entities. Axioms 6—7 specify the state diagram of the causal entities.

4.5 DOMAIN ENVIRONMENT ONTOLOGY

As mentioned in Section 4.1, there could be different kinds of ontologies according to their level of generality, as shown in Fig. 4.2. Apart from top-level environment ontology that describes general concepts, which are independent of a particular domain, there are many domain ontologies as its subontologies. It seems reasonable, at least in theory, to have a unified top-level ontology for large communities of application domains. Domain environment ontologies cover the vocabulary related to a generic domain (such as automobiles or online education) by specializing the terms introduced in the top-level ontology. A domain-dependent ontology provides fine-grained concepts whereas generic ontology provides coarser-grained concepts.

4.5.1 CONCEPTUALIZATION OF ENVIRONMENT ENTITIES

In terms of the top-level environment ontology, the domain environment ontology should consist of a set of environment entities in this particular domain, with phenomena that can be raised by these environment entities. It should also contain all permitted interactions of these environment entities with the to-be systems. The domain environment ontology is important for building the understanding of real-world problems in system development. It is the background knowledge and the context boundary of such problems.

Of course, any particular domain environment ontology can be constructed with the help of domain experts. However, there are already plenty of general domain ontologies ready for use on the Web. For example, Fig. 4.10 depicts the general domain ontology for "*Travel Ticket*." Here, there are five domain entities: person, itinerary, ticket, merchandise, and merchant.

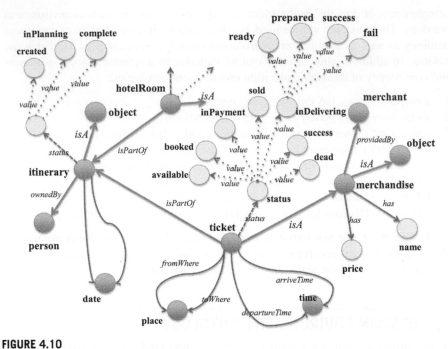

FIGURE 4.10

Fragment of general domain ontology for "budget traveling."

Updated from P. Wang, Z. Jin, L. Liu, G. Cai, Building toward capability specifications of web services based on environment ontology, IEEE Transactions on Knowledge and Data Engineering 20 (4) (2008) 547–561.

In terms of top-level environment ontology, the domain entities are grouped into three categories. For this fragment of ontology, "*person*" and "*merchant*" should be autonomous entities, and "*ticket*," "*merchandise*," and "*itinerary*" should be treated as causal entities.

From the explanations of the three kinds of entities, the conceptualization of the symbolic entity and the autonomous entity are almost similar to the ordinary ontology; in addition, the interpretations of the concepts and the associations have special meaning in system modeling. Whereas the conceptualization of the causal entity is special, that is, apart from the descriptive aspect like other concepts, the causal entity is of causality, which means that the causal entity can be of different states. To capture the causality of causal environment entities, it is assumed that the attributes of a causal environment entity are classified into two groups (Wang et al., 2008):

- characteristic attributes (and their values that describe the states of this entity)
- noncharacteristic attributes. That is, for any entity $e \in Ent$, its characteristic attributes $CAtts(e) \subseteq Atts(e)$ define the set of states of e as:

$$States(e) = \{^{\prime}\langle \alpha_i, v_j \rangle | \alpha_i \in CAtts(e), \ v_j \in vale(a_i)\}$$

This shows that the status of an environment entity is a pair of characteristic attributes of this environment entity and a certain value within its finite value range. For example, in the domain of a travel agency, the environment entity *"ticket"* can be "available," "booked," "sold" and "used" as its "status." Thus, its "status" is a characteristic attribute that has four alternative values.

The autonomous entities and the symbolic entities are not modeled by an internal causal structure. Single-state machines are used as their models to unify the representations of all environment entities. That means any autonomous entity can do anything that has been requested but always stay in its single state. This is also case for the symbolic entity and it will stay in the same state after receiving or storing new data or sending out the available data. Hence, with the general domain ontology, the only burden of constructing the domain environment ontology is building the state machines of the causal entities. To support the different conceptualization granularities, we use the hierarchical state machine. In the following section, we will present how to construct the hierarchical state machines for causal environment entities.

4.5.2 FORMALIZATION OF ENVIRONMENT ENTITY

First, the basic state machine (BSM) is defined (Wang et al., 2008) to formalize the environment entity. Let $e \in Ent$ be an environment entity and $\alpha \in CAtts(e)$ a characteristic attribute of e.

A BSM of e is:

$$\langle S, \ \Sigma, \ \delta, \ \lambda, \ q_0, \ F \rangle$$

in which:

- $S = \left\{ \langle \alpha, v_j \rangle | v_j \in value(\alpha) \right\} \subseteq States(e)$ is a finite set of states of e
- $\Sigma = \Sigma^{in} \cup \Sigma^{out}$. Σ^{in} is the set of input symbols and Σ^{out} is the set of output symbols
- $\delta : S \times \Sigma^{in} \to S$ is the state transition function
- $\lambda : S \to \Sigma^{out}$ is the output function
- $q_0 \in S$ is the initial state
- $F \subseteq S$ is the set of final states

Then, hierarchy is added to the BSM. $\ll$ is a tree-like partial order relation with a topmost point. This relation defines the hierarchy on the states within $States(e)$ $(x \ll y)$ means that x is a descendant of y $(x < y)$, or x and y are equal $(x = y)$. "Tree-like" means that $\ll$ has the property: $\neg(a \ll b \lor b \ll a) \Rightarrow \neg\exists x$: $(x \ll a \land x \ll b)$. If the state x is a descendant of y $(x \prec y)$ and there is no state z such that $x \prec z \prec y$, the state x is a "child" of y (x child y).

According to $\ll$ on $States(e)$, the subdivision from a state s of s to a BSM N of e can be defined. If $s \notin S(N)$, for all $s' \in S(N)$ ($S(N)$ denotes the set of states in BSM N), such that s' *child* s, state s is a superstate of BSM N (or BSM N has a superstate s), and $\langle s, N \rangle$ is a **subdivision**. The initial state λ_0 in sub-BSM N is called the **default**

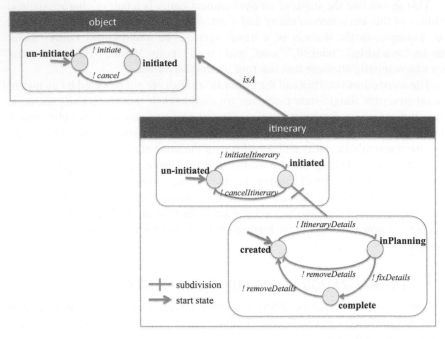

FIGURE 4.11

Hierarchical automation for environment entity "itinerary."

child of superstate *s*. Because ≪ is tree-like, the sub-BSM has no more than one superstate. Fig. 4.11 shows an example of the hierarchical automaton for causal entity "*itinerary*."

4.5.3 DEPENDENCY BETWEEN ENVIRONMENT ENTITIES

Although the environment entities are independent individuals, they should be able to be related with each other to achieve some business requirements. For example, the success for hotel room booking depends on whether the payment can be guaranteed by the bank if the customer uses a credit card. Here, the hotel room, credit card, and even the bank are independent individuals, but they need to be able to be coordinated with some of their own phenomena to fulfil the booking requirements. Fulfilling such a coordination is the to-be-solved problem of the booking system so that the business process can be achieved. That means that such dependencies are supported by the to-be system via interactions between the system and the environment entities according to the environment modeling—based approach.

The idea of capturing the dependency relationship is inspired by the strategical dependency in the I* approach (Yu, 2010). There, dependency exists between intentional actors. Here, we consider the environment entities as actors and then there are dependencies between environment entities. The difference is that in an environment modeling—based approach, we assume that the dependency relationships between environment entities are desired properties for achieving some business purpose, and then guaranteeing the dependency relationships belonging to the problem needing to be solved by the to-be system.

The other difference is the dependum. Any dependum between two environment entities is a phenomenon that is controlled or shared by some environment entities, i.e.,

$$e_1 \cdot phe_1 \to e_2 \cdot phe_2$$

This means that phenomenon phe_2 of e_2 depends on phenomenon phe_1 of e_1 and is realized by two interactions in which the to-be system will be involved:

$$(e_1 \cdot phe_1 \Rightarrow s) \& (s \Rightarrow e_2 \cdot phe_2)$$

The to-be system will guarantee "if $e_1 \cdot phe_1$ occurs, $e_2 \cdot phe_2$ will occur.

Thus, apart from conceptualizing the environment entities, for a software system, locating the problem also asks to identify what relationships between environment entities should be enabled by the system in terms of the business requirements. However, at the stage of the domain environment development, only the dependency relationship can be determined as the common knowledge of this domain.

The formulization of such a dependency relationship can be defined as follows, and then the hierarchical state machines of the environment entities and their dependency relationships constitute a tree-like hierarchical state machine (THSM) (Wang et al., 2008).

Precisely, let $e \in Ent$ be an environment entity, $BSM(e) = \{N_1, \ldots, N_n\}$ ($n \geq 1$) be the set of BSMs of e, and D be the set of subdivisions. A THSM of e is defined as:

$$\langle BSM(e),\ D \rangle$$

in which:

- There is one and only one special BSM in $BSM(e)$ that is called the "object" (denoted by $N(obj) \in BSM(e)$), which is the root of the THSM.
- Other BSMs are partitioned into $m > 0$ disjoint sets $\{B_1, \ldots, B_m\}$, in which each can also constitute a THSM $hsm_i = \langle B_i, D_i \rangle$, $D_i \subseteq D$, $i \in [1, m]$. If $N_{obj}^{B_i} \in B_i$ is the root of hsm_i, there exists $s \in S(N_{obj})$, so that $\left\langle s, N_{obj}^{B_i} \right\rangle \in D$. hsm_i is also called a sub-THSM of s.

The environment ontology in a particular domain is defined as a 6-tuple:

$$\langle Ent, Rel, rel, H, hsm, Dep \rangle$$

in which:

- *Ent* is a set of environment entities in a current domain. An environment entity that can be abstract or concrete is described as $\langle id, Atts, Rans, value \rangle$, in which *id* is the name, $Atts = \{\alpha_1, \ldots, \alpha_n\}$ is a set of attributes, $Rans = \{v_1, \ldots, v_m\}$ is a set of values, and *value*: $Atts \to 2^{Rans}$ is a function mapping attributes to value ranges

- *Rel* is a set of relations, e.g., "is-a," "part-of," etc.
- *r: Rel* → *Ent* × *Ent* is a function that relates environment entities
- *H* is a set of THSMs, each of which has a pair of finite sets of phenomena as its input and output symbols
- *h: Ent* ↔ *H* is a bijective function. For each environment entity *e* ∈ *Ent*, there is one and only one *hsm* ∈ *H*, so that *h(e)* = *hsm*. *hsm* represents the causality of *e* in this domain
- *Dep* is a set of entity phenomena pairs, each of which defines a desired dependency between two phenomena of the environment entities. These relationships in fact represent the business assumptions in a particular domain. There are four kinds of dependences:

  - Relationship represents that an entity instance is created when another entity instance initiates an event:

  $$ins(e_1) \uparrow event(eve) \rightarrow ins(e) \uparrow State = initialState$$

  - Relationship represents that an entity instance is eliminated when another entity instance initiates an event:

  $$ins(e_1) \uparrow event(eve) \rightarrow ins(e) \uparrow State = endState$$

  - Relationship represents that an entity instance is triggered to change its state along its hierarchical state machine when another entity instance initiates an event:

  $$ins(e_1) \uparrow event(eve) \rightarrow ins(e) \uparrow tran(s_1 \rightarrow s_2)$$

  - Relationship represents that an entity instance receives a value phenomenon that depends on shared value phenomena from other entities:

  $$ins(e_1) \uparrow value(val) \rightarrow ins(e) \downarrow f(val)$$

Fig. 4.12 shows a partial domain environment ontology containing two causal entities, "ticket" and "credit card," and one biddable entity, "courier." There are two sets of dependencies: one is for the dependencies between "ticket" and "creditCard" and the other one is for the dependencies between "ticket" and "courier."

Here, for example, the dependencies between "ticket" and "creditCard" contain:

$$ins(ticket) \cdot state = inPayment \Rightarrow \frac{ins(creditCard)}{ins(ticket)} \cdot state = initiated$$

$$\frac{ins(creditCard)}{ins(ticket)} \uparrow !failToBeCharged \Rightarrow ins(ticket) \downarrow creditCardFail$$

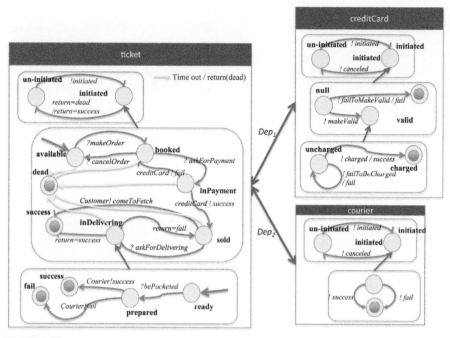

FIGURE 4.12

Partial travel domain environment ontology.

Updated from P. Wang, Z. Jin, L. Liu, G. Cai, Building toward capability specifications of web services based on environment ontology, IEEE Transactions on Knowledge and Data Engineering 20 (4) (2008) 547–561.

$$\frac{ins(creditCard)}{ins(ticket)} \uparrow !BeingCharged \Rightarrow ins(ticket) \downarrow creditCardSuccess$$

The dependencies between "ticket" and "courier" contain:

$$ins(ticket) \cdot state = prepared \Rightarrow \frac{ins(courier)}{ins(ticket)} \cdot state = initiated$$

$$\frac{ins(courier)}{ins(ticket)} \uparrow !fail \Rightarrow ins(ticket) \downarrow courierFail$$

$$\frac{ins(courier)}{ins(ticket)} \uparrow !success \Rightarrow ins(ticket) \downarrow courierSuccess$$

Domain Environment Ontology Construction

5

CHAPTER OUTLINE

This chapter is devoted to presenting the techniques for building domain environment ontologies, i.e., application domain-dependent ontologies, for the purpose of specifying environment modeling based system capabilities.

5.1 DOMAIN ENVIRONMENT MODELING VIA KNOWLEDGE ENGINEERING

Domain environment ontologies are used to capture and specify domain knowledge. Like any other domain knowledge base, domain environment ontologies can be developed manually with the help of domain experts by following knowledge specification regulations. This relates to another research field, i.e., knowledge engineering, referring to all technical, scientific, and social aspects involved in building, maintaining, and using knowledge-based systems. Many knowledge engineering methodologies can be used to help domain experts extract and specify domain knowledge and build the domain knowledge base.

In fact, the goal of knowledge engineering is similar to that of software engineering, i.e., turning the process of constructing knowledge-based systems from an art into an engineering discipline. This requires an analysis of the building and maintenance process itself and the development of appropriate methods, languages, and tools specialized in developing knowledge-based systems.

Environment Modeling-Based Requirements Engineering for Software Intensive Systems
http://dx.doi.org/10.1016/B978-0-12-801954-2.00005-4

Since the 1980s, knowledge engineering has undertaken a paradigm shift from the so-called transfer approach to the so-called modeling approach. In the "knowledge engineering as a transfer process" paradigm, the transformation of problem-solving expertise from a knowledge source to a program is the heart of the process of knowledge-based system development.

This transfer approach was based on the assumption that knowledge required by the knowledge-based system already exists and simply has to be collected and implemented. Most often, the required knowledge was obtained by interviewing domain experts about how they solved specific tasks. With this paradigm, the development of a knowledge-based system has been seen as a transfer process of human knowledge into an implemented knowledge base. This knowledge was implemented so that some kind of production rules were executed by an associated rule interpreter.

However, the transfer approach was feasible only for the development of small prototypical systems; it failed to produce large, reliable, and maintainable knowledge bases. Furthermore, it was recognized that the assumption of the transfer approach, i.e., knowledge acquisition, the collection of already existing knowledge elements, was wrong in some cases because of the important role of tacit knowledge in an expert's problem-solving capabilities.

These deficiencies resulted in a paradigm shift from the transfer approach to the modeling approach, i.e., knowledge engineering as a modeling process. Since then, the overall consensus has been that the process of building a knowledge-based system may be seen as a modeling activity. That means that the development of a knowledge-based system is achieved by building a conceptual model with the aim of realizing problem-solving capabilities comparable to domain experts. It is not intended to create a cognitive-adequate model, i.e., to simulate humans' cognitive processes in general, but to create a model that offers similar results in problem solving in the area of concern. Although the expert may consciously articulate some part of his or her knowledge, he or she will not be aware of a significant part of this knowledge, because it will be hidden within his or her skills. This knowledge is not directly accessible; it has to be built up and structured during the knowledge-acquisition phase. Therefore, this knowledge-acquisition process is no longer seen as a transfer of knowledge into an appropriate computer representation, but rather as a model construction process with the guidance of some metamodel.

The construction of domain environment ontology follows the knowledge-modeling paradigm. The acquisition of knowledge is treated as model construction by following the structure of top-level environment ontology. That is, top-level environment ontology serves as the metamodel for domain environment ontology.

Knowledge modeling of the domain environment ontology refers to a three-layer conceptual structure (Jin, 2006), as illustrated in Fig. 5.1. First, as shown in Fig 5.1A, the concepts of the top-level environment ontology (i.e., the filled rectangles) constitute the upper-most layer of the concept category hierarchy. These concept categories are metacategories. All domain concept categories (i.e., the hollow rectangles) are subtypes of these metacategories. At the bottom level, the application concept categories (i.e., the filled triangles) are instances of the domain concept categories.

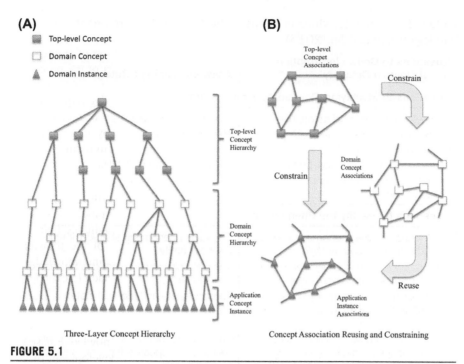

FIGURE 5.1

Three-layer environment ontologies. (A) Three-layer concept hierarchy. (B) Concept association reusing and constraining (Jin, 2006).

Second, the associations in the top-level environment ontology become the description specification for specifying the domain concept categories as well as application concept categories, as shown in Fig 5.1B. The concept categories and their associations in the top-level environment ontology constitute the metamodel of the domain environment model as well as the application environment model.

Thus, there are at least two aspects to top-level environment ontology. First, it is a framework that can be used to steer domain experts and application stakeholders to provide them with knowledge about the domain as well as the application. With an appropriate eliciting tool, the framework helps to generate queries automatically to form questionnaires. By following these queries, domain experts and application stakeholders can be guided to supply relevant information.

On the other hand, top-level environment ontology standardizes the concept categories relevant to the domain and application ontologies. Standard definitions prevent misunderstanding. These standardized concept categories help normalize stakeholders' descriptions so that descriptions from different stakeholders can easily be integrated.

For example, in terms of top-level environment ontology, a questionnaire can be designed to acquire the domain environment ontology as well as the application environment ontologies. Table 5.1 gives examples of some questions. The answers can be understood by their associated concept categories.

Table 5.1 Sample Questions in Terms of the Top-Level Environment Ontology (Chen and Jin, 2016)

Questions to Collect Information About Domain Ontology	Answers' Concept Category
Questions to Identifying Domain/Application Entities	
Who will be the potential actors/users?	The autonomous entities
Which types of physical devices/equipment can be used?	The causal entities
Which external systems can be involved?	The causal/symbolic entities
Are there any data representations that need to be involved?	The symbolic entities
Questions to Identify the Phenomena	
What kinds of value phenomena can be shared with a symbolic entity?	The value phenomena shared with the symbolic entity
For a particular causal entity, can it be in different states? Please name these states.	The state phenomena that can be shared with others
For a causal entity with multiple states, which is its start state and which are its final states?	The start state and the final states
For a causal entity with multiple states, how does it change among its states? Which type of event phenomenon can be shared with others when it makes the changes?	The state transitions of the causal entity as well as the respective trigger events and caused events
Which event phenomena and/or value phenomena can be shared by an autonomous entity?	The event phenomena or the value phenomena shared by the autonomous entity

We take "*car parking control domain*" as an example. In terms of top-level environment ontology, the domain entities should be identified first. In the car parking control domain, the following are some environment entities:

- Car: a causal entity that can be in the state of "*in a parking place*" or "*not in a parking place*"
- Driver: an autonomous entity who can drive a car into or out of a parking place
- Parking Plan: a symbolic entity for recording the occupation state of the parking places
- Display panel: a causal entity for displaying the occupation state of the parking area
- Entry Machine: a causal entity for allowing a car to enter the parking area
- Exit Machine: a causal entity for authorizing a car to go out of the parking area
- Pay Machine: a causal entity for allowing the car driver to pay for parking

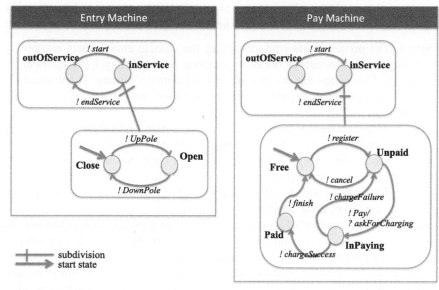

FIGURE 5.2

Hierarchical automata for representing the causality of *Entry Machine* and *Pay Machine*.

- Parking Database: a symbolic entity recording the log of the use of the parking places including registered car information, entry time, exit time, amount of money paid, etc.

Between the two symbolic entities, *Parking Plan* consists of <parking space, location, occupied state> recording whether a *parking space* (in *location*) is "*Occupied*" or "*Available*," whereas *Parking Database* is a table in which each record contains these attributes and their corresponding values.

For each of the five causal entities, a hierarchical automaton is included to characterize their causality. For example, Fig. 5.2A and B show two hierarchical automata of *Entry Machine* and *Pay Machine*, respectively. They represent the behaviors and the causality of *Entry Machine* and *Pay Machine*. For autonomous entity *Driver*, one of its attributes is the set of events that it will share with others, including driving the car, getting a ticket, inserting the ticket, and paying the fee.

5.2 DOMAIN ENVIRONMENT ONTOLOGY CONSTRUCTION

Manual construction of the domain environment ontology from scratch is not easy. It should follow a whole process of knowledge engineering and work closely with domain experts. The construction process is like the process for developing the class hierarchy and should have the guidance of the top-level environment ontology, as shown in Fig. 4.9. The process contains the following steps:

- Step 1. The process starts with identifying the domain environment entities by creating the subconcepts of the entity concepts in the top-level environment ontology. This means that we first identify the domain entities. The domain entities are those that are potential interactors/actors with the to-be systems in this domain.
- Step 2. The identified domain entities are categorized into three types: causal entities, symbolic entities, and autonomous entities. These domain entities are assigned to be the subtype concept categories of the corresponding entity concept category in the top-level environment ontology, as shown in Fig. 5.1A.
- Step 3. For each identified entity concept category, determine its attributes and the value ranges of these attributes.
- Step 4. For each identified autonomous entity concept category, determine its sharable/shared event phenomena and value phenomena, in which a sharable event/value phenomenon is one that the autonomous entity can share with others and a shared event/value phenomenon is one that the autonomous entity would like others to share. These are the sharable/shared event/value phenomena of this autonomous entity concept category.
- Step 5. For each identified symbolic entity concept category, determine the sharable/shared value phenomena. These are the sharable/shared value phenomena of this symbolic entity concept category.
- Step 6. For each identified causal entity concept category, decide its characteristic attributes and define its causality by defining the state transition diagram (or the hierarchical state transition diagram) that captures the state of the causal entity and the state transitions among states to represent the causality of the entity. These states are the sharable state phenomena of this causal entity concept category.
- Step 7. For each identified causal entity concept category and its state transition diagram, collect the sharable/shared event/value phenomena from the transitions of its state diagram. These are the sharable/shared event/value phenomena of this causal entity concept category.
- Step 8. Each sharable/shared phenomenon constitutes a partial interaction with one of the interaction types, i.e., the event propagation, the state detection, or the value transference, as shown in Fig. 4.9, and it becomes the parameters of the associations of an interaction, i.e., "initiate," "receive," and "contain," as shown in Table 4.2.

There might be some axioms defined with top-level environment ontology. These axioms are constraints that should be followed by the domain environment ontology. If there are some violations, the developers are asked to check and correct the concept specification and revise the whole specification.

5.3 AUTOMATIC DOMAIN ENVIRONMENT ONTOLOGY CONSTRUCTION

As mentioned, it is time-consuming to develop a domain environment ontology manually. Currently, there are many general domain ontologies available on the Web. Their general ontological structure includes concept declarations and the relations among these concepts. These domain ontologies based on the general ontological structure are a good start for a domain environment ontology construction.

However, to develop domain environment ontologies, we have to extend the general ontological structure in the following aspects. First, we extend the general ontological structure with state diagrams to include those specifying changeable environment entities with state transitions. Second, the communicating hierarchical state machine (HSM) (Alur, 1999) is used to support the different conceptualization granularities to satisfy the demands of different abstraction levels.

Hence, the construction of domain environment ontologies can be much easier because they can be built semiautomatically from existing general domain ontologies under the guidance of domain experts. Concretely, after identifying of the necessary environment entities, the static description of these entities can be extracted from the available general domain ontologies, as can the relations among the domain concepts. The extra effort is in deriving the state diagrams for causal environment entities. We consider the following relations among environment entities to be derived from the general domain ontology to construct the tree-based hierarchical state machine (THSM) of environment entities.

- These relations represent the characteristics of concepts (called "characteristic relation").
  For example, Fig. 5.3 is a fragment of general domain ontology in an educational domain. **ExploratoryTutorial** is an environment entity, and relation **SituatedIn** associated with it is a characteristic relation.
  The values of this relationship are used to construct the domain THSM of **ExploratoryTutorial**.
- These relations are the components or inheritance relationships between concepts.
  For example, **isA** is an inheritance relation from **ExploratoryTutorial** to **EducationCourse**.

Without a loss of generality, we assume that $O = \{C, R, rel\}$ is an existing general domain ontology in which C is a set of concepts, R is a set of relations, and rel: $R \rightarrow C \times C$ is a function of the relations. We identify the environment entities Ent from the concepts C ($Ent \subseteq C$) and the characteristic attributes of those causal environment entities from the relations in R. After the causal environment entities and their characteristic attributes are identified, the procedure of constructing the domain THSM of each environment entity can be executed. For the sake of unity, the symbolic environment entities and autonomous environment entities are assumed to be associated with one-state automata.

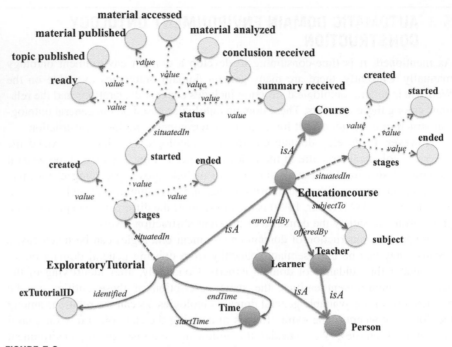

FIGURE 5.3

Fragment of general domain ontology in educational domain.

Updated from P. Wang, Z. Jin, L. Liu, G. Cai, Building toward capability specifications of web services based on environment ontology, IEEE Transactions on Knowledge and Data Engineering 20 (4) (2008) 547–561.

We first construct the basic state machine (BSM) of each environment entities. The BSM construction algorithm (Wang et al., 2008) is given next.

ALGORITHM 5.1. CONSTRUCTING BASIC STATE MACHINES

REQUIRE O is a general domain ontology and e is a concept in O, which is identified to be a causal environment entity (denoted as $e \in Ent$)

    ENSURE set of BSMs of e, i.e., $BSM(e)$

    BEGIN

      $BSM(e) = \phi$; \\ Initialization

      $CAtts(e)$ is the set of characteristic attributes of e which are derived from O;

      FORALL $\alpha \in CAtts(e)$

        Get a value range $value(\alpha)$;

        Create $S = \{\langle \alpha, v_j \rangle | v_j \in value(\alpha)\}$;

        Create a state transition function δ, such that for states s, $s' \in S$ and $m \in \Sigma^{in}$,

          $\delta(s,m) = s'$ is an allowable state transition;

        Create an output function λ, such that for state $s \in S$, and $m' \in \Sigma^{out}$, $\lambda(s) = m'$

          is an output symbol along the state transition;

        Set an initial state $q_0 \in S$;
        Set a set of final states $F \subseteq S$;
        Set $N = \{S, \Sigma, \delta, \lambda, q_0, F\}$ is a BSM of e
        $BSM(e) = BSM(e) \cup N$;
    ENDFOR
  END
RETURN $BSM(e)$

After the BSMs of environment entities are constructed, we shift our focus to the component relationship and the inheritance relationship between environment entities. If there is an inheritance relationship from one environment entity $e_1 \in Ent$ to another environment entity $e_2 \in Ent$, it means that e_1 inherits the attributes from e_2. For example, the environment entity **Education Course** has three attributes {**offeredBy**, **enrolledBy**, and **subjectTo**}. Therefore, the environment entity **ExploratoryTutorial**, which has an inheritance relationship to **EducationCourse**, also has these three attributes plus its own attributes {**identified**, **startTime, end-Time,** and **situatedIn**}. Here, **situatedIn** needs to be inherited and overridden.

During the procedure of constructing the THSM of the child entities, the BSMs and the subdivisions in the HTSMs of the parent entity will be inherited. Similarly, if there is a component relation from e_2 to e_1, e_1 owns attributes of e_2 and the identifiers of these attributes are added to the identifier of e_2 as a prefix.

Algorithm 5.2 (Wang et al., 2008) constructs the THSM of an environment entity $e \in Ent$ in terms of the inheritance relation. Let $e_1, \ldots, e_n \in Ent$ be n environment entities. The domain HSMs of $e_1, \ldots, e_n$ have been constructed, and e has the inheritance relationship to $e_1, \ldots, e_n$. The idea is that e inherits characteristic attributes of $e_1, \ldots, e_n$, because e inherits $e_1, \ldots, e_n$. Therefore, the domain THSMs $(hsm(e_1), \ldots, hsm(e_n))$ are inherited during the construction of $hsm(e)$. The operation semantics of overridden in the algorithm are to create inheritance threads from the BSMs of e to its inherited BSMs from $e_1, \ldots, e_n$.

ALGORITHM 5.2. CONSTRUCTING DOMAIN TREE-BASED HIERARCHICAL STATE MACHINE IN TERMS OF THE INHERITANCE RELATIONSHIP

REQUIRE Domain THSMs $hsm(e_1), \ldots, hsm(e_n)$ and e has the inheritance relationship to $e_1, \ldots, e_n$
  ENSURE $hsm(e) = \{BSM(e), D_e\}$
  BEGIN
    $BSM(e) = \phi$;
    $D_e = \phi$; \\ Initialization
    $BSM(own) = ConstructingBSMs(e, O)$; \\ Creating BSMs of e via Algorithm 5.1
    $BSM(e) = BSM(own)$;
    FORALL $e' \in \{e_1, \ldots, e_n\}$
      $hsm(e') = \{BSM(e), D_{e'}\}$ is the domain THSM of e';

$BSM(e) = BSM(e) \cup BSM(e')$;

$D_e = D_e \cup D_{e'}$; \\ Inheriting domain THSMs of $e_1,\ldots, e_n$

ENDFOR

FORALL $N_i \in BSM(own)$

    WHILE $\exists N_j \in BSM(e) - BSM(own)$, N_i, N_j are constructed in terms of the same characteristic attribute

        Overridden(N_i, N_j);

    ENDWHILE

    IF $\exists s$ is a state in $BSM(e)$, $\langle s, N_i \rangle$ is a subdivision

      $D_e = D_e \cup \{\langle s, N_i \rangle\}$; \\Adding a subdivision

    ENDIF

ENDFOR

RETURN $hsm(e)$

END

Algorithm 5.3 (Wang et al., 2008) constructs the THSM of an environment entity $e \in Ent$ in terms of the component relationship. Let $e_1,\ldots, e_n \in Ent$ be an environment entity. The domain THSMs of $e_1,\ldots, e_n$ have been constructed, and $e_1,\ldots, e_n$ have the component relationship to e. The algorithm is similar to Algorithm 5.2. The domain THSMs ($hsm(e_1),\ldots hsm(e_n)$) are included during the construction of $hsm(e)$ except that it does not need to deal with the problem of overloading and derivation. During the procedure, the root BSMs that are constructed in terms of the characteristic attribute inherited from "*object*" and $e_1,\ldots, e_n$ are combined.

ALGORITHM 5.3. CONSTRUCTING DOMAIN TREE-BASED HIERARCHICAL STATE MACHINE IN TERMS OF THE COMPONENT RELATIONSHIP

REQUIRE Domain THSMs $hsm(e_1),\ldots, hsm(e_n)$ and $e_1,\ldots, e_n$ have the component relationship to e

    ENSURE $hsm(e) = \{BSM_e, D_e\}$

    BEGIN

      $BSM(e) = \phi$;

      $D_e = \phi$; \\Initialization

      $BSM(own) = ConstructingBSMs(e, O)$; \\Creating BSMs of e via Algorithm 5.1

      $BSM(e) = BSM(own)$;

      FORALL $e' \in \{e_1,\ldots, e_n\}$

        $hsm(e') = \{BSM_{e'}, D_{e'}\}$ is the domain THSM of e';

        $BSM(e) = BSM(e) \cup BSM(e')$;

        $D_e = D_e \cup D_{e'}$; \\Including domain THSMs of $e_1,\ldots, e_n$

      ENDFOR

      FORALL $N_i \in BSM(own)$

        WHILE $\exists N_j \in BSM(e) - BSM(own)$, N_i, N_j are constructed in terms of characteristic attributes inherited from "object"

> **Combine**(N_i, N_j);
> ENDWHILE
> IF ∃s *is a state in BSM(e),* ⟨s, N_i⟩ *is a subdivision*
> $D_e = D_e \cup \{⟨s, N_i⟩\}$; \\Adding a subdivision
> ENDIF
> ENDFOR
> RETURN *hsm(e)*
> END

Fig. 5.4 shows a fragment of environment ontology in an online education domain. In this figure, **Teacher**, **Learner**, **Study Materials**, **Education Course**, and **Exploratory Tutorial** are the environment entities. There are inheritance relationships among them: **Exploratory Tutorials** is a kind of **Education Course**. The dependency relationships among them are represented by the phenomena of the same names. The potential functionalities implied by the environment ontology corresponding to different study paths to the final state contain:

- self-education exploratory course, in which a learner can download the study materials
- exploratory course with supervised analysis, in which a learner can obtain the supervision for study analysis

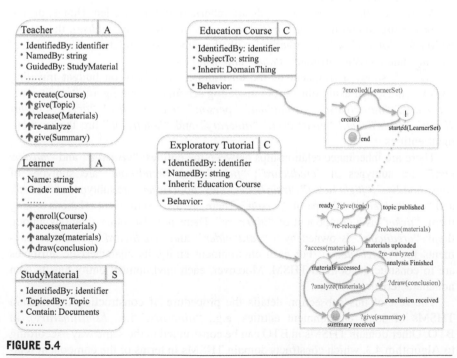

FIGURE 5.4

Fragment of online education domain environment ontology (Wang et al., 2008).

- exploratory course with supervised analysis and evaluation, in which a learner can obtain supervision for study analysis and result evaluation
- fully supervised exploratory course, in which a learner can obtain supervision for study analysis, result evaluation, and advice for further study

5.4 ANOTHER EXAMPLE OF DOMAIN ENVIRONMENT ONTOLOGY

Another example concerns the construction of the *"Budget Traveling"* domain environment ontology. In Chapter 4, we presented the fragment of the *"Budget Traveling"* ontology in Fig. 4.10. The environment entity *"itinerary"* has a characteristic attribute *"status"* with three potential values {*created, inPlanning, complete*}, and two component entities. The environment entity *"ticket,"* which has an inheritance relationship (i.e., *"isA"*) to *"merchandise,"* has its own characteristic attribute *"status"* with seven potential values {*available, booked, inPayment, sold, inDelivering, success, dead*}. Between them, *"inDelivering"* has further potential values {*ready, prepared, success, fail*}. The environment entity *"merchandise"* is an object. Thus, both *"ticket"* and *"merchandise"* inherit the characteristic attributes *"status"* of *"object"* with two alternative values: *"uninstantiated"* and *"instantiated."*

Therefore, attribute *"status"* needs are inherited and overridden. Hence, during the procedure of constructing *hsm(ticket)* as well as *hsm(merchandise)*, the status' BSMs for *"object"* will be inherited with the subdivision relation. Then *"ticket"* has the characteristic attribute *"status"* and *hsm(ticket)*.

Fig. 5.5 shows a fragment of the environment ontology on budget traveling (BTO) represented using object-role modeling schema. In this figure, *"creditcard," "visacard," "mastercard," "cardholder," "person," "merchandise," "ticket," "flightTicket," "trainTicket," "boatTicket," "itinerary"* and *"hotelroom"* are the environment entities.

There are inheritance relationships between the entities: *"visacard"* and *"mastercard"* are subtypes of *"creditcard"*; *"ticket"* and *"hotelroom"* are subtypes of *"merchandise"*; *"flightTicket," "trainTicket,"* and *"boatTicket"* are subtypes of *"ticket"*; and *"cardholder"* is subtype of *"person."* There are also component relations among them: *"ticket"* is a component of *"itinerary."* There are also other relations among them: *"creditcard"* is owned by a *"cardholder"*; and *"creditcard"* guarantees payments for *"merchandise."* For each environment entity, its characteristic attributes are to construct its domain THSM. Moreover, each environment entity has its own noncharacteristic attributes.

The rest of this subsection details the procedure of constructing the domain THSMs of some environment entities, e.g., *"itinerary,"* i.e., *hsm(itinerary)*, in BTO. Other domain THSMs in BTO can be constructed in the same way. According to Algorithm 4.3, which constructs domain THSMs in terms of the component relation, the precondition of constructing *hsm(itinerary)* is that *hsm(ticket)* has been

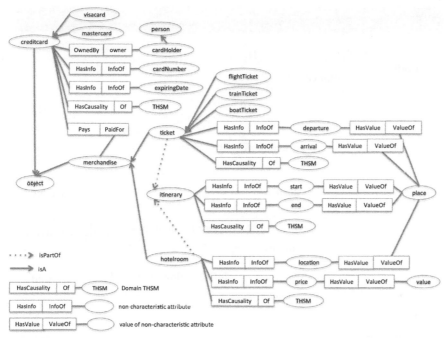

FIGURE 5.5

Budget traveling environment ontology (Wang et al., 2008). *THSM*, tree-based hierarchical state machine.

constructed. For "*ticket*," the construction of its domain THSM under the guidance of domain experts is given as:

Construction of hsm(ticket)

Step 1. (Identifying the characteristic attributes) Seven relationships are associated with "*ticket*" in Fig. 4.10. Among them, "*status*" is a characteristic relationship, i.e., it is a characteristic attribute of "ticket."

Step 2. (Constructing BSMs) Extract value ranges of "*status*" respectively: {*available, booked, inPayment, sold, inDelivering, success, dead*}. Among them, "*inDelivering*" can have four further options: {*ready, prepared, success, fail*}. According to Algorithm 4.1, BSMs N_1, N_2, N_3 are constructed from these characteristic attributes and their values, in which N_1 is a BSM inherited from the root entity "*object*."

Using the same method, BSMs for "*hotelroom*" can be constructed.

Step 3. (Constructing the subdivisions)

"*instantiated*" is the super-state of N_2 and "*inDelivering*" is the superstate of N_3.

$$\langle instantantiated, \ N_2 \rangle, \langle inDelivering, N_3 \rangle \in D_{ticket}.$$

Consequently,

$$hsm(ticket) = \{\{N_1, \ N_2, \ N_3\}, \ D_{ticket}\}$$

which is constructed as shown in Fig. 5.6.

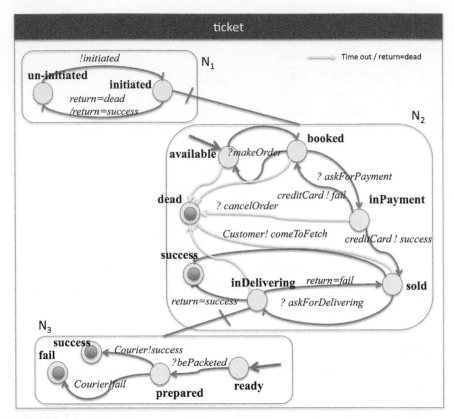

FIGURE 5.6

The domain tree-based hierarchical state machine *hsm(ticket)*.

Updated from P. Wang, Z. Jin, L. Liu, G. Cai, Building toward capability specifications of web services based on environment ontology, IEEE Transactions on Knowledge and Data Engineering 20 (4) (2008) 547–561.

Construction of hsm(itinerary):

Step 1. (Identifying the characteristic attributes) Seven relationships are associated with "*itinerary*" in Fig. 4.10. Among them, "*status*" is a characteristic relationship, i.e., it is a characteristic attribute of "*itinerary*". Moreover, "*itinerary*" is a subtype of "*object*" and has two component relationships to "*ticket*" and "*hotelroom.*"

Step 2. (Constructing BSMs) Extract value ranges of this characteristic attribute. By inheritance, it has: {*uninstantiated, instantiated*}. From the alternative values of the characteristic attribute "*status*," it has: {*created, inPlanning, complete*}. According to Algorithm 4.1, BSMs N_4 and N_5 are constructed from the characteristic attribute and its values.

Step 3. (Including the domain THSM *hsm(ticket)* and *hsm(hotelroom)*) Because "*itinerary*" has component relations to "*ticket*" and "*hotelroom*," according to Algorithm 4.3, the BSMs N_1, N_2, N_3 of "*ticket*" as well as the BSMs of "*hotelroom*" and the subdivisions D_{ticket} and $D_{hotelroom}$ are included in *hsm(itinerary)* as subautomata of "*inPlanning.*"

Step 4. (Constructing the subdivisions):

- "*initiated*" is the superstate of N_4:

$$\langle instantiate,\ N_4 \rangle \in D_{itinerary}$$

- "*inPlanning*" is the superstate of N_2:

$$\langle inPlanning,\ N_2 \rangle \in D_{itinerary}$$

- "*inPlanning*" is the superstate of N_5 of "*hotelroom*":

$$\langle inPlanning,\ N_5 \rangle \in D_{itinerary}$$

Consequently:

$$hsm(itinerary) = \{\{N_2, N_3, N_4,\ N_5, N_6\},\ D_{itinerary}\}$$

is constructed. Fig. 5.7 shows the result.

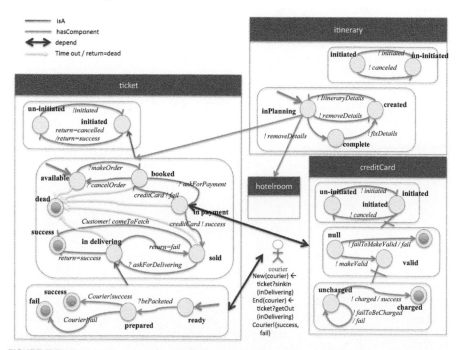

FIGURE 5.7

The domain tree-based hierarchical state machines *hsm(itinerary)*, *hsm(ticket)*, *hsm(hotelroom)*, and *hsm(creditcard)*.

Updated from P. Wang, Z. Jin and L. Liu, Capability description and discovery of internetware entity, Science in China 53 (4) (2010) 685–703.

After the domain THSMs of environment entities are constructed, we identify the dependencies between these domain THSMs. In the environment ontology BTO, there are dependencies between *hsm(creditcard)* and *hsm(ticket)* as well as between *hsm(creditcard)* and *hsm(hotelroom)*, as shown in Fig. 5.7.

5.5 SUMMARY

This chapter has mainly introduced the representation and construction of the environment ontology. For environment ontology, extension to the normal ontology structure is about the state machine—based behavior representation of the causal entities. The next chapter will introduce the second extension to normal ontology structure, which will discuss the goal model of the autonomous entities.

Feature Model of Domain Environment

6

CHAPTER OUTLINE

This chapter presents a feature model-based representation for domain environment ontology. This is for bridging the conceptualized representation and the representation close to system modeling, so that the environment model can be easily integrated into system modeling. This chapter will first briefly introduce the primitive elements in a feature model; then it will present the system environment feature model and the system goal feature model.

6.1 FEATURE MODEL AND FEATURE CONFIGURATION

Feature models were first introduced in the feature-oriented domain analysis (FODA) method proposed by Kang in 1990 (Kang et al., 1990). Since then, feature modeling has been widely used to specify the software capability for decades and has been adopted as a compact product representation of the software product line (SPL). It has demonstrated the characteristics of intuitiveness, understandability, and simplicity.

Features appear to be first-class abstractions in software product line engineering, in which an SPL is defined as "a set of software-intensive systems that share a common, managed set of features satisfying the specific needs of a particular

Environment Modeling-Based Requirements Engineering for Software Intensive Systems
https://doi.org/10.1016/B978-0-12-801954-2.00006-6

market segment or mission and that are developed from a common set of core assets in a prescribed way."[1] When the units of software product construction are features, every software product in an SPL is identified by a unique and legal combination of features.

In the context of FODA, a "feature" is defined as a "prominent or distinctive user-visible aspect, quality, or characteristic of a software system or systems." (Kang et al., 1990) Many other definitions exist in the literature; e.g., a feature is a logical unit of behavior specified by a set of functional and non-functional requirements, a feature is a product characteristic from user or customer views, which essentially consists of a cohesive set of individual requirements, and features are expressions of problems to be solved by the products of the SPL.

Considering the three elements of requirement engineering, i.e., the requirements, the specifications, and the environment assumption, we found that the features in the different definitions have different meanings and scopes. As illustrated in Fig. 3.1 in Chapter 3 of Part 1, the entailment relationship between the requirements, the specifications, and the environment properties is the core concern in requirements engineering for software-intensive systems. Reasoning about requirements involves considering the combined behavior of the to-be system and the environment properties. It is essential to use the same representation to enable reasoning.

This chapter is to use "features" to unify denotation of the characteristics of the three aspects in requirements engineering so that reasoning can be conducted based on feature models. The other advantage of using a feature-oriented approach is to bring the assets of the modeling phase closer to the assets of the design or implementation phase so that requirements models can be a kind of run-time models of the systems. That is essential, especially to system adaptivity.

6.1.1 PRIMITIVE ELEMENTS IN FEATURE MODEL

When discussing feature model and feature-oriented requirements engineering, the following terminologies should be clarified:

- feature model: A feature model is a model that defines features and their dependencies. Basically, there are two kinds of dependencies: the parental relationships, which can be of five types, i.e., mandatory, optional, alternative, AND group cardinality and OR group cardinality; and the cross-tree constraints that can be of two types, i.e., requires and excludes.
- feature diagram: A feature diagram is a visual notation of a feature model. It is basically rooted AND/OR tree. The elements of the tree are illustrated in Fig. 6.1A with cross-tree constraints (Fig. 6.1B). Some extensions exist for the feature diagram, e.g., a cardinalities-based feature model.

---

[1]https://www.sei.cmu.edu/productlines.

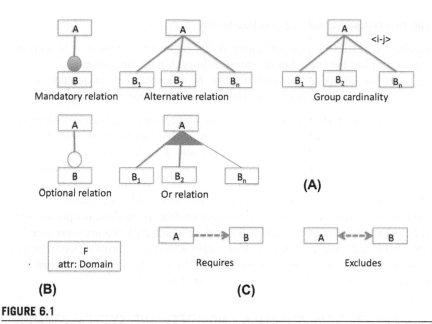

FIGURE 6.1

Propositional feature diagram elements. (A) Parental relationships. (B) Feature attribute, and (C) Cross-tree constraints. *attr*, attribute.

The five parental relationships in Fig. 6.1A are:

- mandatory: Let A and B be two features in which A is the parent of B, in a mandatory relationship. Mandatory feature B has to be included in a configuration if, and only if, its parent feature A is included in the configuration.
- optional: Let A and B be two features in which A is the parent of B, in an optional relationship. If feature A is included in a configuration, the optional child feature B may or may not be included in the configuration.
- OR group cardinality: Let A, B_1, B_2,..., B_n be features in which A is the parent of group features $\{B_1, B_2,..., B_n\}$ in an OR group cardinality relationship. If the group's parent A is included in a configuration, at least one, at most i, of the features in such a group has to be included in the configuration.
- alternative: Let A, B_1, B_2,..., B_n be features in which A is the parent of group features $\{B_1, B_2,..., B_n\}$ in an alternative relationship. If the group's parent A is included in a configuration, exactly one feature in such a group has to be included in the configuration.
- AND group cardinality: Let A, B_1, B_2,..., B_n be features in which A is the parent of group features $\{B_1, B_2,..., B_n\}$ in a decomposition with an AND group cardinality $\langle i - j \rangle$. If the group's parent A is included in a configuration, at least i, at most j, of the features in such a group, it must be included in the configuration.

The two types of cross-tree constraints (Fig. 6.1C) are:

- requires: If feature A requires feature B, the inclusion of feature A in a configuration implies the inclusion of feature B in such a configuration.
- excludes: If feature A excludes feature B, the inclusion of feature A in a configuration implies the exclusion of feature B in the same configuration.

Feature attributes (Fig. 6.1B) are used to supply some additional information about features, i.e., any characteristic of a feature that can be measured. A feature attribute consists of the name of an attribute and a domain that is the space of possible values in which the attribute takes its values. Every attribute belongs to a domain. Relations in one or more attributes of a feature can be associated to that feature. In this way, the nonfunctionalities of features can be identified.

Sometimes to support automated reasoning on feature models, people use logic to express the semantics of the feature diagram, in which each feature corresponds to a Boolean variable and the semantics are represented as a propositional formula (Schobbens et al., 2006). The correspondence between the elements in feature diagram and the propositional formula are listed in Table 6.1.

6.1.2 FEATURE CONFIGURATION AND SOFTWARE SYSTEM FEATURE MODEL

In feature modeling—based SPL, a product (a software system) of the SPL is declaratively specified by selecting or deselecting features according to requirements or preferences, i.e., a set of features the product is required to have, as well as the constraints implied in the feature model. Specifying the features of the product is called the feature configuration for this product.

Feature configuration, which is a set of features, describes a member of an SPL defined by a feature model. More formally, given a feature model with a set of features F, a configuration is a two-tuple of the form (S, R) such that $S, R \subseteq F$ is S the set of features to be selected and R the set of features to be removed such that $S \cap R = \varnothing$. If $S \cup R = F$. The configuration is called full configuration. If $S \cup R \subset F$ the configuration is called partial configuration.

Table 6.1 Proposition Logic-Based Semantics of Feature Models (Schobbens et al., 2006)

Element in Feature Diagram	Semantics
r is the root feature	R
f_1 is an optional subfeature of f	$f_1 \Rightarrow f$
f_1 is a mandatory subfeature of f	$f_1 \Leftrightarrow f$
$f_1, ..., f_n$ are alternative subfeatures of f	$(f_1 \vee ... \vee f_n \Leftrightarrow f) \wedge \bigwedge_{i < j} \neg(f_i \wedge f_j)$
$f_1, ..., f_n$ are or subfeatures of f	$f_1 \vee ... \vee f_n \Leftrightarrow f$
f_1 excludes f_2	$\neg(f_1 \wedge f_2)$
f_1 requires f_2	$f_1 \Rightarrow f_2$

A feature configuration (S, R) of a feature model with the set of features F is permitted if, and only if, the selected set of features S does not violate constraints imposed by the model. That is, this configuration consists of the features that are selected according to the variability constraints defined by the feature model. This means that if all of the features in S are true and all of the features in R are false, each of the propositional formulas representing the semantics of the feature model holds.

A product of the SPL, specified by a feature model with the set of features F, is equivalent to a full configuration in which only selected features are specified and omitted features are implicitly removed.

Product configuration is a feature selection process, taking a feature model fm as input and producing a feature configuration fc that is permitted by fm as output according to variability constraints. This can be reduced to a multistep configuration problem, i.e., the process of producing a series of intermediate configurations, a configuration path going from one feature mode configuration to another.

More formally, this process takes as input a feature model, an initial configuration, and a desired final configuration. As a result, the process provides an ordered list of steps of configuration path K that determines the possible steps, which can be taken to go from the initial configuration to the desired final configuration without violating the global constraints implied by the feature model.

There are already many approaches proposed for automated support (Benavides, 2009). These approaches can be classified into four different groups: propositional logic–based analyses, constraints programming–based analyses, description logic–based analyses, and other ad hoc algorithms, paradigms, or tools.

The following notations can be used to denote the relationships between feature models and feature configurations:

- feature model configuration ($\lhd$): Let fm be a feature model and fc a feature configuration. $fc \lhd fm$ means fc is a derived configuration of fm.
- feature model specialization ($\Subset$): Let fm_1 and fm_2 be two feature models. $fm_1 \Subset fm_2$, i.e., fm_1 is specific to fm_2 if fm_1 is produced by the feature model specification process from fm_2. Let fm_3 be a feature model, $fm_1 \Subset fm_3$ if $fm_1 \Subset fm_2$ and $fm_2 \Subset fm_3$.
- family of feature models: Given a feature model Fm, the feature model family of Fm: $\Theta(Fm) = \{fm_1, \ldots\ldots, fm_n\}$ is a set of feature models in which for all $1 \leq i \leq n$, $fm_i \Subset Fm$.
- family of configurations: Given a feature model Fm, the feature configuration family of Fm: $\Phi(Fm) = \{fc_1, \ldots\ldots, fc_n\}$ is a set of feature configurations in which for all $1 \leq i \leq n$, there is $fm \in \Theta(Fm)$ such that $fc_i \lhd fm$.

6.2 ENVIRONMENT FEATURE MODEL

As explained in the first part of the book, the environment model is an important element for the capability modeling of software-intensive systems because the interactive environment of the system serves as the bridge for the user's requirements (which is about the interactive environment of the systems) to the system specifications (which is about the system behaviors).

6.2.1 FEATURES FOR ENVIRONMENT CONCEPTUALIZATION

Previous chapters in this part of the book introduced environment ontology to show how to conceptualize the environment model. However, ontologies normally focus on the sharable aspect of the domain conceptualization but do not correspond to functional/behavioral features. In previous chapters, we made an extension to the general ontology by including the dynamics of the environment entities when conceptualizing the system environment. The main idea of the extension is to identify and represent the state changes of each environment entity during its life cycle.

This idea implies the need to model each environment entity in terms of the perspective of the system modeling: that is, to treat each environment entity as a small "system." More precisely, it is a physical system that can also react to its own surroundings (e.g., the interactions from the to-be software systems or software-intensive systems) and change its states, such as the reactions based on its own rules or according to its own laws. In this sense, it also shows its functionalities or behavioral capacity. This is one reason to use a feature model in environment modeling.

Furthermore, environment entities may also exhibit some kinds of variability when they are situated in different surroundings or react to different interactions. That may also associate with some constraints. Feature model provides intuitive ways to express variability and constraints. Some research has adopted the feature model to modeling the domain variability and capturing contextual variability. For example, feature model has been used in variability management in the field of the dynamical software product line.

When the software-intensive system and its surrounding environment are both represented, the variability of both the system and the environment can be represented in the same way. This results in a unified representation. Thus, to synchronizing the environment model and the system model easily, this book extends "feature" to represent the characteristics of the interactive environment of the software-intensive systems.

However, the environment feature model has modeling principles that are slightly different from the system feature model:

- A feature in a system feature model is a characteristic of a system relevant to some stakeholders that can be, for example, a requirement, a technical function or function group, or a nonfunctional (quality) characteristic. However, a feature in an environment feature model is a characteristic concerning the real-world entity with which the system will interact.
- Any atom feature in a system feature model represents an atom function of the system that is not able to be decomposed into other smaller-grained functions. But the atom feature in an environment feature model represents a state of an environment entity. The states of the same environment entity form a state diagram that describes the behaviors of the environment entity. Thus, there are state change relations between these atom features.

- The top-level environment feature models are the same for different applications. Applications differ by identifying their own concrete entities below the top-level environment ontology in Fig. 4.9.

6.2.2 HIERARCHY OF ENVIRONMENT FEATURE MODEL

As mentioned earlier, the environment feature model has three levels. In the top-level, along with the Jackson's problem frame approach (Jackson, 2001), Chapter 4 provides an abstraction of real-world entities and their phenomena. It distinguishes six kinds of phenomena: the first three are kinds of individuals, i.e., events, entities, and values, whereas the second three are relations among individuals, i.e., states, truths, and roles. Based on these, two larger categories of phenomena are defined:

- causal phenomena: events, roles, or state-relating entities
- symbolic phenomena: values, truths, or states relating only values

Furthermore, three types of real-world entities are distinguished in terms of the phenomena:

- A causal entity is one whose properties include predictable causal relationships among its causal phenomena. Causal relationships calculate the effect of an interaction with the entity. Any causal entity is directly controllable and detectable and can impose effects onto other environment entities.
- An autonomous entity usually consists of people. It is physical compared with the causal entity, although it lacks positive predictable internal causality. Any autonomous entity is uncontrollable but sensible.
- A symbolic entity is a physical representation of data, that is, of symbolic phenomena. It combines causal and symbolic phenomena in a special way. The causal properties allow data to be written and read. However, the significance of its physical states is that they provide a representation for values and truths. Any symbolic entity is sensible and indirectly controllable via some other causal entities.

Along this line, we developed the environment ontology to model the interactive environment of software-intensive systems in Chapter 5. This chapter adopts the same modeling principles but accommodates the ontology in a feature model using features to represent entities and states or the value of entities.

We explain the extension using an example illustrated in Fig. 6.2, which shows a fragment of the environment feature model for smart home systems. For simplification, Fig. 6.2 uses dotted lines with hollow circles to denote the alternative choices in the rounded rectangle.

The semantics of the environment feature model is slightly different from that of the classical propositional feature model. First, it explicitly stratifies the feature model into three levels, i.e., metalevel, application, and context, to clarify the different semantics of the feature selections.

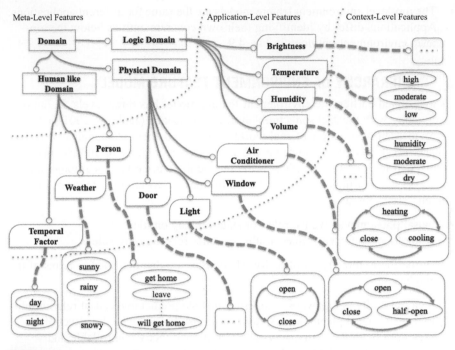

FIGURE 6.2

Example smart home environment feature model.

Second, along with the previously mentioned environment modeling principle in earlier chapters, the real-world entities are categorized into three types: the autonomous, the *causal*, and the symbolic. The metalevel of the feature decomposition is that "real-world entity" (i.e., the root feature) has three subfeatures: the autonomous *entity*, the *causal entity*, and the symbolic *entity*. These three features serve as the type definitions of the application-level features.

The features in the application level contain all of the application entities in smart home applications: "*door*," "*window*," "*air conditioner*" are causal entities; "*person*" and "*weather*" are autonomous entities; and "*brightness*" and "*temperature*" are symbolic entities in the smart home application field. The regulations of the meta-level entities (i.e., the types of entities) are used to guide capturing of the semantics of these concrete application entities.

For example, any symbolic or autonomous entities, such as brightness or the weather, can be detected by certain sensing devices. Any causal entities, e.g., the door or the air conditioner, can be detected to be in some state via detectors and can also be controlled by controllers. An application entity can also be composite, i.e., it contains some (mandatory or optional) parts, the propositional feature elements used to express such semantics.

Context-level features are the phenomena (e.g., the states or the value) of the application entities. At a particular time, any application entity may share with others a particular phenomenon. For example, on a particular day, the weather is sunny, the person is coming home, the air conditioner is open in the heating mode, etc. All pairs of an application entity and its shared phenomenon form the running context of the system at run-time.

6.2.3 ENVIRONMENT FEATURE CONFIGURATION

The corresponding notations for the environment feature models and configurations include: let *Efm* be an environment feature model:

- $\Theta(Efm)$ is the feature model family of *Efm* with regard to the specialization relationship
- $\Phi(Efm)$ is the configuration family of *Efm* with regard to the configuration relationship

The difference is in the configuration process. The normal feature configuration is the feature selection process in which the feature selection is propagated from the root feature to the leaf features in a top-down manner. The environment configuration takes the bottom-up approach. That is, the feature selection is propagated from the leaf features, which will be decided by the sensed data at run-time.

Environment variability represents the diversity of real-world situations in which the to-be software-intensive system will be situated. There are two kinds of variability. The first is diversity in the application-level. Any configuration of the entities may serve as the current surrounding of the to-be software-intensive system in a particular period.

The other diversity is in the context-level. In each configuration of entities, each entity takes one particular state or value. The configuration of states/values for each configuration of domains/entities may serve as the current context of the to-be software-intensive system within that particular period.

6.3 GOAL FEATURE MODEL

Use of the feature model to represent the interactive environment of the to-be software-intensive systems requires a second extension. Besides the functionalities, as well as the environment entities and its states or values, features need to be extended to represent the system goals. These goals are associated with the biddable entities that may be the various stakeholders of the to-be software-intensive systems.

6.3.1 AUTONOMOUS ENTITY AND INTENTIONAL PROPERTY

In Chapter 1, we showed that the goals of the stakeholders were an important concern in requirements modeling of software-intensive systems. Regarding the openness of an interactive environment where there are software-intensive systems, it is highly desirable to include expected and unexpected intentional interactors of to-be software-intensive systems, as shown in Fig. 4.9. Some autonomous entities in the interactive environment of a system may have special intentions for the system, i.e., the goals or purposes for which they join the interactive environment of the system. A goal-oriented approach provides a wealth of modeling strategies and methodologies to deal with the stakeholders' intentions.

However, for systems that will situate in an open and dynamic environment, such as software-intensive systems running on the Internet, some goals of the interactors are that the systems need to achieve and some others need to be avoided or prevented. These two sets of goals need to be treated differently by the system. Hence, the requirements modeling for such systems needs to deal with positive and negative goals at the same time. The positive goals are those that the system needs to achieve.

However, negative goals (e.g., intentional interactors with the malicious intent of attacking the system, stealing private information, etc.) are ones that the system needs to avoid or prevent. The system needs to be equipped with the necessary capacity to resist potential attacks when they detect the purpose of these intentional interactors. This is the concern of security. Part Four will pay attention to the security issue, including the goal model as a run-time model in supporting reasoning at run-time regarding these different intentions.

The other reason for including the goal model as a run-time model is the dynamics of the environment, i.e., the interactive environment may change at run-time. Some autonomous entities may join in and some others may drop off at run-time. The causal entities may change their states. The symbolic entities may change their value. The autonomous entities may have different goal preferences in different scenarios and then change their purpose at run-time, as well as exhibit different behaviors. This results in requirements variability and requirements uncertainty.

6.3.2 INTENTIONAL GOAL AND GOAL FEATURE MODEL

Along with traditional goal-oriented modeling, there are abstract and concrete goal features. The abstract goal feature can be refined into finer goals in terms of the feature-refinement relationship. For the concrete goals, i.e., those goals for which no further refinement is required, three types can be distinguished: hard goals, soft goals, and mixed goals, in which:

- Each hard goal is associated with a condition that needs to be held all of the time. Whenever the condition becomes false, the goal is violated. For example, the goal of "*constant room temperature*" implies the purpose of maintaining constant temperature in a given temperature interval, e.g., the condition:

$$18°C \leq \text{roomTemperature} \leq 23°C$$

should be held. This type of goal can be used to check the violation of the conditions.

- Each soft goal needs to associate with an optimization objective. For example, the goal of "*high performance*" normally implies the expectation that the response time is as fast as possible. That can be specified as an optimization objective:

$$minimize(responseTime)$$

This type of goal will be used to constrain online decision making.

- The mixed goal will be associated with a relaxed condition and also an optimization objective. For example, for the goal "*energy saving*," the energy efficiency standard should be at least 65%, which can be represented as:

$$maximize(energyEfficiency \leq 65\%)$$

Fig. 6.3 shows a goal feature model concerning smartness. We can see that it shares the same model principles of the normal feature model, except that each feature is a goal feature. Different purposes or goals have different refinement strategies and therefore have different goal feature models.

It is understood that a goal feature model *Gfm*, $\Theta(Gfm)$ is the feature model family of *Gfm* and $\Phi(Gfm)$ is the configuration family of *Gfm*.

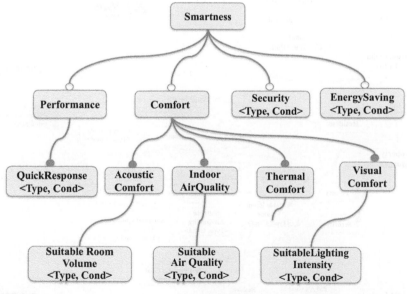

FIGURE 6.3

Goal feature model regarding smartness. *Cond*, condition.

6.3.3 HIERARCHY OF GOAL FEATURE MODELS

Goal model variability represents the diversity of stakeholders' requirements when the system situates in different scenarios. For example, the user may have an intention for different goal models and then may require different application logics or may have different preferences for nonfunctional requirements or have different expectations for quality. That is why different system solutions are needed in different scenarios. The run-time goal model will serve as the reference to select the best system configuration.

Goal feature models will be embedded in the environment feature model as argumentations of the autonomous entities. They are used to represent the purpose of the autonomous entities. Fig. 6.4 shows an environment model fragment with the embedding of a goal feature model of a resident in a smart home application.

As we can see from Fig. 6.4, including the goal feature model extends the environment feature model by appending the intentional annotations, e.g., smartness, security, privacy, etc., to each autonomous entity. The negative intentions may also be appended to malicious interactors, i.e., to ask the system to equip the capabilities to avoid or prevent these intentional goals. The extensions happen in each of the three levels of the environment feature model and then produce the goal-annotated environment feature model:

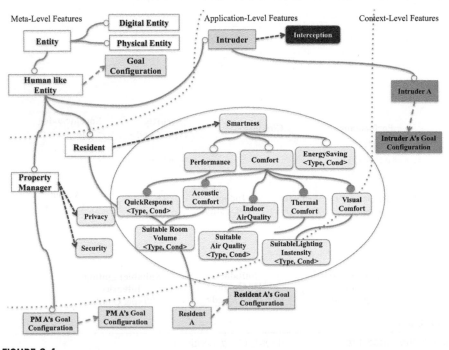

FIGURE 6.4

Goal feature model of smart home. *Cond*, condition.

- First, at the metalevel, to embedding the goal feature model, a new category "*Goal Configuration*" is included. Each autonomous entity will associate with this category (blue dashed arrow in Fig. 6.4). The meaning is:

Autonomous Entity *hasGoalConf* **Goal Configuration**.

This is to capture the observation: "at any time or in any situation, each autonomous entity has a goal configuration. It is the goal of this entity that is desired to be achieved at this time or in this situation."

- Second, at the application level, there are some goal feature models (i.e., the goals and the refinement relationships between goals) to express the potential desires or purpose. For example, in smart home application, some typical goal feature models are concerned with smartness, security, privacy, etc., as the highest-level feature. Each higher-level feature has its own feature refinement patterns to refine a current feature into subfeatures. Multiple refinement patterns mean that there are alternative strategies to realize this feature. In this example, the highest-level feature, "*Smartness*," can be realized by achieving some prescribed subfeatures, e.g., "*energy saving*," "*comfort*," etc. There are also some negative goal feature models, such as interception of private information.

The goal feature models are embedded by the following relationship (dark red dashed arrow in Fig. 6.4):

Role *hasDesire* **Feature**

In which **Role**, a new category specific to the application domain, is a type of autonomous entity. For example, in the smart home application domain, some **Roles** are the resident, the property manager, etc.

Different **Roles** may have different requirements (i.e., the features and their feature refinement patterns). For example, the **resident** may have the purpose of asking for the achievement of "*smartness*." The **property manager** may have the purpose of ensuring "*Security*." The **system intruder** may want to "*intercept private information*." "*Smartness*" and "*Security*" are positive goals that need to be satisfied by the to-be software-intensive system, but the "*Interception of Private Information*" is a negative goal that needs to be prevented by the system.

- Third, at the context level, for each instance of each role, its goal configuration is obtained by using the goal specialization process, as presented earlier. The goal configuration process creates the goal configuration instance, which is currently an interactor in a particular situation. This relationship is represented by
Instance of Role hasGoalConf **Instance of Goal Configuration**.

Fig. 6.4 shows three such relations, i.e., "Resident A has a goal configuration," "Property Manager A has a goal configuration," and "Intruder A has a goal configuration."[2] The collection of positive goal configurations needs to be met by the system, but the collection of negative goal configurations needs to be avoided or prevented by the system.

6.4 SUMMARY

This chapter presented the feature model representation for the environment ontology to unify run-time models. It first presented the environment feature model and introduced its semantics. Then the goal feature model was proposed to express the intentional purposes and goals of the autonomous entities. Then it showed how to embed the goal feature models in the environment feature model to form the goal-annotated environment feature model.

---

[2]Both the positive goal models and the negative goal models may be developed by strategy patterns. Many results in modeling nonfunctional requirements in requirements engineering area can be used here.

Part Two References

R. Alur, R. Kannan, S. Yannakakis, M. Yannakakis, Communicating hierarchical state machines, in: Proceedings of International Colloquium on Automata, Languages and Programming (ICAL'99), vol. 1644, LNCS, 1999, pp. 169–178.

D. Benavides, S. Segura, A. Ruiz-Cortes, Automated Analysis of Feature Models: A Detailed Literature Review, ISA Research Group, 2009.

X. Chen, Z. Jin, Capturing requirements from expected interactions between software and its interactive environment: an ontology-based approach, International Journal of Software Engineering and Knowledge Engineering 26 (1) (2016) 15–39.

T.R. Gruber, A translation approach to portable ontology specifications, Knowledge Acquisition 5 (2) (1993) 199–220.

C.L. Heitmeyer, R.D. Jeffords, B.G. Labaw, Automated consistency checking of requirements specifications, ACM Transactions on Software Engineering and Methodology (TOSEM) 5 (3) (1996) 231–261.

M. Jackson, Problem frames: analyzing and structuring software development problems, Addison-Wesley, 2001.

Z. Jin, Revisiting the meaning of requirements, Journal of Computer Science and Technology 21 (1) (2006) 32–40.

K. C. Kang, S. G. Cohen, J. A. Hess, W. E. Novak, A. S. Peterson, Feature-oriented domain analysis (FODA) feasibility study, Technical Report CMU/SEI-90-TR-021, SEI, Carnegie Mellon University, November 1990.

D.L. Parnas, J. Madey, Functional documentation for computer systems, Science Computing Program 25 (1) (1995) 41–61.

P.Y. Schobbens, P. Heymans, J.C. Trigaux, Feature diagrams: a survey and a formal semantics, in: Proceedings of the 14th IEEE International Requirements Engineering Conference (RE2006), 2006, pp. 139–148.

J. Sowa, Knowledge representation: logical, philosophical and computational foundations, Brooks/Cole, 1999.

P. Wang, Z. Jin, L. Liu, G. Cai, Building toward capability specifications of web services based on environment ontology, IEEE Transactions on Knowledge and Data Engineering 20 (4) (2008) 547–561.

P. Wang, Z. Jin, H. Liu, Capability description and discovery of internetware entity, Science in China 53 (4) (2010) 685–703.

E. Yu, Social Modeling for Requirements Engineering, MIT Press, 2010.

FURTHER READING

L. Bertalanffy, General System Theory: Essays on Its Foundation and Development, George Braziller, New York, 1968.

A. Gomez-Perez, M. Fernandez-Lopez, O. Corcho, Ontological Engineering: With Examples from the Areas of Knowledge Management, E-commerce and the Semantic Web, Springer, 2004.

R. Lu, Z. Jin, Domain Modeling-based Software Engineering: A Formal Approach, Kluwer Academia Publishers, 2000.

R. Studer, V.R. Benjamins, D. Fensel, Knowledge engineering: principles and methods, Data & Knowledge Engineering 25 (1−2) (1998) 161−197.

Environment Modeling-Based System Capability

3

The third part of this book presents the system capability model. The main idea of the system capability model is the grounding of system capability on environment models. The key concept is the "effect" that the system has on the environment. The effects are the changes in the environment that are imposed by the system behaviors.

The effects on the environment capture the semantics of the system capability from the viewpoint of requirements engineering. Requirements are desired effects and system entities are able to impose effects, i.e., change the environment through interactions. All effects are based on the same terminology, i.e., the interactive environment ontology, using the same semantic space. Thus, the capabilities of different parties are comparable and reasoning about the capability is enabled.

This part focuses on the effect-oriented capability model and reasoning about system capability. It contains four chapters, i.e., Chapters 7–10. These four chapters focus on different aspects of capability description and capability reasoning. Chapter 7 introduces the idea of effect-oriented system capability and presents capability profiles and descriptions. It is the basis of the rest of the chapters and also composes the chapters in the next part.

Chapter 8 introduces the matchmaking and composition of capability units in terms of their capability profiles. Matchmaking enables capability unit selection and comparison, and composition enables smaller-grain capability units to be used to fulfil bigger requirements.

Refinement is important to manage requirements/problem complexity in system development. Chapter 9 presents a projection-based approach to refining capability. Using this approach, high-level capability requirements can be systematically refined into subrequirements based on the scenarios. These scenarios are proposed to be those that are used by the desired system to fulfill the requirements.

Chapter 10 discusses an agent-oriented approach for capability aggregation. This is to demonstrate the capability growth model. The research question asks, if there are plenty of elementary capability units, how do they autonomously aggregate to build the capability growth hierarchy to fulfill higher and more general capability requirements via mechanism design? It is assumed to be via the model capturing the crowd-based system development. Individuals in the crowd develop elementary capability units. Once they detect the requirements, these capability units can collaborate with each other to fulfil the requirements and also to obtain the benefits.

Effect-Oriented System Capability

CHAPTER OUTLINE

Before we go straight into the topic of effect-oriented system capability, we need to talk about capability. Dictionaries provide the following definitions:

- Generally, capability means (1) the quality or state of being capable; (2) a feature or faculty capable of development; and (3) the facility or potential for an indicated use or deployment.[1]
- Capability is the state of being able to perform certain actions for achieving certain outcomes. As it normally applied to human capital, it represents the intersection of capacity and ability.[2]
- Capability is often used in the defense industry. Here, it is a domain-specific term and is defined as the ability to execute a specified course of actions that may or may not be accompanied by an intention.
- In the multiagent system area, capability is used to identify the ability to react rationally toward achieving a particular goal. More specifically, an agent has the capability to achieve a goal if its plan library contains at least one plan to reach the goal.

---

[1]http://www.merriam-webster.com/dictionary/capability.
[2]https://en.wikipedia.org/wiki/Capability.

Environment Modeling-Based Requirements Engineering for Software Intensive Systems
https://doi.org/10.1016/B978-0-12-801954-2.00007-8

These explanations imply that any subject that has a certain capability can do something or perform some action. Hence, actions that the systems can take are necessary for capability modeling of software-intensive systems. However, only expressing being able to do something is not enough. We have shown in previous chapters that system requirements analysis and capability modeling need to answer not only what capability the systems are required to have, but why the capability is needed. That is, capability means that the system should be able to do something so that it can impose a direct or indirect effect on the recipients; these effects are for the purpose of building the system.

More precisely, the goals or requirements of building a system are not only about the system but, more important, they are about desired changes on the system's environment and the desired relations between environment entities that need to be maintained, enabled, avoided, or discontinued among the system environment entities or properties. In other words, the motivation for building a system is because of such goals and requirements, and these goals or requirements can be achieved or realized if the system can do something, which will bring about the desired effects on the system's surroundings. In this sense, the answer regarding what is required of the system is derived by these desired effects. Thus, the effects imposed onto the recipients are important when modeling system capability.

In addition, the natural laws that the environment entities should follow are important when considering what the system needs to do. Sometimes particular effects can occur only because of these natural laws, whereas some effects can be avoided because there are natural laws that can be taken advantage of. Thus, building a software-intensive system to enable the desired effects on its surroundings can take advantage of the natural laws that these environment entities satisfy.

To model system capability is to define which are the desired actions that the system should take to enable the desired effects. Effects upon the environment entities are in fact the bridge between the requirements and the system's behaviors. This chapter will explore the effect-based view of system capability and try to answer what capability means when it applies to software-intensive systems, and how to model the capability of software-intensive systems.

This chapter has three sections. Section 7.1 introduces the capability specification of semantic Web services as the background. Section 7.2 discusses the effect-based capability model. Section 7.3 details the system capability profile.

7.1 CAPABILITY SPECIFICATION OF SEMANTIC WEB SERVICES

Determining and specifying the capability that could be implemented by software-intensive systems has been a major concern of many research fields, e.g., software engineering, system engineering, artificial intelligence, and service-oriented computing. In the field of software or system engineering, capability normally refers to functionalities as well as some nonfunctional properties. Artificial intelligence tries to systematize and automate some intellectual tasks and, to a certain extent, to realize the human-level capability of certain problem solving. However, in most cases, the capability of the software, systems, or software agents is only an abstract term whose semantics can only be understood, defined, and dealt with by humans.

Service-oriented computing starts to use semantic Web technologies to describe the capability of Web services. Among different focuses of research in service-oriented computing, automated Web service discovery is the key trigger to service capability modeling and specification. This leads to the attempt to specify the service capability in a machine-understandable way.

Fig. 7.1 illustrates the basic idea of service-oriented computing (Papazoglou et al., 2007), which is about the relationship among three kinds of participants: the service provider, the service requestor, and the service discovery agency. These roles and operations act upon the service artifacts: the service requests (the requirements) and the service implementations (specified as capability descriptions).

As shown in Fig. 7.1, in a typical service-oriented computing scenario, the service provider defines a service capability description (i.e., the implementation of a given service) and advertises it through the service discovery agency. The service requester submits its service request. The service discovery agency stores the service capability descriptions in a service pool. When it receives a service request, it provides help to find available services from its service pool that can potentially fulfill the service requestor's needs. Then the service requester sends a binding operation to the service provider to bind its service request to that service that can fulfill his or her needs.

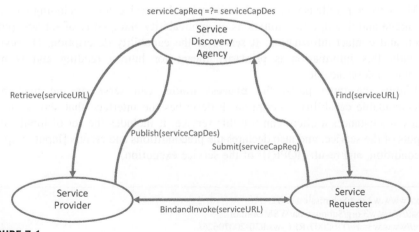

FIGURE 7.1

Service-oriented computing: basic architecture.

Therefore, the central problems to be solved are how to specify the capabilities of Web services as well as the capabilities that are required semantically, so that the service discovery agency can perform matchmaking automatically between the provided service and the service request. Also, with such a specification, the provided service can be invoked properly by the service requester.

For this purpose, researchers propose different kinds of service capability description to enable the machine-understandable capability of services developed by a third party so that they can be identified and invoked properly. Ontologies have been expected to be a tool for building the capability description of Web services with semantics. For example, Web Ontology Language for Services (OWL-S)[3] (formerly DARPA Agent Markup Language for Services), Web Service Modeling Ontology (WSMO),[4] and Web Service Description Language[5] have been proposed to provide a worldwide standard capability specification for semantic Web services.

7.1.1 CAPABILITY DESCRIPTION IN WEB ONTOLOGY LANGUAGE FOR SERVICES[6]

OWL-S is an ontology within the OWL-based framework of the Semantic Web for describing semantic Web services. It aims to enable users and software agents automatically to discover, invoke, compose, and monitor Web resources offering services, under specified constraints.

Fig. 7.2 shows the OWL-S ontology. It has three main components: the service profile, the process model, and the service grounding. The **service grounding** specifies the details a client needs when he or she wants to interact with the service, such as communication protocols, message formats, and port numbers. This group of information instructs how to bind the service to enable the invocation of the service implementation.

The **service profile** is meant to describe what the service does, including the service name and description, limitations on applicability and quality of service, publisher, and contact information. It serves as the capability description. However, currently this information is primarily meant for human reading and is not machine-understandable.

Within the three parts, the **process model** can serve as the machine-understandable capability description. It describes the interface that shows under what circumstances a client can use this service. It includes the set of inputs and outputs of the service, and also declares the preconditions and results [input, output, precondition, and result (IOPR)][7] of the service execution.

---

[3]http://www.w3.org/Submission/OWL-S/.
[4]https://www.w3.org/Submission/WSMO/#mof.
[5]http://www.w3.org/TR/2007/REC-wsdl20-20070626/.
[6]See footnote 3.
[7]See footnote 3.

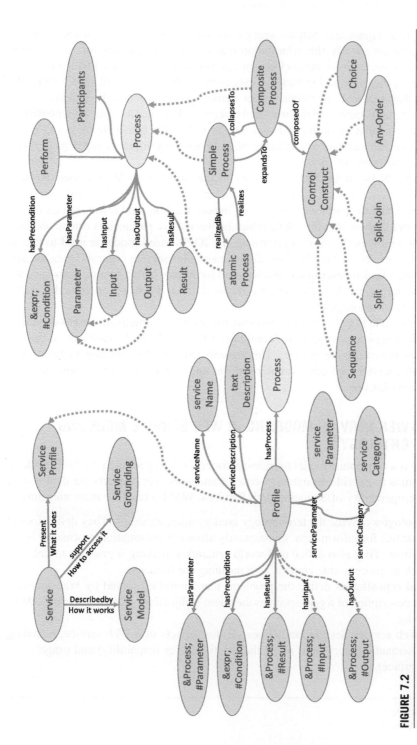

FIGURE 7.2

Components of the Web Ontology Language for Services ontology[8].

As such, inputs and outputs specify the data transformation produced by the service. Inputs specify the information that the service requires for its execution and outputs are the information that can be acquired by the service invoker performing it (i.e., the information that the execution of the service will return when the service has received the inputs under certain preconditions). Preconditions and results are constraints on the use of the service. If a service has a precondition, the service cannot be performed successfully unless the precondition is valid. The results indicate that the performance of a service may mean changes in the state of the world (effects).

The IOPR-based description presents the meanings of the Web service interface with the semantic grounding onto some domain ontologies, i.e., the input and output parameters and the parameters appearing in preconditions and results are terms in a domain ontology so that the relationships between these parameters can be obtained from the ontology. In most applications, the IOPR-based model is used to decide whether a service is capable of fulfilling a particular service request (when the service request is also described in IOPR-based form) or whether two services have the same capability, etc. In both cases, it is required that IOPR has been grounded on the same domain ontologies.

As shown in Fig. 7.2, OWL-S has also provided the formalization of two kinds of services: atomic and composite. It outlines certain predefined constructs for the formation of the composite services. This presents a way to describe how to decompose a complex service into other simpler services and how to compose simpler services into a complex one.

7.1.2 WEB SERVICE MODELING IN WEB SERVICE MODELING ONTOLOGY[9]

WSMO is a conceptual model for relevant aspects relating to semantic Web services. It also aims to provide an ontology-based framework that supports the deployment and interoperability of Semantic Web Services. WSMO has four main elements:

- **Ontologies** provide the terminology used by other elements. They define formal semantics for information, consequently allowing information processing by machine. They also define real-world semantics, making it possible to link machine-process-able content with meaning for humans.
- **Goal repositories** define the problems that should be solved by Web services. The description of a goal specifies the client's objectives when consulting a Web service.
- A **Web service** description defines various aspects of a Web service, including the semantic descriptions about the functionalities (capability) and usage (interface).

---

[8]See footnote 3.
[9]See footnote 4.

- **Mediators** bypass interoperability problems. They are connectors between decoupled and/or heterogeneous components. Different mediators are used to make the connections at different levels, e.g., the mediation of data structure, the mediation of business logic, the mediation of message exchange protocols, and the mediation of dynamic service invocation.

WSMO is presented as four conceptual diagrams in Fig. 7.3. Fig. 7.3A gives the four main elements in WSMO and the relationship between them. Fig. 7.3B is a conceptual model of the ontology. It says that any ontology can have concepts, relations, functions, and instances. These elements have some other relationships with other elements that are included in Fig. 7.3B.

Fig. 7.3D is a conceptual model of the mediator. It shows that there are four types of mediators for mediating different heterogeneous components, i.e., goal-goal mediator (ggMediator), Web-service-goal mediator (wgMediator), ontology-ontology mediator (ooMediator), and Web-service-Web service mediator (wwMediator).

Fig. 7.3C is what we are mostly interested in. It defines the Web service and the capability of the Web services. As we can see from the diagram, any Web service (or any goal) has capability and any capability has four elements: assumption, precondition, postcondition, and effect. The structured description can be represented as:

```
Class capability
      hasNonFunctionalProperties type nonFunctionalProperties
      importsOntology type ontology
      usesMediator type {ooMediator, wgMediator}
      hasSharedVariables type sharedVariables; the variables that are
                                          shared between
                                          preconditions, postconditions
                                          assumptions and effects
   hasPrecondition type axiom; the information space of the Web service
                            before
                            its execution
   hasAssumption type axiom; the state of the world before the execution of the
                          Web service
 hasPostcondition type axiom; the information space of the Web service after
                            the execution of the Web service
      hasEffect type axiom; the state of the world after the execution of the
                          Web service
```

The four elements are defined as an axiom. The comments show that the axioms of "*has precondition*" and "*has postcondition*" are grounded on the information space and the axioms of "*has assumption*" and "*has effect*" are grounded on the state of the world.

For the capability combination compared with OWL-S, whereas the composite service is composed by the constructs, WSMO provides a twofold view of the operational competence of the Web service for describing how the functionality of the Web service can be achieved (i.e., how the capability of a Web service can be

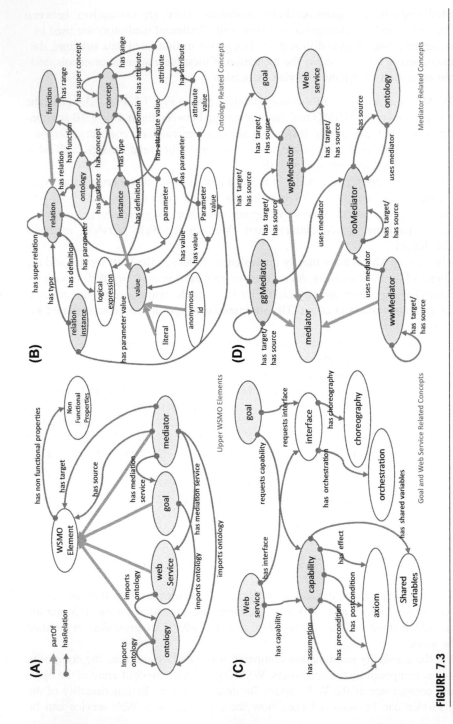

FIGURE 7.3

Web Service Modeling Ontology conceptual diagrams.

fulfilled). First, choreography decomposes a capability in terms of its interaction with the Web service. Second, orchestration decomposes a capability in terms of the functionality required from other Web services. This distinction reflects the difference between communication and cooperation. The choreography defines how to communicate with the Web service to consume its functionality. The orchestration defines how the overall functionality is achieved by the cooperation of a more elementary Web service provider.

7.1.3 SUMMARY OF THE WEB SERVICE CAPABILITY DESCRIPTION

Existing semantic Web service infrastructures describe various aspects related to semantic Web services. However, in these infrastructures, service capability is modeled by the service interfaces. Concretely, the service capability is modeled as the inputs, the outputs, the preconditions, and the results of Web services (referred to here as IOPR).

At a certain abstract level, an example scenario for demonstrating IOPR in real life could be that a regular traveler who wants to have a good travel budget states: "I need a travel agency service that provides flight ticket sales and hotel room reservations, whose service fees are charged by credit card." The following abstract IOPR schema can be used to describe the service request:

```
Capability
  cap-id BudgetTravel
  input (?creditCardNo; ?start; ?end; ?time; ?hotelLocation)
  output (!flightTicketReceipt; !hotelroomReceipt)
  pre-condition (is-valid-creditcard)
  result (is-charged-creditcard)
```

Such a capability model assumes that the capability of a Web service is of atomicity although it can be composite service via service constructs or service orchestration. When it receives the required inputs (input) under certain conditions (precondition), it will return the output (output) with the effect (result). The parameters in IOPR are sharable terminology in a particular domain that is specified in domain ontology. With this, different Web services can exchange information via the interfaces so as to support Web service composition and execution. This specification provides certain semantics on the service capability, based on internal/external domain ontologies referred to by the terms used in IOPR. For example, the Web services for traveling arrangements may refer to travel ontology (refer to Chapter 4 for an example), which contains terms regarding flight, hotel room, price, time, etc.

However, the IOPR-based specification presents the meanings of the Web service interface with semantic grounding onto some external domain ontologies, but the domain ontologies serve only as a general terminology reference. It takes advantage of the terminology reference to compare parameters used in inputs and outputs and derives the semantic similarity between terms. It constrains the capability description within the boundary of terms in the domain ontologies.

However, it fails to model the dynamics and autonomy of the external real-world entities and cannot reason about the relationships between preconditions and post-conditions. As such, the effects that the service invocation have on the domains cannot be specified.

7.2 EFFECT-BASED CAPABILITY MODEL

As mentioned, service capability modeling uses an interface-based capability model. It considers that any Web services are of atomicity and it models the functionality as the input—output relationship with a pair: the preconditions of the service invocation and the postconditions of the service execution. However, because the outside world has not been modeled in Web services, the preconditions and postconditions are not meaningful. In this sense, the IOPR capability specification of a service system in fact mainly describes the structure of information processing executed by Web services following the "input-process-output" pattern. The system separates itself from the environment as one united mechanism thus defining inputs and outputs. Such inputs may be anything or from any source, and the system transforms the inputs into outputs of any kind. In other word, it inputs any data with regard to the environment outside the system, yet in practice the environment contains a significant variety of objects that a system is unable to comprehend.

Effect-based capability (Wang et al., 2008) in a certain sense follows the idea of a subfield of pragmatics, i.e., Austin's Speech Act Theory (Austin, 1976), which is concerned with the ways in which words can be used not only to present information but also to carry out actions. This high-level theoretical framework is developed by philosophers and linguists to account for human communication. The main idea is that the major role of language communication is a kind of action and suggests that speakers do not simply utter sentences that are true or false, but rather perform speech actions such as requests, suggestions, and promises. Speech Act Theory is concerned with language, because action and speech acts are considered the minimal units of human communication. All utterances are speech acts with the primary understanding that all utterances are actions of some sort.

Effect-oriented capability tries to borrow the idea of Speech Act Theory to model the communication or interaction between the system and its surroundings. This is an effort to specify necessary and sufficient conditions for the successful performance of speech acts, involving the user's intentions and requirements.

Previous chapters of this book presented the environment models, in which the general domain ontology has been extended into the environment ontology that specifies the environment entities with their internal state transitions caused by the interactions in which they take part. Such models enable the comprehensibility and reasonability of the environment and they will serve as the fine-grain semantics of system capability compared with the input—output relationship.

7.2.1 EFFECT UPON THE INTERACTIVE ENVIRONMENT

Environment modeling-based approach proposes a new way for capability conceptualization. It makes the system capability more semantic and meaningful by distinguishing three kinds of environment entities, which implies that different effects can be imposed.

For example, a symbolic entity has several attributes with values or value ranges. The effect on this kind of entity can be the value change caused by value assignment. An autonomous entity can initiate events to share with the system. It is autonomous in that it is able to decide the interactions in which it will participate. A causal entity is affected by its state. State transitions of this kind of entity indicate the effect on it imposed by system interactions via the interface. More precisely, we assume that such an environment entity can be represented with its inner states and state transitions. When a system interacts with the environment entities, it in fact triggers the environment entities to change their states along their state transition functions. Consequently, the system's effect can be represented as the running of the state/value changes triggered by the sequence of interactions in which the system is involved.

The key factor of the system's effect upon the interactive environment is the "**interaction**" between the system and the environment entities. The system can initiate the interactions that can trigger the state transitions or value assignments of environment entities, whereas it shares the events or receives messages initiated by environment entities. The system's effect upon its interactive environment is imposed by a sequence of interactions in which the system and its interactive environment entities are involved.

On the one hand, as mentioned in previous chapters, each environment entity is represented as an input—output automaton consisting of states and transitions. The automaton runs on some sequence of inputs (i.e., interactions). That is, it sees a symbol of input (an interaction) and makes a transition to another state, according to its transitional function. A run of an environment entity automaton on a sequence of its input interactions is a sequence of states. It starts from the start state and ends at a final state, and each state transition consumes one input interaction and jumps to the next state along the state transition function. That is, a run of an environment entity automaton is an attempt to accept the sequence of its input interactions.

On the other hand, an interaction sequence in which a system is involved contains its input interactions (initiated by the environment entities) and its output interactions (initiated by the system). Its output interactions become the input interactions of its environment entities and the input interactions of each environment entity make the environment entity change its states. Such a behavioral representation can exhibit the changes caused by the system interactions via the interface. This is the meaning of the effect-oriented capability, i.e., to model the system capability via the state changes of its interactive environment entities.

Here, we would like to include an example to show such a view of system capability. Assume that there is a "Budget Travel Environment Ontology," as shown in Fig. 7.4. It contains three kinds of environment entities: *Credit Card*, *Flight*, and

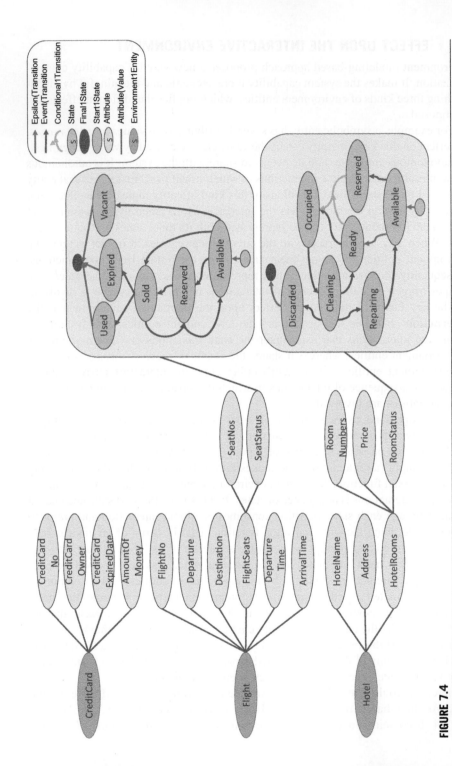

FIGURE 7.4

Example of the budget travel environment ontology.

Hotel. Each has certain attributes and *Flight* and *Hotel* contain causal components that have their own state diagrams regarding seat status and room status, respectively. The states and causal relations come from the domain business logics.

With this environment ontology, different capabilities can be defined as illustrated in Fig. 7.5, in which each path represents a particular effect on an environment entity.

As such, first, as different capabilities are based on the different paths of the same ontology, these capabilities become semantically comparable. Second, as the ontology represents the domain business logics, it becomes possible to check whether the capability is competent.

7.2.2 SYSTEM CAPABILITY CONCEPTUALIZATION

The environmental effect-based perspective reveals whether the systems show how their capability is effective upon their interactive environment. This section is devoted to defining a top-level ontology [Software Capability Upper Ontology (**SCuO**)] for modeling the system capability. This ontology is based on the environment ontology developed in previous chapters but it focuses on the system capability, i.e., how the system exhibits its capability.

Fig. 7.6 presents the ontological structure of the effect-oriented capability conceptualization. First, the system needs to be connected with the environment entities, because both the system and the environment entities will participate in the interactions (i.e., the event propagation, value transfer, and state detection) by sharing phenomena (i.e., the event, value, and state, respectively). The environment entities have been specified in the environment ontology in Part Two. As such, **SCuO** is related to the conceptualization of the system environment, i.e., the environment ontology, via **interactions**. This is the first component.

The second component of the capability conceptualization is the **scenarios**. Each scenario is a sequence of interactions to complete a particular business task for fulfilling a part of requirements. Here, the scenarios act as a "cognitive prosthesis" (Sutcliffe, 2003). They are examples to stimulate the system designer's imagination regarding how to satisfy the business requirements.

Based on the environment-based viewpoint mentioned in previous chapters, the capability of a system can be revealed by its imposed effects onto its environment entities, which are exhibited by the changes that happened on by these environment entities and the interactions between them and the system that cause these changes. Hence, the third component of the capability conceptualization is **effect**. The effect is imposed by the interactions between the systems and their environment entities and exhibited by the changes of the environment entities. In this way, the capabilities of the system are designated upon the environment entities.

The main constituents of **SCuO** are the interactions, the effects upon the environment entities, and the scenarios capturing the meaningful interaction sequences according to the requirements. After examining the applications of software-intensive systems in different domains as well as summarizing the results in books on system

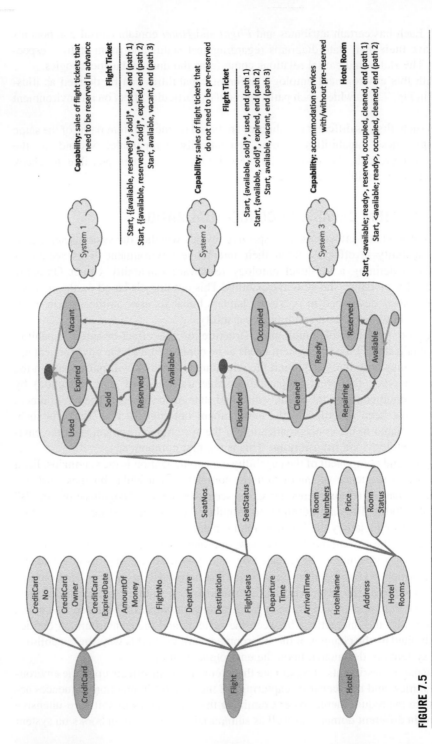

FIGURE 7.5

Three capability specifications.

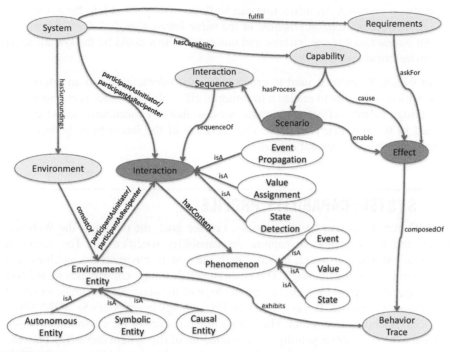

FIGURE 7.6

Ontological structure of effect-oriented capability conceptualization.

analysis and modeling, we extract a set of concept categories for building **SCuO**. These categories are related to each other to capture their context. They illustrate the basic understandings of the environment-based perspective on system capability:

- Any *system* shows one or more *capabilities*, each of which is exhibited by the *effect* upon a set of environment entities.
- Any system is developed to fulfil a set of requirements. Any part of the requirements can be instantiated as an effect upon the environment entities and will be realized by a certain *scenario*.
- Each *effect* is represented as a behavior trace graph of environment entities but is a result along with a *scenario*, which enables the *behavior trace graph* via an *interaction sequence* between the system and the environment entities.
- Each *scenario* is conducted by an *interaction sequence*, which consists of a set of *interactions* and the order relationship between them.
- The environment entity is further categorized into the *autonomous entity*, the *causal entity*, and the *symbolic entity*. Different entity categories can show different behaviors based on their own characteristics.
- Each *interaction* is a shared *phenomenon* between a software entity and an environment entity and represents one individual action in which the software

entity is involved. An interaction can be further categorized into the *event interaction*, the *state interaction*, or the *value interaction*.

- An *interaction* has one initiator and one receiver that could be the system or an environment entity.

In which, *Scenario* is used to group individual interactions into an interaction flow, which is the way to realize a meaningful effect. In this sense, *scenario* serves as a bridge between effects and interactions, so that any meaningful effect can be related to the way that realizes it, i.e., the trace of the interactions between the system and the environment entities.

7.3 SYSTEM CAPABILITY PROFILE

WSMO introduces four building blocks, i.e., the goal, the ontology, the Web services, and the mediator, to capture the capability specification. The proposed environment-based approach includes both the system environment ontology and the system capability ontology. The environment ontology corresponds to WSMO ontology, which gives the sharable terminology of the application domain in which the system will situate. The system capability ontology corresponds to WSMO Web services capability description. The distinguished feature of the environment-based perspective on system capability is the grounding of the system capability onto the environment entities, so that the different system entities' capabilities can be comparable in terms of the sharable environment entities. The environment modeling-based system capability is proposed as a way to obtain a more elaborate system capability specification than that found in an interface-based description for semantic Web services.

7.3.1 CAPABILITY PROFILE

How is the capability profile of a system entity defined? In answering this question, we first need to explore the kind of the effects that the environment ontology can show. An intuitive idea is to use the behaviors of the environment entities that can be caused by the system entity. We are trying to use the notion of ***running paths*** as the formalization tool, in which a running path describes possible behaviors of an environment entity.

Then, let e be an environment entity instance, and $h(e)$ the tree-like hierarchical state machine (THSM) of e with δ_e the state transition function and λ_e the output function. A finite effect path ρ of e is an alternative sequence of states and shared/sharing phenomena[10] starting from an initial state $e \cdot s_0$ ending with a final state $e \cdot s_n$;

---

[10]A shared phenomenon is an input symbol and a sharing phenomenon is an output symbol.

$$\rho =:= e \cdot s_0 \frac{phe_{1,e}^{in}}{phe_{1,e}^{out}} e \cdot s_1 \cdots e \cdot s_{n-1} \frac{phe_{n,e}^{in}}{phe_{n,e}^{out}} e \cdot s_n$$

so that in $h(e)$, $\delta_e\left(e \cdot s_i, phe_{i+1,e}^{in}\right) = e \cdot s_{i+1}$ and $\lambda_e\left(e \cdot s_i, phe_{i+1,e}^{in}\right) = phe_{i,e}^{out}$ for all $0 \leq i < n$. Note that we can also define the infinite effect path in the same way. However, to make things easier to understand, we only use the finite effect path in this book.

Normally, a capability may involve multiple environment entities. Hence, a capability profile may refer to more than one environment entity. Then a combined effect path is needed. Let $e_1, e_2, \cdots, e_n$ be n environment entities, and ρ_{e_i} be one of the effect paths of e_i ($0 \leq i < n$). A combined effect path is:

$$\Omega =:= \langle \rho_1, \cdots, \rho_n \rangle$$

Furthermore, we need to introduce the feasible effect path, because only feasible effects can happen in reality. But in which sense can the effect path be feasible? That is the system entity's duty. The system entity will make these effects happen. That is the essence of the capability of system entity. Next, we are at the step of defining the capability profile of system entity.

Let se be a system entity, $Ent = \{e_1, e_2, \cdots, e_n\}$ be the set of its environment entity instances, ρ_{e_i} be one of the effect paths of e_i ($1 \leq i \leq n$), and $\Omega = \langle \rho_{e_1}, \cdots, \rho_{e_n} \rangle$ a combined effect path. Then, along each ρ_{e_i} ($1 \leq i \leq n$):

- state $e_i \cdot s_0$ is reachable by the interaction with se if $e_i \cdot s_0$ is the start state of e_i
- output phenomena $\lambda_{e_i}(e_i \cdot s) = e_i \cdot s \cdot phe^{out}$ is enabled by the interaction with se if state $e_i \cdot s$ is reachable
- state $e_i \cdot s_j$ ($1 \leq j \leq i_n$) is reachable by the interaction with se if:
  - state $e_i \cdot s_{j-1}$ is reachable by the interaction with se and
  - input phenomenon phe_{j,e_i}^{in} is available and
  - $\delta_{e_i}\left(e_i \cdot s_{j-1}, phe_{j,e_i}^{in}\right) = e_i \cdot s_j$

The availability of the input phenomenon may depend on (or the composition of) the output phenomena of other environment entity instances. These dependence relations have been acknowledged in the environment ontology (as shown in Chapter 4). Essentially, with regard to the dependence relations, the role of the system entity is to establish the dependencies, i.e., to transform the dependees' output phenomena into the desired dependers' input phenomenon. For a system entity, the dependees' output phenomena are input and the dependers' input phenomenon is the output. We structure the dependence relations from the angle of the system entity as follows.

For any system entity se, its input phenomenon $\widetilde{phe}$ can be:

- an atomic phenomenon phe, which is an output phenomenon of an environment entity instance. It can be:
  - an event $event(phe)$ that occurred upon the dependee and is notified to se
  - a dependee's current state $state(phe)$ that is detected by se

- a dependee's attribute value $value(phe)$ that is passed to se
- a composite phenomenon phe. It can be:
  - $phe = phe_1 \succ phe_2$ if phe_1, phe_2 are phenomena and phe_1 precedes phe_2
  - $phe = phe^n$ if phe is a phenomenon and phe occurs n times ($n \in \mathbb{N}$)
  - $phe = phe_1 \otimes phe_2$ if phe_1, phe_2 are phenomena and either phe_1 or phe_2 occurs
  - $phe = phe_1 \otimes phe_2$ if phe_1, phe_2 are phenomena and both phe_1 or phe_2 occurs

As for any input phenomenon, there could be more than one dependee, and we denote the transformation on the set of environment entity instances that the system entity se will realize as:

$$\Im(se): \left(\wp\, Ent.\widetilde{phe} \right) \rightarrow \left(e.\widetilde{phe} \right)$$

in which $\widetilde{phe}$ is the output phenomenon of se and thus the input phenomenon of e. Fig. 7.7 illustrates the role of the system entity, which is obviously to establish the dependencies in domain business logics.

Then we can figure out the effect on the environment by the interactions with the system as follows. Let se be a system entity, $Ent = \{e_1, e_2, \cdots, e_n\}$ is the set of its

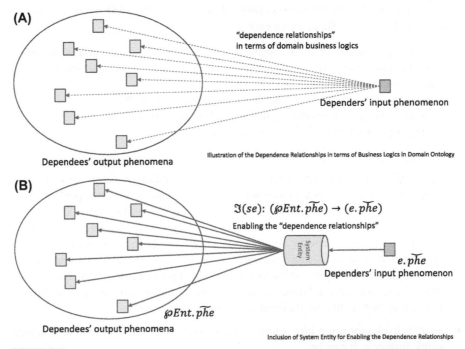

(A)

"dependence relationships" in terms of domain business logics

Dependers' input phenomenon

Dependees' output phenomena

Illustration of the Dependence Relationships in terms of Business Logics in Domain Ontology

(B)

$\Im(se): (\wp Ent.\widetilde{phe}) \rightarrow (e.\widetilde{phe})$

Enabling the "dependence relationships"

System Entity

$e.\widetilde{phe}$

Dependers' input phenomenon

$\wp Ent.\widetilde{phe}$

Dependees' output phenomena

Inclusion of System Entity for Enabling the Dependence Relationships

FIGURE 7.7

Purpose of including the system entity and the assigned transformation of the system entity.

environment entities, ρ_i is an effect path of e_i $(0 \le i < n)$, and $\Omega = \langle \rho_1, \cdots, \rho_n \rangle$ is a combined effect path. Let

$$\Phi = \{\{dom(\mathfrak{J}(se)), \; range(\mathfrak{J}(se))\} | \mathfrak{J}(se) \text{ is } se\text{'s function}\}$$

be a set of transformations on $\wp \, Ent$ that se can realize. Ω is feasible if all final states in Ω are reachable by the transformation set Φ. That effect Ω can be imposed by se upon Ent and can be written as $\Phi \Vvdash \Omega$. We call Ω a feasible combined effect path via the transformation set Φ of se.

Then let se be a system entity and $Env = \{e_1, e_2, \cdots, e_n\}$ the set of environment entity instances with which se interacts. Define

$$effs(se) =:= \{\Phi_1 \Vvdash \Omega_1, \cdots, \Phi_m \Vvdash \Omega_m\}$$

as the effect set that se can impose onto its environment, in which each Ω_i, $1 \le i \le m$, is a feasible combined effect path of se via the transformation set Φ_i.

The capability profile of a system entity se is defined as:

$$cap(se) =:= \langle ent(se), effs(se) \rangle$$

in which:

- $ent(se) = \{e_1, \cdots, e_n\}$ is a sct of environment entity instances of se
- $effs(se)$ is the effect set that se can impose onto its environment

7.3.2 AN EXAMPLE CAPABILITY PROFILE

This section gives an example to illustrate the environment ontology-based capability description. This is an online education system which delivers education courses designed by teachers to the learners through the Internet. One system entity is Intelligent Acquisition of Topic and Materials (called "ITAM") is able to configure topics and materials for an exploratory tutorial of Chinese geography (Wang et al., 2010). Its environment entities include "*teacher*", "*help entity*", "*study entity*", and "*exploratory tutorial[name?Chinese-geography]*". In an exploratory tutorial, "*help entity*" provides topics of Chinese geography for "*teacher*", and "*teacher*" obtains materials from "*study entity*". Fig. 5.4 in Chapter 5, gives the environment ontology for an education course (ECO).

In this example, there are several kinds of dependences in terms of the types of environment entity instances and the possible interaction contents. To be precise, let e_1 and e_2 be two environment entity instances. The dependence relations between e_1 and e_2 have the following categories:

1. <Event, Event > Dependence:

$$\langle e_1 \uparrow event(eve'), \; e_2 \downarrow event(eve) \rangle$$

when e_1 notifies an event eve', and it should be shared by e_2. This means: se needs to be aware event eve' and then share it with e_2 as an input event of e_2.

2. <Value, Value > Dependence:

$$\langle e_1 \uparrow value(attr'.val'), \quad e_2 \downarrow value(attr.val \infty val') \rangle$$

e_1 owns a symbolic attribute and its value is $attr'.val'$. When e_1 passes this value, e_2 needs to update its own symbolic attribute with val'. This means: se needs to send e_2 a value assignment by updating its attribute value $attr.val$ with val', when receiving $attr'.val'$ from e_1.

3. <Value, Event > Dependence:

$$\langle e_1 \uparrow value(val) \odot \vartheta, \quad e_2 \downarrow event(eve) \rangle$$

e_1 owns a symbolic attribute; its value is val. $value(val) \odot \vartheta$, which is a condition expression. When this condition expression becomes true, e_2 needs to receive event eve. This means: se needs to send to e_2 a value assignment by updating its attribute value $attr.val$ with val', when receiving $attr'.val'$ from e_1.

4. <State, Event > Dependence:

$$\langle e_1 \uparrow state(sta), \quad e_2 \downarrow event(eve) \rangle$$

when e_1, a causal entity, changes its state into state sta, e_2 needs to receive event eve. This means: se needs to issue an event eve when it detects that e_1 has changed its state to sta.

5. <State, Value > Dependence:

$$\langle e_1 \uparrow state(sta), \quad e_2 \downarrow value(attr = val) \rangle$$

when e_1, a causal entity, changes its state into state sta, e_2 needs to get a value assignment $attr = val$. Here, val is a value. This means: se needs to assign a value val to e_2's attribute $attr$, i.e., $attr = val$, when it detects that e_1 has changed its state to sta.

6. <Event, Value > Dependence:

$$\langle e_1 \uparrow event(eve), \quad e_2 \downarrow value(attr = val) \rangle$$

when e_1 notifies an event eve, e_2 needs to get a value assignment $attr = val$. Here, val is a value. This means: se needs to assign a value val to e_2's attribute $attr$, i.e., $attr = val$, when it is notified of an event eve from e_1.

Because the dependencies need to be established by se, the lightweight capability profile of se contains all of the dependencies. The lightweight capability description of IATM is shown in Table 7.1.

We can see from this example that the lightweight capability profile explicitly declares the dependencies that need to be established by the system entity. For example, dependences between teacher and exploratory tutorial are that:

1. *Teacher* creates a new exploratory tutorial named "*Chinese Geography*". As a result, an instance of *exploratory tutorial* is "*created*". When there are learners who have enrolled in this tutorial, the substate machine is initiated and the state is set to "*ready*"

Table 7.1 Lightweight Capability Profile of Intelligent Acquisition of Topic and Materials

---

Capability Profile of Intelligent Acquisition of Topic and Materials
> **Environment Entities**
>> {ECO:teacher; ECO:learner; ECO:help-Entity; ECO:study-Entity; ECO:exploratory-tutorial}

> **Dependences:** {
>> <teacher↑create(exploratory-tutorial[name?Chinese-geography]),
>>> Exploratory-tutorial[name:Chinese-Geography]: {state = created, enrNum = 0}>
>> <learner↑enroll(exploratory-tutorial[name:Chinese-geography]),
>>> Exploratory-tutorial[name:Chinese-Geography]: {enrNum ++}>
>> <teacher↑*requestTopic(Topic)*, Help-entity↓*request(Topic)*>
>> <help-entity↑*share(description)*, teacher↓*receive(Topic Description)*>
>> <teacher↑*offer(Information)*, Exploratory-tutorial↓*offer(Information)*>
>>> <teacher↑*requestMat(Topic)*, Study-entity ↓*request(topic)*>
>>> <study-entity↑get(content), teacher↓receiveMat(Content)>
>>> <teacher↑*re-give*, Exploratory-tutorial↓*reset*>
>>> <exploratory-tutorial↑push(Information), learner↓access(Information)>
>>> ......

> }

---

2. *Teacher* can request to obtain the "*topic description*" and the "*study material*" from *help entity* and the *study entity*, respectively
3. *Teacher* shares a phenomenon "↑*offer(topic description)*" and the state of the exploratory tutorial changes from "*ready*" to "*topic published*"; at the same time, the exploratory tutorial shares the phenomenon "*push(topic description)*". This is a transitional dependence. As a result, learners will access the "*topic description*"
4. *Teacher* shares a phenomenon "↑*offer(study materials)*" and the state of the exploratory tutorial changes from "*topic published*" to "*materials published*". This is also a transitional dependence. As a result, learners will access the "*study material*"
5. *Teacher* shares the phenomenon "↑*regive*" and the exploratory tutorial is the shared phenomenon "↓*reset*" and changes its state from "*materials published*" or "*topic published*" to "*ready*" for the next round

The effects that need to be imposed have not been explicitly given.

7.3.3 CAPABILITY SPECIFICATION GENERATION

With these dependencies, a forest-structured hierarchical state machine (FSHM) is formed, which can be defined as:

$$chm =:= \{ \mathcal{M}, dep_{\mathcal{M}} \}$$

in which:

- $\mathcal{M} = \{k_1, \cdots, k_n\}$ is a set of specific THSMs corresponding to an effect set
- $dep_{\mathcal{M}}$ is a set of dependencies among the specific hierarchical state machines (Alur et al., 1999) in $\mathcal{M}$.

The full capability specification of the system entity *se* is captured by an Forest-structured Hierarchical State Machine (FHSM), which consists of a set of specific THSMs with those phenomenon pairs that can be enabled by these specific HSMs.

Any specific THSM is a fragment of the domain THSM of one environment entity and each state transition in this fragmented domain THSM can be enabled by the system entity. The fragmented domain THSM represents the effect that the system entity can impose on this environment entity. According to the principle of effect-based assumption, all effects that the system entity can impose onto its environment entities represent the capability of the system entity. This means that the system entity can coordinate its environment entities to behave as desired. If we call each fragmented domain THSM, this can be executed by a specific system entity interacting with a specific THSM. A set of specific THSMs and the dependencies among them that need to be enabled by the system entity constitute the capability specification, i.e., the FHSM, of the system entity.

The capability of a system entity coordinates its environment entities by realizing the dependencies among these environment entities to enable the behaviors of these environment entities. The effects on the set of environment entities with the dependencies form a forest-structured hierarchical partial state machine. Here, "forest" means there could be more than one state diagram when the system entity needs to interact with multiple causal environment entities. "Partial" means that this state diagram is partial to the corresponding state diagram in the environment ontology.

Table 7.2 shows an algorithm for generating the FHSM from a lightweight capability profile based on the environment ontology.

Fig. 7.8 is a screenshot showing the FHSM *fhm*(*ITAM*) that is generated based on the capability profile of *IATM* and the environment ontology *ECO*. The state space is part of the environment ontology *ECO*.

7.4 SUMMARY

This chapter proposed an approach to the capability description of a system entity based on environment ontology. The main idea is that system capabilities can be grounded on their effects on environment entities. The main contributions of the chapter are:

- A capability description based on the environment ontology is proposed. On the basis of the environment ontology, the system's capabilities are described by its environment, the interactions with the environment, and the state transitions of the environment entities. With this capability description, the capabilities of two

Table 7.2 Algorithm for Generating a Forest-Structured Hierarchical State Machine

---

Algorithm Forest-Structured Hierarchical State Machine Generation

Input: Environment Ontology $\{Ent, Rel, rel, HSM, ksm, Dep\}$

   Capability Profile $\{ent(se), effs(se)\}$, in Which:

   $ent(se) = \{e_1, \cdots, e_n\} \subseteq Ent,$

   $effs(se) = \{InterSet_1 \odot TranSet_1, \cdots, InterSet_m \odot TranSet_m\}$. \\ $InterSet_i$ is a set of
                        interactions, and $TranSet_i$ is a set of transitions

Output: FHSM $fhm = \{K, inter_K\}$

1. Get $hsm(e_1), \cdots, hsm(e_n)$ which are domain HSMs of $e_1, \cdots, e_n$ from HSM, respectively,
2. Let $runhsms = \{hsm(e_1), \cdots, hsm(e_n)\}$; \\ to deposit the original THSMs to be *processed*
3. Let $readyhsms = \varnothing$;
4. **while** $(runhsms \neq \varnothing)$
5. $hsm(e) = GetFrom(runhsms)$; \\ *Getting a tree-like hierarchical state machine hsm(e) from runhsms*
6. $runhsms = runhsms - \{hsm(e)\}$;
7. $Interaction(e) = GetInteractionFrom(e, effs(se))$
8. $Transition(e) = GetTransitionFrom(e, effs(se))$; \\ obtaining the set of interactions that e involves and the set of e's state changes from the set of effects
9.   Let $k(e) = buildSpecificTHSM(hsm(e), Interaction(e), Transition(e))$;
      \\ **buildSpecificTHSM** is a procedure to build a specific THSM from original THSM according to the interaction set that e takes part and the state transitions that e undergo
10. $readyhsms = readyhsms \cup \{k(e)\}$
11.   Let $depIn(k(e)) = Interaction(e)$ keep the set of interactions that e take part in the specific THSM $k(e)$
12. **end while**
      \\ when $runhsms$ is empty, the THSMs in $readyhsms$ are the specific THSMs and dependencies between these specific THSMs are also created
13. FCHM, $chm = \{K, inter_K\}$ then is built as:
    $K = readyhsms = \{k(e_1), \cdots, k(e_n)\}$;
    $inter_K = \{depIn(k(e_1)), \cdots, depIn(k(e_n))\}$;
14. Return chm

---

systems, the required capability, and the provided capability become comparable. This enables capability reasoning about matchmaking that will be presented in Chapter 8.

- Another point is about capability decomposition. Capability decomposition becomes increasingly important as the system becomes more complex. With the capability description that has been grounded onto the environment entity state space, capability decomposition is transferred into the capability projection. This issue will be discussed in Chapter 9.

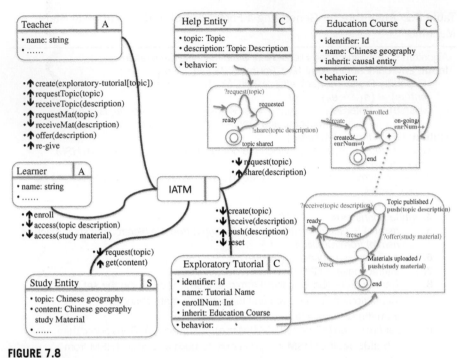

FIGURE 7.8

Capability specification of Intelligent Acquisition of Topic and Materials.

- Furthermore, such a capability description makes it possible to allow system entities to be aggregated autonomously for capability composition. Chapter 9 will present a mechanism to enable requirements-driven system entity collaboration, in which self-interested system entities actively and autonomously search for the required capability and compete to collaborate with each other to fulfill the required capability.

Reasoning I: System Capability Comparison and Composition

8

CHAPTER OUTLINE

Reason is the capacity to make sense of things consciously, apply logic, establish and verify facts, and change or justify practices, institutions, and beliefs based on new or existing information. Capability reasoning discussed in this part consists of three main reasoning capacities in requirements engineering: capability comparison, capability refinement, and capability aggregation. This chapter discusses capability comparison and composition. Capability comparison involves checking whether two pairs of capability descriptions are equivalent. Capability composition means composing simpler capability to construct a composite capability.

Concerning capability comparison and composition, the typical scenario as the first attempt is service discovery and service composition. Hence, in the following discussion, we will first present some related work in service-oriented computing.

8.1 RELATED WORK IN SERVICE-ORIENTED COMPUTING

As mentioned, service-oriented computing (Papazoglou et al., 2007) highlights a new paradigm in which three parties constitute the ecosystem of Web services on the Internet. As a computing paradigm, service-oriented computing promises a world of cooperating services that are loosely connected, creating dynamic business processes and agile applications that span organizations and platforms. From the viewpoint of software engineering, the main issue is that it uses services as fundamental elements to support the rapid, low-cost development of distributed applications in heterogeneous environments.

Research issues about capability discovery and matchmaking originate in service-oriented computing. When service providers advertise their services by publishing the services' capability description, service requesters ask for the desired capability via submitting the requirements descriptions. Service broker agencies find services that can potentially fulfill the requesters' needs by making judgments about the equivalence between the provided capability and the required capability. Achieving automated Web service discovery highlights the need for automated capability comparisons.

8.1.1 STANDARD LANGUAGES ENABLING MATCHMAKING

There are many available research efforts in this field. Earlier efforts include Extensible Markup Language (XML)-based standards such as Web Service Description Language (WSDL[1]). It is built on a Universal Description Discovery Integration (UDDI),[2] which provides a registry of Web services.

WSDL is an XML format for describing network services as a set of end points operating on messages containing either document-oriented or procedure-oriented information. The former is for abstract description and the latter is for physical binding. Only the abstract description part is interesting to service discovery and matchmaking; it uses the following elements:

- types: a container for data type definitions. It contains all data type definitions for elements that are required in the message definition.
- message: an abstract, typed definition of the data being communicated. It contains a set of part elements, each of which is an integral part of the final message. Each part will refer to a data type to represent its structure.
- port type: an abstract set of operations supported by one or more end points. It defines the type of service access entry, i.e., the mode and structure of the incoming/outgoing messages. Four modes are supported in WSDL, i.e., the one-way mode, the request-response mode, the solicit-response mode, and the notification mode. A port type can contain several operations, and an operation refers to an abstract description of an action supported by the service.

Without XML-based profiles, the **keyword-based search** is conducted against service in WSDL, which describes Web services in terms of their physical attributes, such as name, address, and services interface. Information retrieval and relevance assessment techniques are used for best match.

---

[1]http://www.w3.org/TR/2007/REC-wsdl20-20070626.
[2]http://uddi.org/pubs/uddi-v3.0.2-20041019.htm.

However, service capabilities in WSDL are scarcely represented semantically. Ontology-based Web service descriptions have made considerable progress in describing service capability from multiple perspectives. Major initiatives to be mentioned are Web Ontology Language for Services (OWL-S)[3] and Web Service Modeling Ontology (WSMO),[4] which were discussed in the previous chapter. The OWL-S capability model is based on a one-step process, i.e., the Input/Output/Precondition/Result (IOPR) schema. However, IOPR-based approaches fall short of logical relationships for underlying the inputs and the outputs. WSMO differentiates from OWL-S in that it specifies internal and external choreography by using abstract state machines. The external choreography also represents the service capabilities to some extent. The WSMO Mediator handles heterogeneity among the requesters and providers.

There are also some lightweight approaches annotating WSDL documents with semantic descriptions, such as WSDL-S.[5] WSDL-S uses semantic concepts analogous to those in OWL-S. However, similar to OWL-S, WSDL-S does not overcome the obstacles of the IOPR schema mentioned earlier.

8.1.2 SYNTACTIC SIMILARITY-BASED MATCHMAKING

Some extensions have been proposed to overcome such obstacles, to achieve automated and intelligent service discovery. Among others, Language for Advertisement and Request for Knowledge Sharing (LARKS) (Sycara et al., 2002) represents a typical effort along this line. It is an agent capability description language that aims to enable advertising, requesting, and matching agent capabilities. Compared with OWL-S and others, the main feature of LARKS is that it includes logical constraints on input/output variables via the Horn clause and attaches each variable that appears in the specification to a concept of the domain ontology. With these settings, LARKS allows reasoning on the service specification based on the domain ontology.

The capability specification in LARKS is written via a frame language, as shown in Table 8.1.

Reasoning for service matchmaking in LARKS includes context matching, profile comparison, similarity matching, signature matching, and constraints matching. However, all five steps are based on the comparison and the similarity measurement of the "terms" or "variable" in corresponding slots.

For example, context matching compares the "context" section by checking whether the contexts in the advertised capability specifications and in the requested capability description are the same or similar. After context matching, advertised capability specifications that have the same or similar context of the required capability description are selected as candidate services for further matchmaking.

---

[3]http://www.w3.org/Submission/OWL-S/.
[4]http://www.w3.org/Submission/WSMO/.
[5]http://www.w3.org/Submission/WSDL-S/.

Table 8.1 Frame Language in Language for Advertisement and Request for Knowledge Sharing (Sycara et al., 2002)

Context[6]	Context of Specification
Types	Declaration of used variable types (optional)
Input	Declaration of input variables
Output	Declaration of output variables
InConstraints	Logical constraints on input variables in Horn clause
OutConstraints	Logical constraints on output variables in Horn clause
ConcDescriptions	Ontological descriptions of used words (optional)
TextDescription	Textual description of specification (optional)

The profiles, similarity, and signature matching compare the requested capability description with the capability specifications of the candidate services. The profile matching uses a weighted keyword representation for the specifications and a given term frequency-based similarity measurement.

Computation of similarity relies on a combination of distance values as calculated for pairs of input/output declarations and input/output constraints. Each distance value is computed in terms of the distance between concepts and words that occur in their respective specification section.

The signature filter considers the declaration parts of the requested capability description and the advertised capability specification, and determines according to each pair whether their signatures of the (input/output) variable types match following the subtyping inference rules based on the domain ontology.

The constraint matching focuses on the (input/output) constraints and declaration parts of the specifications. It checks whether the input/output constraints of any pair of requested capability description and advertised capability specification logically match.

LARKS are mainly of a syntactic reasoning by the subtyping rules and the term similarity based on a domain ontology. The semantic reasoning relies on the constraints matching via the reasoning on the Horn clause specified in the input/output constraints.

8.1.3 BEHAVIOR-BASED INTELLIGENT MATCHMAKING

Behavior-based service capability description tries to model service behaviors and conduct matchmaking via behavior equivalence. Various behavioral models including extended finite-state automata, process algebraic notations, graph formalism, and logic formalism are studied.

---

[6]Here, context means a set of related keywords or topics about the capability specification.

For example, (Shen et al., 2005) assumed that the capability of a Web service is modeled as an extended automaton. Two kinds of state (i.e., the messaging state and the activity state) in the automaton can be distinguished, because any run of a Web service process can be explained in terms of receiving or sending messages and performing activities. Here, the messages are observable conversations between cooperating services or between activities within a Web service and the activities that are performed inside the service.

With the automaton representation, the capability of a Web service can be denoted as a language of the automaton. Then the required capability is a capability query regarding the properties of behavior signatures. The output for a query is a set of services whose behaviors satisfy these constraints.

Such a behavior-based service description is more expressive than the interface-based description, because behaviors can be captured as the same semantic descriptions, even though Web services are developed by different teams and are described in different conceptual frameworks without prior agreement.

In addition, some other efforts focus on the service contextual information. It has also been modeled with the purposes of coordinating and collaborating Web services in their actual implementation. WS-Resource[7] and WS-Context[8] are proposed to promote interoperability among Web services and their state interactions. For example, many researchers focus on defining context by categorizing the context, e.g., the computing category, user category, and physical category to enhance systems with context-aware capabilities.

8.1.4 SERVICE COMPOSITION

Web service composition is a combination of several existing services to create a value-added composite service. It aims to combine and coordinate a set of services with the purpose of achieving functionality that cannot be realized through existing services. The efforts in the service community assume that all services follow an interface-based model. That is, any service is defined as an activity that can be invoked by its interface. Then two mechanisms are provided to describe the sequence of activities that make up the composite business process: service **orchestration** and service **choreography** (Peltz, 2003).

In orchestration, the logic is specified from the local viewpoint of one single participant, called the orchestrator. That is, service orchestration represents a single executable business process that coordinates interaction among the different services by describing a flow from the perspective and under the control of a single end point. Orchestration can be considered a construct between an automated process and the individual services that enact the steps in the process. Orchestration

---

[7]http://docs.oasis-open.org/wsrf/wsrf-ws+resource-1.2-spec-os.pdf.
[8]http://docs.oasis-open.org/we-caf/ws-context/v1.0/wsctx.html.

includes the management of transactions between the individual services, including any necessary error handling, as well as a description of the overall process. The standard for Web services orchestration is Web Services Business Process Execution Language.[9]

However, service choreography is more collaborative and allows each involved party to describe its part in the interaction. In choreography, the logic of message-based interactions between the participants is specified according to a global perspective. Choreography represents a global description of the observable behavior of each service participating in the interaction, which is defined by the public exchange of messages, rules of interaction, and agreements between two or more business process end points. Choreography is typically associated with interactions that occur among multiple Web services rather than a specific business process that a single party executes. The choreography mechanism is supported by the standard Web Services Choreography Description Language.[10]

8.2 ENVIRONMENT MODELING-BASED CAPABILITY COMPARISON

Now, back to the capability reasoning in the environment modeling-based approach. Capability comparison is needed to find a suitable system entity for a particular piece of requirements. Here, requirements represent the required capability, and the system has designed capability. Capability comparison is like a conformance test for checking whether the designed capability can actually satisfy the requirements.

According to an environment-based view on capability modeling, the capability of a designed system entity is a set of effects that the system entity can impose on its environment. It is specified as a set of interactions with environment entities and the changes that will happen in those entities. Thus, in the following section, we will see what the required capability is and how we may compare it with the designed capability.

8.2.1 REQUIRED CAPABILITY

As shown in the first part, requirements are about the properties of the environment and are considered to be the required effects on the environment, but are not relevant to implementation. From such a perspective, requirements can be represented in the same way as the designed capability. That is, requirements concern a set of expected environment entities and a set of expected changes imposed on those entities.

This section shows such requirements to explain the meaning of the required effects. The following example is also from the online education system (Wang et al., 2010). It needs a system entity, the "Intelligent Exploratory Tutorial of Geography" (IETG), which can allow teachers to offer *geography exploratory tutorials*. Specifically, in

---

[9]http://www.oasis-open.org/committees/download.php/23964/wsbpel-v2.0-primer.htm.
[10]https://www.w3.org/TR/ws-cdl-10/.

Table 8.2 Required Capability Description of Intelligent Exploratory Tutorial of Geography[11]

```
Required Capability Profile IETG
   Environment Entities:
      {teacher, learner, exploratory-tutorial[name?geography], help-entity, study-entity}

   Effect Set:
         {teacher↑create(exploratory-tutorial[name?Geography])}
            ⊙{exploratory-tutorial[name?Geography]: null→ready}
         {learner↑enroll(exploratory-tutorial[name?Chinese-geography])}
            ⊙{exploratory-tutorial[name?Geography]: enrollNum++}

         {teacher↑request(info), help-entity↓request(info),
          help-entity↑share(topic), teacher↓shared(topic),
          teacher↑give(topic), exploratory-tutorial[Geo] ↓obtains(topic)}
            ⊙{help-entity: ready→topic sent,
               exploratory-tutorial[Geo]: ready→topic published}

         {study-entity↑get(materials), teacher↓(materials),
          teacher↑give(materials), exploratory-tutorial[Geo] ↓obtain(materials)}
            ⊙{exploratory-tutorial[Geo]: topic published→materials published}

         {teacher↑re-give, exploratory-tutorial[Geo] ↓re-obtain}
            ⊙{exploratory-tutorial[Geo]: materials published→topic published}

         {learner↑access(materials), exploratory-tutorial[Geo] ↓access(materials)}
            ⊙{exploratory-tutorial[Geo]:materials published→materials accessed}

         {learner↑submit(Study Result), exploratory-tutorial[Geo] ↓analyze(Study Result),
            teacher↓askForAnalysis(Study Result)}
            ⊙{exploratory-tutorial[Geo]: materials uploaded→Analysis Asked}

         {learner↑draw(conclusion,learner.name.val),
            exploratory-tutorial[Geo] ↓draw(conclusion,learner.name.val)}
            ⊙{exploratory-tutorial[Geo]: materials analyzed→conclusion received}

         {teacher↑provide(summary),
          exploratory-tutorial[Geo]↓provide(summary)}
            ⊙{exploratory-tutorial[Geo]: conclusion finished→end}
   }
```

this exploratory tutorial of geography, *teacher* obtains topic descriptions from *help entity* and obtains study materials from *study entity*. *Learner* can enroll in the tutorial and access information about the tutorial. When *learner* finishes the study and submits the study results, *teacher* can analyze the results to draw a conclusion. Finally, *teacher* summarizes these conclusions. Obviously, the environment entities mentioned in the requirements include *teacher*, *learner*, *help entity*, *study entity*, and *exploratory tutorial*. Table 8.2 presents a description of the requirements.

---

[11] ↑ means the environment entity on the left is sharing the phenomenon on the right; ↓ means the environment entity on the left is shared with the phenomenon on the right; → means the path from the left-hand side state to the right-hand side state.

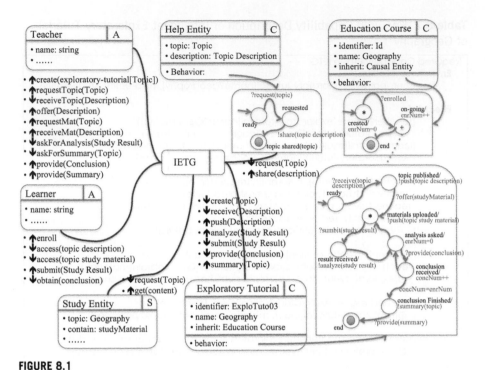

FIGURE 8.1

Required capability specification of Intelligent Exploratory Tutorial of Geography.

Based on the requirement description, the required Forest-structured Hierarchical State Machine (FHSM) is generated via Algorithm 7.3 by reasoning on the environment ontology for the education course. Fig. 8.1 shows the FHSM of the required capability.

8.2.2 CONTEXT SIMILARITY

The capability comparison for system entity discovery includes a two-step process. To compare a required capability with a provided capability, first we need to measure the similarity of their environments, because two capabilities are meaningful only when the system entities are in their own environments. Environment comparison is easy. It is mainly based on the similarity of terminology in terms of the environment ontology. Formally, let

$$Cap(req) = \{Ent^{req}, \ Effs^{req}\}$$

be a required capability profile and

$$Cap(ava) = \{Ent^{ava}, \ Effs^{ava}\}$$

be an available capability profile. The first step is to compare their environments to see whether they have similar environment entity sets, i.e., compare Ent^{req} and Ent^{ava}.

First, for any two environment entities:

$$e_1 = id_1[s.attr_{11}?v_{11}, \ldots s.attr_{1n}?v_{1n}]$$

$$e_2 = id_2[s.attr_{21}?v_{21}, \ldots, s.attr_{2m}?v_{2m}]$$

in which $s.attr_{1i} \in NAttrs(e_1)$, $i \in [1, n]$ and $s.attr_{2j} \in NAttrs(e_2)$, $j \in [1, n]$. For values of a noncharacteristic attribute, $v_{1i} \sqsubseteq v_{2j}$ means that v_{1i} is a subtype of v_{2j}. When values of noncharacteristic attributes are not designated here, the values are universal and are denoted as $\top$ (for any value $v \sqsubseteq \top$). If e_1 and e_2 are the same environment entity, $id_1 == id_2$, or if e_1 is a subtype of e_2, $id_1 \sqsubseteq id_2$.

Thus, three kinds of relationships between two environment entities, e_1 and e_2, can be defined (Wang et al., 2008, 2010):

- (subsumption) $e_1 \sqsubseteq e_2 \Leftrightarrow$

  $(id_1 \sqsubseteq id_2 \ \vee \ id_1 == id_2) \wedge$
  $\forall s.attr_{1i} \in NAttrs(e_1), \exists s.attr_{2j} \in NAttrs(e_2)$
  $\quad (s.attr_{1i} == s.attr_{2j} \wedge (v_{1i} == v_{2j} \ \vee \ v_{1i} \sqsubseteq v_{2j}))$

  e_1 is a subtype of e_2 or they are the same environment entity, and their noncharacteristic attributes and values match inclusively.

- (equivalence) $e_1 == e_2 \Leftrightarrow e_1 \sqsubseteq e_2 \wedge e_1 \sqsupseteq e_2$

  e_1 and e_2 are the same environment entity, and their noncharacteristic attributes and values match exactly.

- (intersection) $e_1 \sqcap e_2 \Leftrightarrow$

  $(id_1 \sqsubseteq id_2 \ \vee \ id_1 \sqsupseteq id_2 \ \vee \ id_1 == id_2) \wedge$
  $\exists s.attr_{1i} \in NAttrs(e_1), \exists s.attr_{2j} \in NAttrs(e_2)$
  $\quad (s.attr_{1i} == s.attr_{2j} \wedge (v_{1i} == v_{2j} \ \vee \ v_{1i} \sqsupseteq v_{2j} \ \vee \ v_{1i} \sqsubseteq v_{2j}))$

  e_1 is a subtype of e_2 or e_2 is a subtype of e_1, or they are the same environment entity, and they have some equal values of noncharacteristic attributes.

Second, in consideration of their inheritance relations, noncharacteristic attributes, and corresponding values, Ent^{req} and Ent^{ava} are compared using a set-based approach (Wang et al., 2008, 2010):

- $\forall e^{req} \in Ent^{req}, \ \neg \exists e^{ava} \in Ent^{ava}$

  $e^{req} \sqsubseteq e^{ava} \ \vee \ e^{req} \sqsupseteq e^{ava} \ \vee \ e^{req} \sqcap e^{ava}$

  There is a "_non-match_" between Ent^{req} and Ent^{ava} ($Ent^{req} \cap Ent^{ava} = \phi$). The environment entities in the required capability profile and the environment entities that the available capability profile refers to are irrelevant. In this situation, the comparison process terminates.

- $\forall e^{req} \in Ent^{req}, \ \exists e^{ava} \in Ent^{ava} e^{req} \sqsubseteq e^{ava}$

  There is a "_plug-in match_" between Ent^{req} and Ent^{ava} ($Ent^{req} \subseteq Ent^{ava}$). The environment entities in the required capability profile form only a subset of the environment entities' set to which that available capability profile refers.

- $\forall e^{ava} \in Ent^{ava}, \exists e^{req} \in Ent^{req} e^{req} \sqsupseteq e^{ava}$
  There is a "*subsume match*" between Ent^{req} and Ent^{ava} ($Ent^{req} \sqsupseteq Ent^{ava}$). The relevant environment entities in the required capability profile form a superset of the environment entities' set to which that available capability profile refers.
- $Ent^{req} \subseteq Ent^{ava} \wedge Ent^{req} \sqsupseteq Ent^{ava}$
  There is an "*exact match*" between Ent^{req} and Ent^{ava} ($Ent^{req} == Ent^{ava}$). The environment entities in the required capability profile and the set of environment entities to which the available capability profile refers match perfectly.
- $\exists e^{req} \in Ent^{req}, \exists e^{ava} \in Ent^{ava} e^{req} \sqsubseteq e^{ava} \vee e^{req} \sqsupseteq e^{ava} \vee e^{req} \sqcap e^{ava}$
  There is an "*intersection match*" between Ent^{req} and Ent^{ava} ($Ent^{req} \cap Ent^{ava} \neq \phi$). The environment entities in the required capability profile and the set of environment entities to which the available capability profile refers have a "nonempty" intersection.

Back to the example, on the basis of the environment ontology for an education course, a comparison of the set of environment entities in the user requirements (IETG) and that in the system entity for the Intelligent Acquisition of Topic and Materials (IATM) can be performed:

The environment entities in the requirements are:

$$IETG : \{\text{teacher, learner, help entity, study entity, exploratory}$$
$$\text{tutorial [name? geography]}\}$$

The environment entities in the system entity are:

$$IATM : \{\text{teacher, exploratory tutorial [name? Chinese} - \text{geography]},$$
$$\text{help entity, study entity}\}$$

Moreover, Chinese geography is a subclass of geography

$$(\text{Chinese} - \text{geography} \sqsubseteq \text{geography})$$

Therefore,

$$IETG : Ent^{req} \sqsupseteq IATM : Ent^{ava}$$

This means that there is a subsume match between the environment entities in the requirement description and the capability description of the system entity.

8.2.3 EFFECT COMPARISON

After the sets of environment entities are compared, the fact that there is relevancy (no nonmatch) between Ent^{req} and Ent^{ava} means that they have some common or relevant environment entities. Thus, a comparison of their effects on the common or relevant environment entities can be performed. Because the FHSM is generated according to an effect set grounded on the environment ontology (see Algorithm.7.2), the comparison of effects is regarded as one between FHSMs generated on the effects. Therefore, the problem is how to compare the two FHSMs. We perform the comparison in terms of the equivalence, the inclusion, or the intersection relations between the FHSMs.

Back to the example, Fig. 7.8 shows the capability specification of system entity IATM, and Fig. 8.1 shows the required capability profile. The relevant environment entities of IETG: Ent^{req} and IATM: Ent^{ava} are same, i.e.,

$$\{teacher, learner, exploratory\ tutorial, help\ entity, study\ entity\}$$

This step is to compares their FHSMs.

How do we compare the two FHSMs? It is known that comparing the general communicating hierarchical state machines (CHM) (Alur et al., 1999) consumes extra exponential space. This is because of arbitrary nesting of the concurrency and hierarchy constructs. However, the forest communicating hierarchical state machine (FHSM) is a well-structured subclass of the general CHM in which arbitrary nesting of the concurrency and hierarchy constructs is not allowed. We also perform a comparison in terms of the equivalence, inclusion, or intersection relations between FHSMs.

Before performing the comparison of two FHSMs, some basic notations are given. Let $chm = \{\{k_1, \ldots\ldots, k_n\}, inter_K\}$ be an FHSM, $S(k_i)$ be the set of states in $k_i \in \{k_1, \ldots\ldots, k_n\}$, and $S(chm)$ be the set of all states in $chm(S(k_i) \subseteq S(chm))$.

States $a, b \in S(chm)$ are simultaneous $(a|b)$, iff $a \in S(k_i)$, $b \in S(k_j)$, $i, j \in [1, n], i \neq j$. States a and b are simultaneous if they are in different specific tree-like hierarchical state machines (THSMs). For example, the FHSM in Fig. 8.1 states that *"help entity: requested"* and *"exploratory tutorial: topic published"* are simultaneously pairwise because they are in different THSMs.

A set $A \in 2^{S(chm)}$ is said to be consistent if $\forall a, b \in A : a|b$. It means that all elements in A are pairwise simultaneously. The set *{help entity: requested, exploratory tutorial: topic published}* is an example consistent set.

The global state of FHSM *chm* is defined as a maximal consistent set: $A \in 2^{S(chm)}$, $\forall x \in S(chm) - A : \neg consistent(A \cup \{x\})$

For example, in Fig. 8.1, *{help entity: requested, exploratory tutorial: topic published}* is a global state. If we add an arbitrary state, e.g., *"help entity: topic shared"*, into the set, the set will become inconsistent because *"help entity: requested"* and *"help-entity: topic shared"* are not simultaneous. After defining the global state, we can define a next-state relation, which is referred to as the global state transition under triggers of FHSM.

The next-state relation of FHSM is defined as $F \subseteq G \times 2^{\Sigma^{in}} \times G$, in which G is the set of global states of the FHSM and Σ^{in} is the set of inputs to the FHSM.

For example, in Fig. 8.1,

$$g_1 = \{help\ entity: ready, exploratory\ tutorial: ready\},$$

$$g_2 = \{help\ entity: topic\ shared, exploratory\ tutorial: topic\ published\}$$

are two global states.

$$\langle g_1, \{teacherrequest(topic), help\ entity?request(topic),$$
$$help\ entityshare(topic\ description),$$
$$teacherreceiveTopic(topic\ description),$$
$$teacheroffer(topic\ description),$$
$$exploratorytutorialreceive(topic\ description)\}, g_2\rangle$$

is a global state transition in which *"teacher"* sends out a message.

↑*request(topic)*, "*help entity*" then receives the message and stops at state topic "*requested*", "*help entity*", sends out a message "*share(topic description)*", and stops at state "*topic shared*". Then, *teacher* receives the message.

"↓*receiveTopic (topic description)*". This means that *teacher* obtains a topic description from *help entity*. Afterward, *teacher* sends out a message "*offer(topic)*". *Exploratory tutorial* receives this message, and its state changes from *ready* to *topic published* and then sends out "*push (topic description)*" to the enrolled *learner*s. This means that *teacher* configures a topic description about the education course and delivers the description to enrolled *learner*s.

Given that the two FHSMs chm_1 and chm_2 and a binary relation $\varphi \subseteq G_1 \times G_2$ (G_1 is the set of global states of chm_1 and G_2 is the set of global states of chm_2), let F_1 and F_2 be the next state relations of chm_1 and chm_2, and $\Sigma^{in}(g)$ be the set of inputs to global state g. We give the following four conditions (Wang et al., 2008; 2010):

1. $<\sigma_1, \sigma_2> \in \varphi, \sigma_1, \sigma_2$ are the initial global states of chm_1 and chm_2 respectively
2. $<g_1, g_2> \in \varphi \Rightarrow \forall i \in 2^{\Sigma^{in}(g_1)} g_1' < g_1, i, g_1' > \in F_1 \Rightarrow \exists g_2' < g_2, i, g_2' > \in F_2 \land <g_1', g_2'> \in \varphi$
3. $<g_1, g_2> \in \varphi \Rightarrow \forall i \in 2^{\Sigma^{in}(g_2)} g_2' < g_2, i, g_2' > \in F_2 \Rightarrow \exists g_1' < g_1, i, g_1' > \in F_1 \land < g_1', g_2'> \in \varphi$
4. $<g_1, g_2> \in \varphi \Rightarrow \exists i \in s^{\Sigma^{in}(g_1)} g_1' < g_1, i, g_1' > \in F_1 \Rightarrow \exists g_2' < g_2, i, g_2' > \in F_2 \land <g_1', g_2'> \in \varphi$

If φ satisfies conditions 1 and 2, and does not satisfies condition 3, φ is an inclusion relation and we say that chm_1 is included by chm_2 under φ, $chm_1 \sqsubseteq^\varphi chm_1$. Symmetrically, if φ satisfies conditions 1 and 3 and does not satisfies condition 2, we say that chm_1 includes chm_2 under φ, $chm_1 \sqsupseteq^\varphi chm_2$. If φ satisfies conditions 1, 2, and 3, φ is an equivalence relation, and chm_1 and chm_2 are equal under φ, $chm_1 =^\varphi chm_2$. If φ satisfies condition 4 and does not satisfies condition 2 and 3, φ is an intersection relation and we say that chm_1 intersects with chm_2 under φ, and $chm_1 \sqcap^\varphi chm_2$. If φ does not satisfy any of these conditions, we say that chm_1 is irrelevant to chm_2 under φ, and $chm_1 \nleftrightsquigarrow^\varphi chm_2$. The matching degrees between two FHSMs chm_{req} and chm_{ava} are listed in Table 8.3.

Table 8.3 Match Degrees Between chm_{req} and chm_{ava} (Wang et al., 2008; 2010)

Type of Capability Match	Meaning
Exact Match	$chm_{req} =^\varphi chm_{ava}$
Plug-in Match	$chm_{req} \sqsubseteq^\varphi chm_{ava}$
Subsume Match	$chm_{req} \sqsupseteq^\varphi chm_{ava}$
Intersection Match	$chm_{req} \sqcap^\varphi chm_{ava}$
Nonmatch	$chm_{req} \nleftrightsquigarrow^\varphi chm_{ava}$

The comparison between IETG: Eff^{req} and IATM: Eff^{ava} can be presented. According to Table 8.3, there is a subsume match between them. Moreover, in the first step there is a subsume match between IETG: Eff^{req} and IATM: Eff^{ava}. In other words, system entity IATM only partially satisfies the requirements. To satisfy the requirements completely, system entity IATM needs to collaborate with other system entities.

8.3 ENVIRONMENT MODELING-BASED CAPABILITY COMPOSITION

Capability composition combines some available capability units to create a new capability unit so that it can satisfy the user's complex requirements. First, the capabilities of available capability units are specified by using their effects on the environment entities; second, the piece of requirements is also specified by using the desired effects on the environment entities; thus, capability composition finally can be performed by reasoning on the effects of the candidate capability units to achieve the desired effects of the requirements.

This section uses an example to illustrate the effect-based capability composition (Wang and Jin, 2006). We assume that there are four capability units: ticket selling (TS), ticket delivery (TD), hotel service (HS), and payment service (PS). They have three shared environment entities, *ticket[departure?China, destination?China]*, *hotelroom[location?China]*, and *creditcard[type?MasterCard]*, derived from the environment ontology, budget traveling ontology (BTO). Given the requirements G_{travel} that needs a budget traveling capability for travelers, this goal can be represented as a set of desired effects on the three environment entities. Obviously, any one of the four capabilities cannot satisfy G_{travel} on its own. There should be a possibility of combining the four capability units together to fulfill G_{travel}. The composition is conducted by combining their effects on the three environment entities in terms of the satisfaction of the desired effects of G_{travel}. The desired effects of G_{travel} are given in Table 8.4.

Table 8.4 Desired Effects

Required Capability Profile Budget Traveling (BTA)
Environment Entities:
{ticket, hotelroom, creditcard}
Effect Set:
{ticket[departure?China,destination?China] ↑({orderInfo,orderCancelInfo, reAvailableInfo,accountInfo,deliveryInfo},{deliveredInfo}) ⊙ ticket[departure?China,destination?China]: available→{ordered,cancelled}→delivered}
{hotelroom[location?China] ↑({orderInfo,orderCancelInfo,reVacancyInfo, accountInfo},{paidInfo}) ⊙ hotelroom[location?China]:vacancy→{ordered,cancelled}→paid}
{creditcard[type:MasterCard] ↑({chargeInfo},{chargedInfo}) ⊙, creditcard[type:MasterCard]:valid→charged}

Table 8.5 Effects of Four Available Capability Units

Ticket-Selling (*TS*)

{ticket[departure?China,destination?China] ↑({orderInfo,orderCancelInfo, reAvailableInfo,accountInfo},{soldInfo})

⊙ ticket[departure?China,destination?China]:

available→{ordered,cancelled}→sold}

Ticket-Delivery (*TD*)

{ticket[departure?China,destination?China] ↑({deliveryInfo},{deliveredInfo})

⊙ ticket[departure?China,destination?China] : sold→delivered}

Hotel Service (*HS*)

{hotelroom[location?China] ↑{{orderInfo,orderCancelInfo,reVacancyInfo, accountInfo},{paidInfo})

⊙ hotelroom[location?China] :vacancy→{ordered,cancelled}→paid}

Payment Service (*PS*)

{creditcard[type:MasterCard] ↑{{chargeInfo},{chargedInfo}}

⊙ , creditcard[type:MasterCard] :valid→charged}

Moreover, the effects of the four available Web services (TS, TD, HS, and PS) are listed in Table 8.5.

According to the budget traveling environment ontology shown in Fig. 5.5, the four capability units are generated based on their effects. They are viewed as the capability specifications of the four available capability units.

Given the four available capability units $CU = \{TS, TD, HS, PS\}$, a composition of CU is an FHSM chm_{bta} such that chm_{bta} delegates all state transitions in the FHSMs chm_{ts}, chm_{td}, chm_{hs}, and chm_{ps} of the four capability units. Given requirements G_{travel}, which cannot be satisfied by any available capability units, the capability composition for satisfying G_{travel} is required to check whether a composition chm_{bta} exists that realizes G_{travel}.

Formally, given two FHSMs chm_1 and chm_2, the task to obtain a desired composition chm of chm_1 and chm_2 can be decomposed to the following two sub-tasks. First, we compose the specific THSMs in chm_i ($i=1, 2$), which are of same environment entity. For example, in the two FHSMs, $chm_{ts} = \left\{ \left\{ k_{ticket}^{ts} \right\}, \varnothing \right\}$ (Fig. 8.2A) and $chm_{ts} = \left\{ \left\{ k_{ticket}^{td} \right\}, \varnothing \right\}$ (Fig. 8.2B), k_{ticket}^{ts} and k_{ticket}^{td} are of the same environment entity "*ticket*". We need to check whether there exists a target THSM k_{ticket}^{bta} by composing k_{ticket}^{ts} and k_{ticket}^{td}. Second, state—trigger—transitions among these composed specific THSMs are constructed according to the environment ontology. For example, we suppose that $k_{creditcard}^{bta}$ is a composition of $k_{creditcard}^{bta}$ and $\varnothing$ (there is no other specific THSM of *creditcard* except for $k_{creditcard}^{bta}$ in elementary FHSMs). It is described in the environment ontology BTO that a state valid in $k_{creditcard}^{bta}$ can trigger a state transition from ordered to

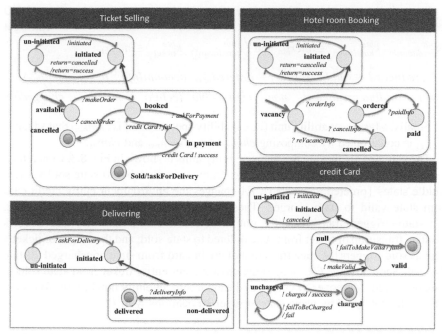

FIGURE 8.2

Four available capability units.

sold in k_{ticket}^{bta}. Therefore, there is a state–trigger–transition relation between $k_{creditcard}^{bta}$ and k_{ticket}^{bta}.

Concretely, we present here how to compose the chm_{ts}, chm_{td}, chm_{hs}, and chm_{ps} of four available capability units to obtain the desired chm_{bta}. First, we present how to check whether a target THSM k_{ticket}^{bta} exists by composing k_{ticket}^{ts} and k_{ticket}^{td}. The technique for composing finite state machines in terms of satisfying a formula of deterministic propositional dynamic logic (DPDL) can be used here (Berardi et al., 2003). The process could be:

- translating k_{ticket}^{bta}, k_{ticket}^{ts}, and k_{ticket}^{td} into a set of DPDL formulas, and a DPDL formula Φ_{ticket} that captures the composition can be built as a conjunction of these formulas
- formulating the problem of composition existence of the target THSM k_{ticket}^{bta} as the DPDL proposition. The DPDL formula Φ_{ticket} is satisfiable if and only if there exists the target THSM k_{ticket}^{bta} by composing k_{ticket}^{ts} and k_{ticket}^{td}.
- constructing the target THSM k_{ticket}^{bta} by composing k_{ticket}^{ts} and k_{ticket}^{td} after validating the satisfaction of formula Φ_{ticket} based on the standard tableau algorithm
- because there is only one $k_{creditcard}^{ps}$, which is a specific THSM of *creditcard*, $k_{creditcard}^{bta}$ is $k_{creditcard}^{ps}$. Similarly, $k_{hotelroom}^{bta}$ is also $k_{hotelroom}^{hs}$.

Second, the two state—trigger—transitions in the environment ontology BTO between "*ticket*" and "*creditcard*" are given as follows. We can get $\left\langle k_{creditcard}^{bta},\ k_{hotelroom}^{bta} \right\rangle \in inter_{bta}$ and $\left\langle k_{creditcard}^{bta},\ k_{ticket}^{bta} \right\rangle \in inter_{bta}$.

$$creditcard - valid_{bta} \uparrow \langle ticket - ordered_{bta},\ accountInfo,\ ticket - sold_{bta} \rangle$$
$$ticket - soldbta\ creditcard - non - chargedbta,\ feeInfo,\ creditcard - chargedbta$$

Finally, a target capability unit (its capability specification is chm_{bta}) that satisfies G_{travel} is constructed by composing chm_{ts}, chm_{td}, chm_{hs}, and chm_{ps}.

The result of composing the four capability units is shown in Fig. 8.3. Concretely, *TS* changes the environment entity ticket from state available to state sold via two middle states {ordered, cancelled}. *PA* changes the environment entity credit card from state valid to state charged. These two services are synchronous by using two state—trigger—transitions: the output of credit card's state as valid triggers the state transition of ticket from state ordered to state sold, and the output of ticket's state as sold triggers the state transition of credit card from state noncharged to state charged. Sequentially, *TD* changes the environment entity ticket from state sold to state delivered. Moreover, *HS* changes the environment entity hotel room from state ordered to state paid by using state—trigger—transitions with *PS*.

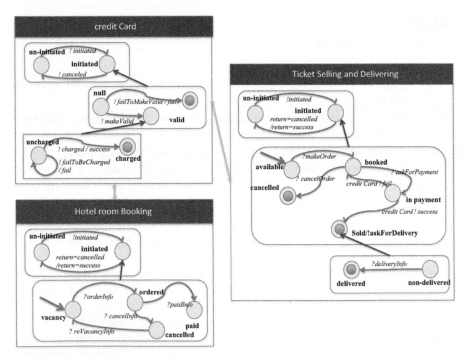

FIGURE 8.3

Composite capability units.

Table 8.6 Composite Capability Schema

```
<capability_composition>
  <capability unit name="TS">
    <input>orderInfo,orderCancelInfo,reAvailableInfo,accountInfo</input>
    <output>soldInfo</output>
  </capability unit>
  < capability unit name="TD">
    <input>deliveryInfo</input>
    <output>deliveredInfo</output>
  </capability unit >
  < capability unit name="HS">
    <input>orderInfo,orderCancelInfo,reVacancyInfo,accountInfo</input>
    <output>paidInfo</output>
  </capability unit >
  < capability unit name="PS">
    <input>chargeInfo</input>
    <output>chargedInfo</output>
  </capability unit >

  <sequence>
    <invoke partnerName="TS"/>
    <invoke partnerName="TD"/>
  </sequence>
  <synchronization>
    <invoke partnerName="TS"/>
    <invoke partnerName="PS"/>
    <state_trigger_transition ID="pay_ordered_ticket">
    <state_trigger_transition ID="ticket_charge_creditcard">
  </synchronization>
  <synchronization>
    <invoke partnerName="HS"/>
    <invoke partnerName="PS"/>
    <state_trigger_transition ID="pay_ordered_hotelroom">
    <state_trigger_transition ID="hotelroom_charge_creditcard">
  </synchronization>
</capability composition>
```

From here, we can learn how the four capability units collaborate to realize G_{travel}. *TS* provides the ticket-selling capability. Sequentially, *TD* provides the ticket-delivery capability. *TS* and *PS* are synchronous by using state−trigger−transitions, i.e., the ticket is paid by the credit card. *HS* provides the hotel room booking capability. *HS* and *PS* are also synchronous by using state−trigger−transitions, i.e., the hotel room is paid by the credit card. The result of composition is thus given in XML style, as shown in Table 8.6.

8.4 SUMMARY

The Internet is an open system in which heterogeneous system entities or software agents can appear and disappear dynamically. As the number of system entities on the Internet increases, there is a need to compare the capabilities of these system entities so that they can be used, invoked, and deployed on demand. Capability comparison is necessary. Because these system entities are provided by different parties, normally they are black boxes to the user. Their internal structures, algorithms, implementation strategies, and so on are not knowable. The users can only observe their behaviors, i.e., which environment entities they are making contact with and which effects can be imposed on the environment entities. Because the environment entities are sharable, such an effects-based capability specification makes capability comparison possible.

Reasoning II: System Capability Refinement

Refinement is an important design principle for mastering complexity. It is used to simplify the development and maintenance of a software system. Most requirements engineering approaches have had their own refinement strategies. For example, the goal-oriented approach (Lamsweerde, 2009) introduces a set of goal patterns to decompose high-level abstract goals into low-level operational goals. The problem-frames approach (Jackson, 2001) proposes "problem projection" as the refinement relationship between the problem and its subproblems from a functional angle.

The basic idea of refinement in requirements engineering is to refine high-level (functional) requirements (i.e., the system-level requirements) into more operational requirements (i.e., the constituent-level requirements) so that the original requirements can be reconstructed from these parts by composition. In system development, the refinement process is also undertaken for the purpose of gaining insight into the identity of the constituent components.

Capability refinement is proposed in environment modeling-based requirements engineering. It is conducted for a situation in which there is a need to obtain a capability profile that is too complex to be matched with an available capability or to be understood and analyzed to find an implementable solution. In a concrete manner, along with the idea of problem projection proposed in Jackson's problem-frames approach, capability refinement tries to perform the projection on the capability profile. The purpose is to obtain subcapabilities so that they can fulfill the whole capability via collaboration.

Environment Modeling-Based Requirements Engineering for Software Intensive Systems
https://doi.org/10.1016/B978-0-12-801954-2.00009-1

Essentially, capability refinement is used to convert an abstract capability profile into implementable capability specifications. It reduces the nondeterminism in the abstract profile and separates the concerns. After capability refinement, the capability requirements will be elaborated and divided into distinct parts so that each addresses a simpler capability and all parts collaborate with each other to realize the whole capability.

The principle and methodology of the capability refinement depend on the capability description. As mentioned earlier, in environment modeling-based requirements engineering, we assume that system capability is exhibited through its interactions with its environment entities. Thus, capability refinement is conducted according to the scenarios, which is a meaningful (in terms of the effects required by application business logics) sequence of interactions. This chapter will introduce how to extract and represent the business scenarios and then how to refine the capability in terms of the scenarios.

9.1 GUIDED PROCESS FOR SCENARIO DESCRIPTION

Conducting an application development requires collecting and specifying the required capability. Chapter 7 presented the ontological structure of the effect-oriented capability conceptualization, which serves as a model for the capability profile. As illustrated in the conceptual diagram shown in Fig. 7.6, a *system* is associated with four concept categories: *environment*, *interaction*, *requirements*, and *capability*, in which the environment, interaction, and requirements are obtained from the application domain knowledge and/or stakeholders, whereas the capability will be the derived result in the requirements phrase.

To conducting capability refinement, we first need to obtain information about the three aspects:

$$< Env, Inter, Req >$$

where:

- *Env* (environment) is a finite set of environment entities that are expected to interact with the desired system
- *Inter* (interaction) is a finite set of interactions in the direct interface of the desired system and its environment entities
- *Req* (requirements) is a set of constraints about the interactions that need to be satisfied by the desired system and its environment entities

When the information is interrelated, a process is needed to acquire the information systematically. After such information is obtained, the capability can be refined with some strategies in the second step. This section will discuss the process and include an example.

9.1.1 **THE PROCESS**

As mentioned in Chapter 7, the key issue in effect-oriented capability modeling is connecting the requirements (i.e., the desired environment states and environment changes) to the sequences of behaviors (i.e., the interactions in which the desired system will be involved). The ontological structure in Fig. 7.6 includes "scenarios" to relate the requirements to the interactions.

The main idea of including scenarios is to justify whether any piece of requirements in *Req* can be realized by the behaviors. According to Fig. 7.6, a scenario is a flow of interactions, i.e., it is an interaction sequence. The link between a scenario and a piece of requirements captures the meaning of realizing the piece of requirements by following the process of interactions prescribed in the interaction sequence. Thus, to allow description and analysis, the process is to identify and prescribe the scenarios to attain the requirements.

The problem frame approach inspires some practical techniques. The process of capturing and specifying the capability profile takes six steps (Jin et al., 2009; Chen and Jin, 2016):

Step 1. (Name a system): assigning a name *sysN* to the desired system. This leads to the assertion:

$$System(sysN,\ Description)$$

Step 2. (Identify the set of environment entities): identifying environment entities, $env_1, \ldots, env_{n_{env}}$, that are needed to interact with the desired system. Then we can have environment entity set:

$$Env = \{envN_1,\ \ldots,\ envN_{n_{env}}\}$$

In terms of the ontological structure, each environment entity may be of different types, i.e., *causal*, *autonomous*, or *symbolic*. Any environment entity is of at least one type. That leads to following assertions. Let *envN* ∈ *Env*:

$$EnvEnt(envN,\ Description,\ EnvTypeSet)$$

Step 3. (Determine the phenomena of concern): identifying the shared phenomena, $pheN_1, \ldots,$ and $pheN_{n_{phe}}$, that will be involved in the direct interfaces between the desired system and the environment entities:

$$Phe = \{pheN_1,\ \ldots,\ pheN_{n_{phe}}\}$$

In terms of the ontological structure, each phenomenon is of one and only one type: i.e., *PheType* can be *event*, *state*, or *value*. That leads to following assertions: Let *pheN* ∈ *Phe*, *PheType* ∈ {*event*, *state*, *value*}:

$$Phenomenon(pheN,\ Description,\ PheType)$$

Step 4. (Determine the interactions): identifying the interactions, $intN_1, \ldots,$ and $intN_{n_{int}}$, that can happen between the desired system and the environment entities.

According to the effect-oriented capability modeling, any phenomena of the environment entities are shared phenomena with the desired system in the sense that:

- a state can be sensed by the desired system
- a value can be retrieved or assigned by the desired system
- an output event can be detected by the desired system and an input event will be triggered by the desired system

Hence, the phenomena can be deduced into the interactions between the desired system and the environment entities. Then:

$$Inter = \{intN_1, \ldots, intN_{n_{int}}\}$$

Each is represented by an assertion. Let $pheN \in Phe$, $intN \in Inter$:

$$Interaction(intN, Ini, Rec, pheN)$$

This means that $intN$ is an interaction, its initiator and receiver are Ini and Rec respectively, either Ini or Rec is $sysN$, and the other is an environment entity in $EnvEnt$, vice versa. Its content is $pheN \in Phe$.

Step 5. (Determine the initial requirements): Requirements are constraints on the phenomena (and hence on the interactions) according to business logics. These constraints are often grouped together, forming clusters. Each cluster may represent a separate part of business logics.

This step is to identify the clusters of constraints on interactions, $reqN_1$, ..., and $reqN_{n_{req}}$. Each cluster of constraints represents a piece of requirements. Recording $ReqC$ as the set of clusters of constraints:

$$Req = \{reqN_1, \ldots, reqN_{n_{req}}\}$$

How to acquire and represent the cluster of constraints reflects the basic idea about what requirements are. Answers to this question differ according to the methodology. Following the idea of requirements reference in the problem frame approach, we consider that any constraints are interaction references of two types: **"as-is"** interaction is the only occurrence that can be referred and **"to-be"** interaction is referred but asks for some relationships and behaviors to make it. Then, this step is, for each $reqN \in Req$, identifying the set of interactions that is referred by reqN. Assertion:

$$Reference(reqN, intN, refType)$$

is used to represent one of the interactions referred by $reqN$. Here, $intN \in Inter$, and $refType \subseteq \{\text{'to-be', 'as-is'}\}$.

Step 6. (Organize the scenarios): According to the effect-based capability model, any piece of the requirements (in terms of business logics) is about the state changes of the environment entities. The way to satisfying the requirements is through the state transition graph. Now, each cluster of constraints $reqN \in Req$, identified in the previous step, has associated with a set of interactions. This step organizes all referred interactions into an interaction flow connected by order relations to form scenario *sceN* so that *sceN* can realize *reqN*.

Within a cluster of constraints, the referred interactions are divided into two groups: one is to group the "as-is" interactions (denoted by *asIsInt*); the other is to group the "to-be" interactions (denoted by *toBeInt*). All are referred by the requirements but with a difference in mood. The "as-is" interaction means that it is observable, whereas the "to-be" interaction means that it is expected to be observable. Thus, the latter implies that the desired system needs to be involved and take some action so that the phenomena can happen.

Two notations are used to denote order relations among the interactions. Assume *a* and *b* are interactions:

- $a > b$: *a* precedes *b*
- $a <> b$: *a* is synchronized with *b*

We define five types of order relations:

- ("as-is" order) *asIsOrd* : *asIsInt* $>$ *asIsInt*: the order of "as-is" interactions. This means that the referred interaction on the right-hand side occurs after the referred interaction on the left-hand side.
- ("to-be" order) *toBeOrd* : *toBeInt* $>$ *toBeInt*: the order of "to-be" interactions. This means that the required interaction on the right-hand side is stimulated after the required interaction on the left-hand side.
- ("as-is" enabling) *asIsEna* : *asIsInt* $>$ *toBeInt*: the "as-is" interaction enables the "to-be" interaction. The referred interaction enables the required interaction.
- ("to-be" enabling) *toBeEna*: *toBeInt* $>$ *asIsInt*: the "to-be" interaction enables the "as-is" interaction. The required interaction enables the referred interaction.
- (synchronization) *sync*: *asIsInt* $<>$ *toBeInt*: the synchronicity of the "as-is" interaction and the "to-be" interaction. The required interaction occurs at the same time as the referred interaction.

A scenario is formed as:

$$sceN = < intSet, assSet >$$

Here,

$$intSet(\subseteq Inter) = asIsInt \cup toBeInt$$

is the set of interaction nodes and

$$assSet = \{ < int_1, int_2 > | int_1, int_2 \in intSet \text{ and } (int_1 > int_2 \text{ or } int_1 <> int_2) \}$$

contains a set of order relations (i.e., edges) between interactions.

After specifying the scenario, asserting:

$$Realize(sceN, reqN)$$

to denote that *sceN* can realize *reqN*.

In mapping onto the environment entity models, we can see that scenarios capture the desired system's behaviors. Scenarios show how the desired system can run on the models to enable the required state changes stimulated by business logics and regulated by the environment physical laws.

The initial information acquisition can be finished. In the following section, an example is presented showing how to conduct the process. However, to allow the automated capability refinement, scenarios need to be well formed. This issue will also be discussed in the next section.

9.1.2 AN EXAMPLE

This section uses the example of a package routing controller to illustrate the information acquisition process. This example is extracted from Jackson's "problem frames" book (Jackson, 2001) and Hall's paper (Hall et al., 2008), in which the package routing controller is used to discuss problem decomposition. The schematic picture and the initial context diagram are given in Fig. 9.1A and 9.1B. To make the illustration more understandable, we use Jackson's abbreviations to denote the original modeling elements. The narrative description about the required capability is as follows:

"A *package router* is a large mechanical device used by postal and delivery organizations to sort packages into bins according to their destinations. The *packages* carry bar-coded labels. They move along a *conveyor* to a reading station

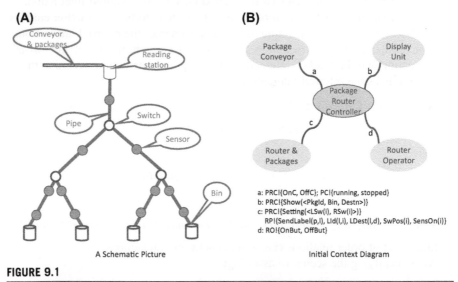

(A)

A Schematic Picture

(B)

Initial Context Diagram

a: PRC!{OnC, OffC}; PC!{running, stopped}
b: PRC!{Show(<PkgId, Bin, Destn>)}
c: PRC!{Setting(<LSw(i), RSw(i)>)}
   RP!{SendLabel(p,l), LId(l,i), LDest(l,d), SwPos(i), SensOn(i)}
d: RO!{OnBut, OffBut}

FIGURE 9.1

Schematic picture and context diagram of package routing controller (Hall et al., 2008).

where their *package ID*s and *destinations* are read. They then slide down pipes fitted with *sensors* at top and bottom. The pipes are connected by two-position *switches* that the computer can flip. At the leaves of the tree of pipes are destination bins corresponding to the bar-coded destinations. A misrouted package may be routed to any bin with an appropriate **message being displayed**. There are control buttons by which an **operator** can command the controlling computer to stop and start the conveyor.

The problem is to build the controlling computer (1) to *obey the operator's commands*, (2) to *route packages* to their *destination bins* by *setting the switches* appropriately, and (3) to *report misrouted packages*."

From the initial context diagram and narrative description, the environment entities and related phenomena can be summarized as:

- **router operator** is a person, an autonomous entity. He or she can click on two buttons and share two events: *OnBut* (by clicking on the "*On*" button) and *OffBut* (by clicking on the "*Off*'" button) to start and stop the conveyor
- **display unit** is a display screen, a causal entity in the sense that it will display the appropriate message about the misrouted package when receiving such a message
- **package conveyor** is a causal entity. It can be shared with two events: *OnC* (when the conveyor starts) or *OffC* (when conveyor stops), and it can be in one of its two states, *Running* or *Stopped*
- **Route & Package** is also a causal entity. It is a composite entity consisting of a reading station, a set of switches and sensors, a set of bins, and pipelines. Its causality is exhibited in the following aspects:
  - Its reading station can detect the incoming package and capture and share information (i.e., *PkgID, Destn*) about the package
  - Its layout is that of a binary tree. Each nonleaf node is equipped with a two-position switch. Each switch can be set as "*to the left*" or "*to the right*" i.e., $< LSw(i), RSw(i) >$ (i is the identifier of a certain switch). When it is shared with a setting to these switches, this setting will be deployed. As a result, the setting can decide the package's traveling path

It is asked that the delivery should ensure the package is being delivered to the bin that corresponds with the package's destination.

If requirements are rewritten in a more structured way, we obtain the following constraints:

- **Obey the operator's command**:
  - Constraint 1
    - When: **route operator** presses the "**OnBut**"
    - Then: it is expected that **package conveyor** will be in state of **running**

- Constraint 2
  - When: **route operator** presses the "**OffBut**"
  - Then: it is expected that **package conveyor** will be in state of **stopped**
- **Route package**s to their **destination bins** by **setting the switches**
  - Constraint 1
    - Assume: Assoc(Destn, Bin), Layout(Bin, <LWs(i), RWs(i)>)
    - When: **router & packages** detects the **package** (its ID is **$PkgID,** its destination is **$Destn)**
    - Then: it is:
      - if Assoc($Destn, $Bin)
        - if Layout ($Bin, <LWs(i), RWs(i)>), set Router with <LWs(i), RWs(i)>
      - and: **package** (with ID **$PkgID**) reaches bin (with number **$Bin**)
- **Report misrouted package**
  - Constraint 1
    - Assume: Assoc(Destn, Bin)
    - When:
      - **package** (with ID **$PkgID** and destination **$Destn**) reaches bin with number **#Bin** and
      - Assoc($Destn, $Bin); and
      - #Bin ≠ $Bin
    - Then: it is expected that **display unit** receives a message of **show(<$PkgID, $Destn, #Bin))**

In terms of the process introduced in Section 9.1.1, in **Step 1**, a name is given to the desired system. The name is chosen to be package router controller (PRC). Thus, asserting:

$$System(sys, \ Package \ Router \ Controller \ (PRC))$$

In **Step 2**, from the initial context diagram, four environment entities are identified: are (eve_1) *package conveyor* (PC), (eve_2) *router & packages* (RP), (eve_3) *display unit* (DU), and (eve_4) *router operator* (RO). Recording:

$$Env = \{eve_1, \ eve_2, \ eve_3, \ eve_4\}$$

Among the four environment entities, *PC* and *DU* are *causal*, *RP* is *causal* and *symbolic*, whereas RO is *autonomous*, so the following assertions can be written:

EnvEnt(eve_1, PC, {causal})
EnvEnt(eve_2, RP, {causal, symbolic})
EnvEnt(eve_3, DU, {causal})
EnvEnt(eve_4, RO, {autonomous})

In **Step 3**, the shared phenomena between the desired system and the environment entities are identified based on the constraints. That is, extracting the referred phenomenon in the constraints:

Phenomenon(phe_1, OnBut, {event})

Phenomenon(phe_2, OffBut, {event})

Phenomenon(phe_3, running, {state})

Phenomenon(phe_4, *stopped*, {state})

Phenomenon(phe_5, *Detect*(<*$PkgID, $Destn*>), {event, value})

Phenomenon(phe_6, Setting($<$ LSw(i), RSw(i) $>$), {event})

Phenomenon(phe_7, "PagArr"($<$ $PkgID, #Bin $>$), {event, value})

Phenomenon(phe_8, Show($<$ $PkgId, $Bin, $Destn $>$), {event, value})

Phenomenon(phe_9, *OnScreen*(<*$PkgID, $Destn, #Bin*>), {state})

In **Step 4**, these shared phenomena are assigned to the direct interfaces between the desired system and the environment entities to represent the interactions:

Interaction(int_1, RO, RC, phe_1)

Interaction(int_2, RO, RC, phe_2)

Interaction(int_3, PC, RC, phe_3)

Interaction(int_4, PC, RC, phe_4)

Interaction(int_5, RP, RC, phe_5)

Interaction(int_6, RC, RP, phe_6)

Interaction(int_7, RP, RC, phe_7)

Interaction(int_8, RC, DU, phe_8)

Interaction(int_9, DU, RC, phe_9)

In **Step 5**, three clusters of requirements are recognized. That is, *sys* is for realizing *req*, which obviously includes three pieces of requirements: (*req*$_1$) *obeying the operator's commands*, (*req*$_2$) *routing packages,* and (*req*$_3$) *reporting misrouted packages*, in terms of the narrative statements. Thus:

$$Req = \{req\} = \{req_1, req_2, req_3\}$$

The shared phenomena referred by each piece of requirements are identified. Use *req*$_1$ (*obeying the operator's commands*) as an example. Obviously, it refers to *RO*'s event phenomena, *OnBut* or *OffBut* (when that happens), PC's state phenomena, *running* and *stopped* (then it is expected and continues in its current state until a predefined interrupt). The following assertions can be obtained:

Reference(req_1, int_1, {as-is})

Reference(req_1, int_2, {as-is})

Reference(req_1, int_3, {to-be, as-is})

Reference(req_1, int_4, {to-be, as-is})

req_2 and req_3 can be analyzed in the same way. For example, req_2 refers to phenomenon $Detect(<\$PkgID, \$Destn>)$, $Setting(<LSw(i), RSw(i)>)$, and $PkgArr(<\$PkgID, \#Bin>)$. It is expected that the corresponding bin ($\$Bin$) with $\$Destn$ can be known and $\#Bin$ is equal to $\$Bin$. This results in correct package routing:

> Reference(req_2, int_5, {as-is, to-be})
> Reference(req_2, int_6, {to-be})
> Reference(req_2, int_7, {as-is})

For req_3, when the package is misrouted, the display unit needs to receive a message that contains information about the misrouted package, and then the information will be displayed on the screen:

> Reference(req_3, int_7, {as-is, to-be})
> Reference(req_3, int_8, {to-be})
> Reference(req_3, int_9, {to-be})

Step 6 is organizing the interactions into scenarios to realize requirements. Currently recognized requirements are used as the thread to organize scenarios. Finally, three initial scenarios are captured corresponding to the three pieces of requirements, as shown in Fig. 9.2. The three assertions are recorded:

> Realization(sce_1, req_1)
> Realization(sce_2, req_2)
> Realization(sce_3, req_3)

9.2 SCENARIO-BASED CAPABILITY PROJECTION

Realistic capability requirements are often complicated. They need to be decomposed into simpler capability requirements so that the subcapabilities can be realized more easily. However, capability refinement is not straightforward. Jackson suggests in the problem frame approach that "problem projection" is an effective technique for analyzing and structuring problems (Jackson, 2001). The idea is that each subproblem is a projection of the full problem and concerns only phenomena that are relevant to that subproblem. This would allow subproblems to be overlapped in some way so that information about one domain can be distributed over several subproblems. We use this idea as the basic means for capability refinement.

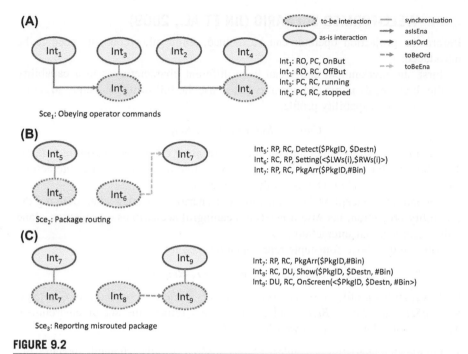

FIGURE 9.2

Package router controller: initial scenarios. *Sce*, scenario; *Int*, interaction.

9.2.1 PRELIMINARY

This section explores capability projection. First, recall the projection in relational algebra. It is formally defined as:

$$\pi\{a_1, \ldots, a_n\}(R) = \{t[a_1, \ldots, a_n] | t \in R\}$$

where $t[a_1, \ldots, a_n]$ is the restriction of the tuple t to the set $\{a_1, \ldots, a_n\}$ so that

$$t[a_1, \ldots, a_n] = \{(a', v) | (a', v) \in t, a' \in \{a_1, \ldots, a_n\}\}$$

The result of projection $\pi_{\{a_1, \ldots, a_n\}}(R)$ is defined only if $\{a_1, \ldots, a_n\}$ is a subset of the header of R.

Second, capability projection takes a similar form. Because the purpose of capability projection is to identify subcapabilities in terms of scenarios, the formation of capability projection will be:

$$\pi_{sce}^{req}(Cap) = SubC$$

Here, *Cap* is a capability profile and *sce* is a scenario for realizing requirement *req* of *Cap*. *SubC* is a set of the subcapability profiles of *Cap* so that the subcapabilities in *SubC* can collaborate to realize *Cap*.

9.2.2 WELL-FORMED SCENARIO (JIN ET AL., 2009)

Before the projection operator can be defined, some other concepts need to be introduced.

First, an environment entity can have different characteristics in a capability profile. It can be dynamic and/or static. Let us use the following four-tuple structure to represent the capability profile:

$$Cap =< Sys, Env, Inter, Req >$$

Each $eve \in Env$ is either an initiator or a receiver of an interaction $int \in Inter$. Thus, eve is dynamic in Cap if int is an event interaction or a state interaction, and eve is static in Cap if int is a value interaction.

Second, the concept of the "well-formed scenario" is needed when defining the capability projection, because it needs a meaningful scenario as a projection plane rather than a casual interaction flow.

Rewrite the above four-tuple representation, i.e., let

$$Cap\,(Sys) =< Env, Inter,\ Req >$$

be the capability profile of Sys and $sce =< intSet,\ assSet >$ a scenario for Cap (Sys) and $intSet = asIsInt \cup toBeInt$, and assume $\rho(sce)$ returns the set of environment entities involved in sce: sce is well-formed if:

- (single characteristics principle): All $eve \in \rho(sce)$ is either dynamic or static, but not both
- (feasibility principle): Let $int \in toBeInt$:
  - If int is an event interaction and is controlled by the desired system, there is an "as-is enabling" relation: $asIsEna(int', int)$, int' is an event or state interaction controlled by an environment entity
  - If int is a value interaction and is controlled by the desired system, there is a "to-be order" relation: $toBeOrd(int', int)$, int' is a value interaction controlled by an environment entity
  - If int is a state interaction and is controlled by a causal entity, there is a "to-be order" relation: $toBeOrd(int', int)$, int' is an event interaction controlled by to-be system

Intuitively, the scenarios being well-formed are to ensure the completeness of the scenarios. Normally, the initial scenarios built from the initial requirements constraints are not complete. Based on these principles, they can be elaborated on using some heuristic strategies.

9.2.3 HEURISTIC STRATEGIES FOR SCENARIO ELABORATION (JIN ET AL., 2009)

The initial scenarios are rarely well-formed. That is normally because some phenomena are missing from the original capability profile or some designed environment entities need to be included to realize the capability. The following are some strategies for elaborating the capability profiles:

Strategy I. (Elaboration by introducing new elements): Sometimes the scenarios contain some infeasible interactions because they lack "as-is" enabling, "to-be" enabling, etc. In this case, some new elements need to be introduced to enable the missing relations to hold. Normally, new elements can be introduced by domain knowledge, i.e., the environment model.

Strategy II. (Elaboration by introducing model entity): A scenario may involve real-world entities that are both dynamic and static. In this case, a model entity needs to be introduced that corresponds by analogy to a real-world entity to separate the two concerns. The model entity is a map of the original real-world entity. It will be engaged where a static entity is needed, whereas the real-world entity is used where a dynamic entity is needed. The interaction that happens in dynamic mode will synchronize with the interaction that happens in static mode. Thus, the scenario can be split into two: one builds the model (in dynamic mode) and the other uses it (in static mode).

When a model entity $\sigma(eve)$ ($\sigma(eve)$ represents the model entity of eve) is included to separate the two concerns of the same entity, the capability profile:

$$Cap(Sys) =< Env, Inter, Req >$$

can be elaborated using the following steps:

Step 1. Introducing a model domain $\sigma(eve)$ into Env:

$$Env = Env \cup \{\sigma(eve)\}$$

Then two means can be adopted to accomplish model building. One is to introduce an autonomous entity as the model builder, which results in another new entity to be added in Env. The other is to develop an automatic model builder whose functionality needs to be included in the model-building requirements.

Step 2. Identify new phenomena and interactions involving $\sigma(eve)$ and other newly introduced entities. Add them into $Inter$; change $Inter$'s original phenomena and interactions so that those two concerns are separated because of the introduction of $\sigma(eve)$.

Step 3. Split the original requirements statements into two separate subrequirements. One is to build $\sigma(eve)$ and the other to use $\sigma(eve)$ to realize the rest of the functionality of the original requirements.

Step 4. The elaboration results in scenario separation. After that, the original scenario can be elaborated accordingly and projection can be performed.

In the following, we will use the package router controller as an example to show where and how to use these strategies.

The first case is for **routing package**, the package & router, which is a real-world entity that is both dynamic and static. It is static because it is a router layout for each package so that the package can go through to the destination bin. It is dynamic because the packages to different destinations may need different router layouts

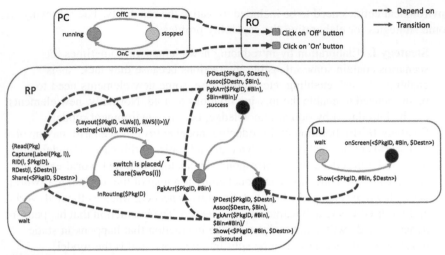

FIGURE 9.3

Environment entity models and dependences.

triggered by an event, $Setting(< LSw(i), RSw(i) >)$. Thus, a router layout model needs to be included to separate the two concerns in terms of **Strategy II**.

The second case needs to have domain knowledge. Fig. 9.3 is a fragment of the package router domain knowledge, which describes the physical laws of the environment entities and also business logics. Any capabilities can be realized only when the interactions follow them.

As shown in Fig. 9.2A, Scenario I is not well-formed. req_1 refers to and constrains PC's state interaction, *running* or *stopped* (this means that is expected to be detected) to reflect the meaning of "obeying". Based on the environment model, two to-be event interactions are required, to be included and shared by RC and PC, to enable the state interactions:

Phenomenon(phe_{10}, OnC, {event})
Phenomenon(phe_{11}, $OffC$, {event})
Interaction(int_{10}, RC, PC, phe_{10})
Interaction(int_{11}, RC, PC, phe_{11})

With these phenomena and interactions, in terms of PC's model, PC needs the signal OnC or $OffC$ to be enabled in the state of *running* or *stopped*, and then two new references are captured:

Reference(req_1, int_{10}, {to-be})
Reference(req_1, int_{11}, {to-be})

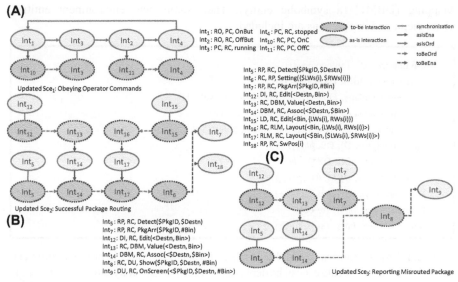

FIGURE 9.4

Package router controller: updated scenarios (*Sce*). *Int*, interaction.

The well-formed scenario for realizing req_1 is shown in Fig. 9.4A.

Extending scenarios by introducing new elements may demand eliciting further environment entities, phenomena, interactions and requirements in terms of the environment model. Sometimes, this case needs to combine the above two strategies.

Referring to Fig. 9.2B, sce_2 is not well-formed as the "to-be" interaction int_6 and misses an "as-is" enabling relation that can enable the setting of the switches. In a concrete manner, to enable the switch to be set, it is necessary to know the destination bin. It is obvious that the destination bin can be determined by the destination, i.e., association $Assoc(<Destn, Bin>)$ is needed. Furthermore, the association between the bin and the switch settings, i.e., $Layout(<Bin, \{LWs(i), RWs(i)\}>)$, is missing. In fact, the two missing interactions have been mentioned in the structured requirements statements. They are the assumptions in the requirements statements.

Strategy I suggests including the enabling relations. For association $Assoc(<Destn, Bin>)$, one way to do this is to allow a "Destination Informant (DI)" (an autonomous entity) to assign the association by building "Destination-Bin

Mapping (DBM)" (a symbolic entity). Then some new environment entities, phenomena and interactions are included:

EnvEnt(eve_5, DI, {autonomous})

EnvEnt(eve_6, DBM, {symbolic})

Phenomenon(phe_{12}, $Edit(<Destn, Bin>)$, {event, value})

Phenomenon(phe_{13}, $Value(<Destn, Bin>)$, {value})

Phenomenon(phe_{14}, Assoc($<Destn, Bin>$), {event, value})

Interaction(int_{12}, DI, DE, phe_{12})

Interaction(int_{13}, DE, DBM, phe_{13})

Interaction(int_{14}, DBM, RC, phe_{14})

Reference(req_2, int_{12}, {as-is, to-be})

Reference(req_2, int_{13}, {to-be})

Reference(req_2, int_{14}, {as-is, to-be})

Upon further examination of the problem, package & router is both dynamic and static. It is dynamic because it can be deployed to a certain layout dynamically. It is static because the package will travel along the setting path. Strategy II suggests including a model entity, i.e., $Layout(< Bin, \{LWs(i), RWs(i)\}>)$ ($RLM = \sigma(PR)$), and allows a layout designer (LD) to develop the model. Then, when delivering the package, the model can be used to let the package go through the layout. Also, some new environment entities, phenomena, and interactions are identified:

EnvEnt(eve_7, LD, {autonomous})

EnvEnt(eve_8, RLM, {symbolic})

Phenomenon(phe_{15}, $Edit(<Bin, \{LWs(i), RWs(i)\}>)$, {event, value})

Phenomenon(phe_{16}, $Value(<Bin, \{LWs(i), RWs(i)\}>)$, {value})

Phenomenon(phe_{17}, $Layout(<Bin, \{LWs(i), RWs(i)\}>)$, {event, value})

Interaction(int_{15}, LD, RC, phe_{15})

Interaction(int_{16}, RC, RLM, phe_{16})

Interaction(int_{17}, RLM, RC, phe_{17})

Reference(req_2, int_{15}, {as-is, to-be})

Reference(req_2, int_{16}, {to-be})

Reference(req_2, int_{17}, {as-is, to-be})

With these identified entities, phenomena, and interactions, Scenario III can also be extended. The updated scenarios are given in Fig. 9.4A–C.

9.2.4 PROJECTION UPON WELL-FORMED SCENARIO

When a well-formed scenario is constructed, the capability projection can be performed. Let $Cap =< Sys, EnvEnt, Inter, Req >$ be the capability profile, and sce a well-formed scenario for Cap for realizing $req \in Req$. Then a subcapability

SubCap of capability *Cap* upon *sce* for *req* (i.e., *subCap(SubCap, Cap, sce, req)*) can be obtained by:

$$SubCap = \pi_{sce}^{req}(Cap) = < \pi_{sce}^{req}(Sys),\ \pi_{sce}^{req}(EnvEnt),\ \pi_{sce}^{req}(Inter), \pi_{sce}^{req}(Req) >$$

The auxiliary projection operators are defined:

- The projection of a capability upon a scenario for realizing a piece of requirements is a partial capability:

$$\pi_{sce}^{req}(cap(Sys)) = cap(Sys')$$

so that *Sys'* is a subsystem of *Sys*.

- The projection of an environment entity set upon a scenario for realizing a piece of requirements is an environment entity set that contains all environment entities involved in this scenario:

$$\pi_{sce}^{req}(EnvEnt) = \{eve \in EnvEnt \wedge (eve = ini(int) \vee eve$$
$$= rec(int)) \wedge (int \in N(sce))\}$$

- The projection of an interaction set upon a scenario corresponding to a machine is an interaction set that contains all interactions in this scenario:

$$\pi_{sce}^{req}(Inter) = \{int|(int \in Inter) \wedge (int \in N(sce))\}$$

- The projection of a requirement set upon a scenario corresponding to a machine is a requirement set that contains all requirements realized by this scenario:

$$\pi_{sce}^{req}(Req) = \{req|req \in Req\}$$

Going back to the package routing example, for the package router controller, the capability profile is:

$$Cap(PRC) = < EnvEnt, Inter, Req >$$

whereas $Req = \{req_1, req_2, req_3\}$ and sce_1, sce_2, and sce_3 are three scenarios to realize req_1, req_2, and req_3 respectively. It is easy to justify that updated sce_1 to realize req_1 is well-formed. Thus the subcapability upon sce_1 is:

$$\pi_{sce_1}^{req_2}(PRC) = Cap(CO) = < CO_{EnvEnt},\ CO_{Inter},\ CO_{Req} >$$

whereas:

- $CO = \pi_{sce_1}^{req_1}(PRC) = Command\ Obeyer$ is the name of the subcapability
- $CO_{EnvEnt} = \pi_{sce_1}^{req_1}(EnvEnt) = \{PC, RO\}$

- $CO_{Inter} = \pi_{sce_1}^{req_1}(Inter) = \{int_1, int_2, int_3, int_4, int_{10}, int_{11}\}$
- $CO_{Req} = \pi_{sce_1}^{req_1}(Req) = \{req_1\}$

The updated scenario sce_2 is well-formed. However, with the inclusion of the new entities, new phenomena, and new interactions, this scenario can be split into three scenarios:

- sce_4 for realizing the editing of the association between the destination and the destination bin (req_4)
- sce_5 for realizing the creation of the router layout model to decide the routing path (req_5)
- sce_6 for realizing the delivery of the package to a certain bin along the deployed routing path (req_6)

This means that req_2 is refined into three subrequirements: req_4, req_5, and req_6. The splitting edges are $< int_{13}, int_{16} >$ and $< int_{16}, int_{17} >$ because both are the two interactions with entities, i.e., destination bin mapping (DBM) and routing layout model (RLM), both of which are dynamic and static. int_{13} and int_{16} create the entities to deal with the dynamics and int_{14} and int_{17} use the entities treating them in static mode. Splitting separates the concerns. Fig. 9.5 shows these three scenarios.

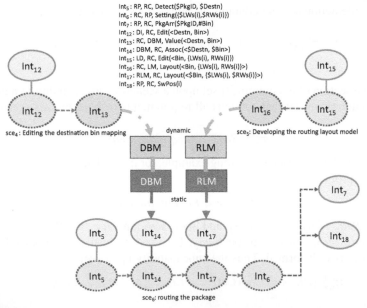

Int_5: RP, RC, Detect($PkgID, $Destn)
Int_6: RC, RP, Setting({$LWs(i),$RWs(i)})
Int_7: RP, RC, PkgArr($PkgID,#Bin)
Int_{12}: DI, RC, Edit(<Destn, Bin>)
Int_{13}: RC, DBM, Value(<Destn, Bin>)
Int_{14}: DBM, RC, Assoc(<$Destn, $Bin>)
Int_{15}: LD, RC, Edit(<Bin, {LWs(i), RWs(i)})
Int_{16}: RC, LM, Layout(<Bin, {LWs(i), RWs(i)}>)
Int_{17}: RLM, RC, Layout(<$Bin, {$LWs(i), $RWs(i)}>)
Int_{18}: RP, RC, SwPos(i)

FIGURE 9.5

The split scenarios. *DBM*, destination bin mapping; *Int*, interaction; *RLM*, routing layout model; *Sce*, scenario.

By following the projection operators, the profile of three subcapabilities can be obtained as:

System(sys_4, 'Destination Editor (DE)')
Scenario(sce_4, 'editing destination-bin mapping')
EnvEnt(eve_5, DI, {autonomous})
EnvEnt(eve_6, DBM, {causal})
Phenomenon(phe_{12}, Edit(<Destn, Bin>), {event, value})
Phenomenon(phe_{13}, Value(<Destn, Bin>), {event})
Interaction(int_{12}, DI, DE, phe_{12})
Interaction(int_{13}, DE, DBM, phe_{13})
Requirement(req_4, 'destination editing')
Reference(req_4, int_{12}, {as-is, to-be})
Reference(req_4, int_{13}, {to-be})
Realization(sce_4, req_4)

System(sys_5, "Router Layout Model Editor (RLME)")
Scenario(sce_4, "building router layout model")
EnvEnt(eve_7, LD, {autonomous})
EnvEnt(eve_8, RLM, {causal})
Phenomenon(phe_{15}, Edit(<Bin, {LWs(i), RWs(i)}>), {event, value})
Phenomenon(phe_{16}, Value(<Bin, {LWs(i), RWs(i)}>), {event})
Interaction(int_{15}, DI, DE, phe_{15})
Interaction(int_{16}, DE, DBM, phe_{16})
Requirement(req_5, "router layout model building")
Reference(req_5, int_{15}, {as-is, to-be})
Reference(req_5, int_{16}, {to-be})
Realization(sce_5, req_5)

System(sys_6, "Package Router (PR)")
Scenario(sce_6, "routing the package")
EnvEnt(eve_6, DBM, {symbolic})
EnvEnt(eve_8, RLM, {symbolic})
EnvEnt(eve_2, RP, {causal, symbolic})
Phenomenon(phe_5, Detect(PkgID, Destn), {event, value})
Phenomenon(phe_{14}, Assoc(<Destn, Bin>), {value})
Phenomenon(phe_{17}, Layout(<Bin, {LWs(i), RWs(i)}>), {event})
Phenomenon(phe_6, Setting(<LWs(i), RWs(i)>), {event}
Phenomenon(phe_7, PkgArr(PkgID, Bin), {event, value})
Interaction(int_5, RP, RC, phe5)
Interaction(int_{14}, DBM, RC, phe_{14})

Continued

Interaction(int$_{17}$, RLM, RC, phe$_{17}$)
Interaction(int$_6$, RC, RP, phe6)
Interaction(int$_7$, RP, RC, phe7)
Requirement(req$_6$, "package routing")
Reference(req$_6$, int$_5$, {as-is, to-be})
Reference(req$_6$, int$_{14}$, {as-is, to-be})
Reference(req$_6$, int$_{17}$, {as-in, to-be})
Reference(req$_6$, int$_6$, {to-be})
Reference(req$_6$, int$_7$, {as-is})
Realization(sce$_6$, req$_6$)

Finally, we reduce the capability refinement for req_3. Examining Fig 9.4C, the updated scenario sce_3 can be refined into two scenarios. One is for editing destination bin mapping, as illustrated in Fig. 9.5. The other one is for reporting the misrouted package. The capability profile is:

System(MRR, "Mis-Routed Reporter")
EnvEnt(eve$_2$, RP, {causal, symbolic})
EnvEnt(eve$_3$, DU, {causal})
EnvEnt(eve$_6$, DBM, {causal, symbolic})
Phenomenon(phe$_5$, Detect(PkgID, Destn), {event, value})
Phenomenon(phe$_{14}$, Assoc(<Destn, Bin>), {value})
Phenomenon(phe$_7$, PkgArr(PkgID, #Bin), {event, value})
Phenomenon(phe$_8$, Show(PkgID, Destn, #Bin), {event, value})
Phenomenon(phe$_9$, OnScreen(<PkgID, Destn, #Bin>), {state})
Interaction(int$_5$, RQ, MRR, phe$_5$)
Interaction(int$_{14}$, DBM, MRR, phe$_{14}$)
Interaction(int$_7$, RP, MRR, phe$_7$)
Interaction(int$_8$, MRR, DU, phe$_8$)
Interaction(int$_9$, DU, MRR, phe$_9$)
Requirement(req_7, "reporting misrouted package")
Reference(req_7, int5, {as-is, to-be})
Reference(req_7, int14, {as-is, to-be})
Reference(req_7, int7, {as-is, to-be})
Reference(req_7, int8, {to-be})
Reference(req_7, int9, {to-be, as-is})
Scenario(sce_7, "reporting misrouted package")
Realization(sce_7, req_7)

After the capability elaboration, the capability refinement of the package router controller is shown in Fig. 9.6.

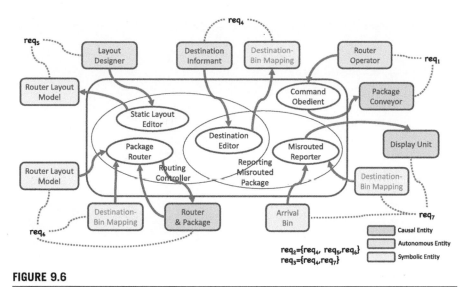

FIGURE 9.6

Package router controller: capability projection.

9.3 SUMMARY

This chapter proposes scenario-based capability projection for refining complex capability. The main contributions are threefold:

- Using concepts from the problem frames approach and extending them with scenarios, a conceptual model has been developed for a scenario-extended problem description. This ontological approach to problem description represents a novel technique for describing different classes of software problems.
- The proposed conceptual modeling process provides details of the problem description process. These guidelines are particularly useful for analysts during requirements elicitation because they give step-by-step instructions on how to elicit requirements though scenarios and how to describe software problems.
- A formal treatment of scenario-based projection has been provided with the problem frames and illustrates the rigor of the approach with a case study. This much-needed formality provides the potential for automated support for problem analysis and projection.

Reasoning III: System Capability Aggregation

CHAPTER OUTLINE

Capability composition was proposed in component-based design and service-oriented computing. In component-based design, the main concern is proposing a reuse-based approach to defining, implementing, and composing loosely coupled independent components into systems. All system processes are placed into separate components so that all of the data and functions inside each component are semantically related. Component-based capability composition is conducted via predefined interfaces. When a component offers capabilities to the rest of the system, it provides interface that specifies the capabilities that others can use and tells how they can do so, whereas when a component needs to use another component's function, it invokes an interface that specifies the capabilities that it requires.

In service-oriented community, the efforts of capability composition normally focus on checking the composability of services and then composing simple services to fulfil the request of complex services in a centralized manner. For example, workflow-based composition builds or creates (statically or dynamically) a workflow or process model and selects an atomic service for each task. Artificial intelligence planning—based composition grounds the requested service on a possible state space and the provided services as the state change triggers. A planner is

Environment Modeling-Based Requirements Engineering for Software Intensive Systems
https://doi.org/10.1016/B978-0-12-801954-2.00010-8

designed to make plans to reach the target state from the initial state by the invocations of atomic services.

This chapter discusses capability composition from another angle, which we call capability aggregation. Different from component composition and service composition, capability aggregation adopts a decentralized manner to make a composed capability, i.e., an agent-based manner (Maamar, et al., 2005). In capability aggregation, a software entity is considered as a capability agent. The capability profile of the software entity is the capability description of the agent. As in service composition, any capability aggregation is triggered by a capability request. The capability request is also treated as a capability agent. The difference is the former is the real agent and the latter is a virtual agent. All real agents and virtual agents are self-interested and autonomous.

The situation in which capability aggregation occurs is when a virtual agent comes out because there is a capability request. The capability request is normally associated with a payment. That means that the virtual agent would like to offer this payment if others can realize the required capability. When recognizing the capability request, the real agents may apply to make a contribution to the capability request with the desired payoff expectation. These real agents and the virtual agent may need to negotiate with each other so that an agreement about the capability realization and the balance of the payment and payoff can be achieved. Then the real agents will form a coalition (Kraus, et al., 2003) to realize the required capability collaboratively and each will obtain the expected payoffs. We call this framework the requirements-driven agent aggregation.

This chapter considers the modeling issues in this framework, including modeling the capability aggregation as a capability assignment problem and presenting a negotiation-based method to allow the agent coalition.

10.1 PRINCIPLES AND ARCHITECTURE
10.1.1 GENERAL PRINCIPLES

Four general principles are followed when the framework is developed: the autonomy principle, the abstract principle, the explicitness principle, and the competence principle.

The autonomy principle states that all software entities are autonomous, active, and persistent. They can control their own resources and their own behaviors and can even show social ability by collaborating with each other through dynamic discovery and negotiation. They can autonomously search for each other and choose the roles that they will have in collaboration to satisfy a piece of desired requirements so that interactions between them can be established dynamically and connected flexibly. In this sense, the autonomous software entities can be treated as agents.

The abstraction principle states that any complicated capability has its own abstract realization patterns. Each abstract realization pattern defines a way to decompose a complicated capability into a set of simpler capabilities. It also assigns the simpler capabilities to a set of roles and allows them to realize the complicated capability collaboratively. These roles can be taken by competent autonomous software entities.

The explicitness principle states that all aspects of autonomous software entities must be explicitly specified, covering both the syntax and semantic. This enables the semantic correctness of software entity interactions and capability reasoning to be assessable.

The competence principle states that for an autonomous software entity to be able to join dynamically in an abstract realization pattern to collaborate with each other meaningfully and correctly, it must be competent to understand the capability required and to follow the interaction protocols instructed by the roles' specifications, which, according to the explicitness principle, is accessible.

10.1.2 **ARCHITECTURE**

Following general principles, the first abstraction we make is to figure out three kinds of parties in the computing style. We use three types of agents to represent the different parties. They are capability-providing agents, capability-planning agents, and capability-consuming agents. Different parties have different responsibilities:

- Virtual capability agents are the initiators. When a software consumer has capability requirements that need to be realized, he or she creates and deploys a virtual capability agent to ask for the realization of the required capability.
- Capability planning agents are planners for the required capability. When observing a required capability, they produce realization plans. Each plan contains a decomposition of the required capability into a set of scenarios. A role model is also generated that consists of a set of collaborative roles. This plan is in fact an abstract capability realization coalition that is responsible for assigning the part capabilities to the roles and ensuring these roles can collaboratively realize the required capability.
- Real capability agents are the realization bodies of the required capabilities. When observing a capability realization plan, they first determine whether they are competitive with one or more roles based on their own capabilities. If so, and if they are willing to be the capability realizer, they make a bid applying to join the capability realization coalition.

When all of the roles in an abstract coalition have been taken by available capability-providing agents, the concrete coalitions consisting of these agents will be formed into the candidate realization bodies of the required capability. Then the virtual capability agent will negotiate with the real capability agents in the coalitions to make the role allocation.

Fig. 10.1 shows the architecture of this framework. There are three agent pools to contain three types of agent. The real capability agents can realize certain capabilities. The virtual capability agent is initiated by a capability-consuming request. It is

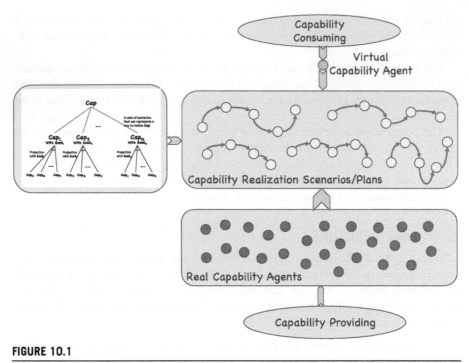

FIGURE 10.1

Architecture of agent aggregation framework. *Cap*, Capability; *SceS*, Scenario Set.

specified as the required capability that needs to be realized. The capability-planning agent produces capability realization patterns guided by predefined capability refinement knowledge.

Among the three types of agents, both the real capability agents and the capability-planning agents are predefined and relatively stable during the computing process. However, the virtual capability agents are dynamically initiated and undergo a five-state life cycle (Zheng, et al., 2010):

- initiated: the virtual capability agent is initiated by a capability consuming requester
- planned: the capability realization patterns for realizing the required capability have been proposed by capability-planning agents
- coalition-formed: the coalitions of the capability realization patterns have been formed. Each coalition consists of a set of available real capability agents
- role-allocated: a stable feasible coalition has been selected as the realization body of the required capability
- destroyed: the required capability has been realized and then the virtual capability agent is destroyed

10.2 REQUIREMENTS-DRIVEN AGENT AGGREGATION

This section discusses requirements-driven agent aggregation (Tang and Jin, 2010). As mentioned, the agent aggregation is triggered by a capability-consuming request. The required capability normally is not an atomic capability.[1] In this case, the capability projection presented in Chapter 9 is adopted to refine the capability into a set of finer-grain capabilities. This refinement can be done by the capability-planning agent. It also produces candidate capability realization patterns. This is to expend the opportunity of realizing the capability. Here, we first rephrase the capability projection.

10.2.1 CAPABILITY PROJECTION REPHRASING

Chapter 9 presented the reasoning on projection to refine the capability. There, the information acquisition and capability elaboration process for ensuring the projection and the projection operations were introduced. This chapter will use the results of the capability projection.

More formally, the capability projection can be redefined as: Let Cap be a capability profile and Cap have m kinds of projections, Cap_1, Cap_2, ..., Cap_m, each of which, Cap_i ($1 \leq i \leq m$), represents a strategy of the application business logics realization corresponding to a set of scenarios (i.e., $SceS_i$). The capability refinement tree can be built as:

- Cap is the root
- Cap_1, Cap_2, ..., Cap_m are the OR children of Cap corresponding to m complete sets of scenarios $SceS_1$, $SceS_2$, ..., $SceS_m$ respectively
- For each i ($1 \leq i \leq m$), each:

$$Cap_i = \pi_{SceS_i}(Cap) = \left\{ cap_{i_1}, cap_{i_2}, ..., cap_{i_l} \right\}$$

is a projection of Cap upon scenario set $SceS_i$. The projected capabilities in $\pi_{SceS_i}(Cap)$ are AND children of Cap_i;

- Each Cap_i ($1 \leq i \leq m$) is a capability split strategy of Cap. It says that Cap can be realized by using strategy Cap_i if all cap_{i_j} ($1 \leq j \leq l$) can be realized

The structure of the capability refinement tree is shown in Fig. 10.2. The capability refinement tree offers knowledge about the application logics. The intuitive explanation for this structure is: "A complex capability may have multiple ways to realize, each of which realizes it through a set of scenarios. On each set of scenarios, the capability can be projected. A projection on a certain set of scenarios produces a capability split."

---

[1]If it is, the capability matching mechanism presented in Chapter 8 will be used to support matching between a real agent and the virtual agent with the required capability.

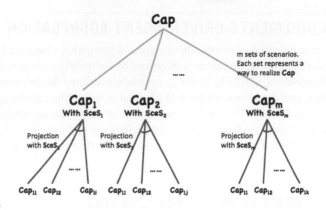

FIGURE 10.2

Illustrated structure of the capability refinement tree. *Cap*, Capability; *SceS*, Scenario Set.

10.2.2 CAPABILITY REALIZATION PATTERN

Within the framework of requirements-driven capability aggregation, the capability refinement tree serves as background knowledge to allow real capability agents to know what capabilities are demanded by the required capability agents. With this knowledge, real capability agents know whether they can contribute to a certain required capability.

We also assume that all agents need incentives, e.g., receiving benefits, to motivate them. For this purpose, we associate an offered payment with each virtual capability agent and an expected payoff with each real capability agent. We rewrite these capabilities as follows:

Let $\mathbb{C} = \{c_1, c_2, ..., c_{|\mathbb{C}|}\}$ be a set of capabilities. For any nonelementary capability $c \in \mathbb{C}$, c has at least a capability realization pattern $pat(c)$ that represents a way to realize c. Any capability realization pattern consists of three parts: the scenarios of its elementary capabilities, the role model to realize these elementary capabilities, and an assignment of the elementary capabilities to its roles, i.e.,

$$pat(c) = \; < Scen(c), \; RMod(c), \; Assig(c) >$$

is a capability realization pattern of c, in which:

$$Scen(c) = (Cap, \; COrd, \; Scap, \; Ecap, \; CapWs, \; \tau)$$

is a set of scenarios to realize c. It is a directed acyclic graph with the elementary capabilities as the nodes and the control flow as the edges. $Cap \subseteq \mathbb{C}$ is the set of elementary capabilities of c. $COrd$ expresses the control flow among the capabilities in Cap. $Scap$ is the start node and $Ecap$ is the final node. Apart from capability decomposition, the scenarios assign weights to the elementary capabilities. Each weight attached to a particular elementary capability represents the degree of importance of this elementary capability in the scenarios.

$$CapWs = \{\omega_1, \omega_2, ..., \omega_{|Cap|}\}$$

is a set of weights in which $\sum_{i=1}^{|Cap|} \omega_i = 1$

$$\tau: Cap \rightarrow CapWs$$

is an injective function from *Cap* to *CapWs*. Thus, $\tau(c_i) = \omega_j$ ($c_i \in Cap$ and $1 \leq i,j \leq |Cap|$) means that the weight of c_i in this pattern is ω_j.

$$RMod(c) = (Roles, Prots)$$

is a role model for realizing *c*. It consists of a set of roles and a set of interaction protocols. Here, the roles are abstract constructs in capability realization bodies. All roles are atomic constructs and cannot be defined in terms of other roles:

- Roles: names all of the roles that will take part in the realization of *c*
- Prots: specifies the interactions among roles during the realization. It details the flow of interaction as well as the messages that will be exchanged in interactions.

$$Assig(c) = assign(Scen(c), RMod(c))$$

$$= \{assign(c_i, r_j) | c_i \in Cap(Scen(c)), r_j \in Roles(RMod(c))\}$$

is a set of the assignment of a task with an elementary capability in *Scen* to a role in *RMod*. All tasks in scenarios need to be assigned to one role for implementation.

Fig. 10.3 exemplifies a capability realization pattern concerning the capability of land-based shipping. The upper part shows a weighted scenario, and the lower part, a role model. It demonstrates an assignment by using the long dotted lines regarding elementary capabilities of the roles between the two parts.

10.2.3 CAPABILITY AGGREGATION: NOTATIONS

This section presents the mechanism of the coalition formation. Before going into detail, some notations are introduced. First, a virtual capability agent is a tuple:

$$Req\ VirtAgt = < Cap, Payment >$$

in which:

- *Cap* is the required capability
- *Payment* $= \phi \in \mathbb{N}$ is a maximum payment that the virtual capability agent can offer for the realization of *Cap*. That is, this agent will give $\phi' \leq \phi$ as the payment if the required capability can be realized

Generally speaking, any virtual capability agent can ask for more than one capability and offer different payments for each capability. To simplify the description, we limit it to only one required capability in this book

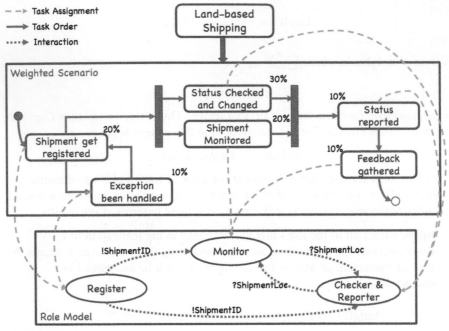

FIGURE 10.3

Capability realization pattern.

Second, the real capability agents can be specified using the same terminology. The difference is that they ask for payoffs when they contribute the realization of the capability instead of offering payment. That is, let *agt* be a real capability agent, and then *agt* can be described as a triple:

$$CapAgt \; RealAgt \; = \; < Cap, \; ExpPay, \; ECP >$$

in which:

- *Cap* is a set of elementary capabilities that can be realized by *RealAgt*
- *ExpPay* is a set of the minimum prospective payoffs of *RealAgt*'s elementary capabilities
- *ECP*: *Cap* → *ExpPay* is a minimum prospective payoff function of the set of elementary capabilities. That is, for $cap \in Cap$, $\rho \in ExpPay$, $ECP(cap) = \rho$ means that the agent wants to get a payment $\rho' \geq \rho$ when it contributes to realizing *cap*

Third, the capability-planning agent is responsible for producing the abstract capability realization pattern for a required capability. Each abstract capability realization pattern defines a set of its elementary capabilities as well as the relationship (i.e., the interaction flow) among these elementary capabilities. It also designs a role model (with interaction protocol) and assigns each elementary capability to a role. The selected abstract capability realization plan will become the proposal for allowing the real capability agents to join in and then form a concrete capability realization coalition.

The capability realization pattern can be represented as:

$$CapPattern\ pat = <\ Cap,\ CapS,\ Scen,\ RoleS,\ Coll,\ CapToRole\ >$$

in which:

- Cap is the capability that needs a realization pattern
- $CapS = \{< cap, \omega > | cap$: *an elementary capability and* ω: *weight*$\}$ is a capability-weight set. Each element is an elementary capability with its weight; $\sum \omega = 1$
- $Scen$: $CapS \cup \{Scap\} \times CapS \cup \{Ecap\}$ is a scenario of elementary capabilities. It defines the processes of the capability realizations
- $RoleS$ is a set of participants that will be involved to realize the capabilities
- $Coll$: $RoleS \times RoleS$ defines interactions between participants during the capability realization
- $CapToRole$: $CapS \rightarrow RoleS$ is a surjective function that assigns each elementary capability to a role

10.2.4 CAPABILITY AGGREGATION: MECHANISM DESIGN

When a capability request arises, a virtual capability agent is initiated by the capability consumer. If it is an elementary capability, there is no need to form a coalition. Instead, it can be directly allocated to a real capability agent via capability comparison introduced in Chapter 8. On the contrary, if the required capability is composite, the capability planning agent will propose a capability realization pattern. With the capability realization pattern, we assume that the real capability agents will can autonomously apply to join the pattern to form coalitions that are competent to realize the required capability.

As we know, a coalition is an alliance of individuals. But how can the real capability agents temporarily form such a coalition upon the proposed pattern for a required capability? And why do they want to join the coalition? Let us build the explanation:

Let

$$ReqVirtAgt = <\ Cap, Payment\ >$$

be the virtual agent, and let the pattern of realizing Cap be:

$$<\ Cap,\ CapS,\ Scen,\ RoleS,\ Coll,\ CapToRole\ >$$

To form a feasible coalition, the real agents need to know whether they are effective upon this pattern.

How do they know this? Without loss of generality, let $RealAgt$ be a real agent that is willing to take part in the coalition and let $rol \in RoleS$ be a role in the pattern.

With the capability-role assignments in *CapToRole*, *RealAgt* can judge whether it can be competent to *rol*, i.e., it is competent to a role if it has all of the capabilities that have been assigned to this role. Real capability agents that are competent to roles in the pattern are effective agents.

Formally, let *CapAgt RealAgt* be a real capability agent and *Role rol* a required role. For any $\forall rol \in Role$, if $Cap(rol) \subseteq Cap(RealAgt)$, *CapAgt RealAgt* is an effective capability agent for *Role rol*. The equivalence of two elementary capabilities can be conducted by the capability comparison introduced in Chapter 8.

Let

$$RealAgtS = \{RealAgt_1, ..., RealAgt_m\}$$

be a set of real agents;

$$Coal = \langle VirtAgt, RealAgtS \rangle$$

will form a coalition upon the pattern:

$$\langle Cap, CapS, Scen, RoleS, Coll, CapToRole \rangle$$

to realize *VirtAgt* if there exists a one-to-many mapping from *RealAgtS* to *RoleS*, such that:

- Any role $rol \in RoleS$ has been applied by one and only one effective real capability agent $agt \in RealAgtS$
- Each agent $agt \in RealAgtS$ has applied at least one role $rol \in RoleS$ for which it is competent

We call $Coal = \langle VirtAgt, RealAgtS \rangle$ a coalition upon the capability realization pattern:

$$\langle Cap, CapS, Scen, RoleS, Coll, CapToRole \rangle$$

Because agents are self-interested, sometimes for some purpose they may pretend to have certain capabilities. In this case, the formed coalition may not competent for the required capability. Such a coalition will be not feasible. Here, some mechanism is needed to ensure the formed coalition is feasible for the required capability.

Originally from a multiagent area, mechanism design is the art of designing the mechanism so that agents are motivated to indicate their preference truthfully and the mechanism can choose the desirable outcome from the perspective of some objective.

Traditionally, mechanism design is a manual endeavor in which the designer uses experience and intuition to hypothesize that a certain rule set is desirable in some way and then attempts to prove that this is the case. Automated mechanism design was introduced in (Sandholm, 2003); in this design, the mechanism is automatically created for the setting and objective. Sandholm in this paper formulates the mechanism design problem as a computational optimization problem as follows.

"We are given an automated mechanism design setting, an *IR* (individual rationality) notation (ex interim, ex post, or none), and a solution concept (domain strategies or Bayesian Nash equilibrium). Also, we are told whether payments are possible and whether randomization is possible. Finally, we are given a target value *G*. We are asked whether a mechanism exists of the specified type that satisfies both the *IR* notation and the solution concept, and gives an expected value of at least *G* for the objective."

By applying the automated mechanism design into the requirements-driven capability aggregation, its setting needs to be instantiated as follows:

- A meaningful outcome is a realization pattern for the required capability.
- The type of real capability agent is the set of elementary capabilities that it can realize. The type of required capability agent is the set of elementary capabilities that it wants to realize. That is, we call the set of elementary capabilities the agent type.
- The objective function is defined to be benevolent, i.e., to pursue the contentment of both the virtual capability agents and the real capability agents.

Thus, first, we need to name the types of capability agents. To simplify the description, let $\ddot{\Theta}$ be the set of all elementary capabilities derived by the capability projections introduced in Chapter 9. The types of capability agent are subsets of $\ddot{\Theta}$, i.e., that capability agent *agt* is of the type $\Theta = \{cap_1, cap_2, \ldots, cap_n\} \subseteq \ddot{\Theta}$ means *agt* is able to propose the set of elementary capability Θ.

Then the problem of forming the coalition of capability agents for a given capability request can be figured out as follows. Let a finite set of elementary capabilities be $\ddot{\Theta}$. Let *Req req* be the requirements and $\delta = Cap(req) \subseteq \ddot{\Theta}$ be the type of virtual capability agent. The setting contains:

- a finite set of outcomes $OAgt$ produced by capability planning agents, each of which is a capability realization pattern of δ
- a finite set of real capability agents $\ddot{A} = \{agt_1, agt_2, \ldots, agt_n\}$;
- each agent $agt_i \in \ddot{A}$ has
  - sets of elementary capabilities $\Theta_i \in \wp\left(\ddot{\Theta}\right)$ as its types
  - probability distribution γ_i over Θ_i
  - utility function $u_i \colon \Theta_i \times O \to \mathbb{R}$
- an objective function $g \colon \Theta \times O \to \mathbb{R}$ that maximizes both the satisfaction degree of the virtual capability agent and all real capability agents

For simplicity, the deterministic mechanism in automated mechanism design is used. This means that one certain capability set corresponds to one certain outcome. Different from the general deterministic mechanism with payments, the requirements-driven mechanism contains two types of agents and thus needs to consider two kinds of payments. With a fixed cost, the virtual agent cares about the quality that the required capability can realize, whereas the real agents care about the payments that they can obtain when taking part in the capability realization. Thus, the requirements-driven mechanism design consists of:

- an outcome selection function:

$$o: \Theta_1 \times \dots \times \Theta_N \to O$$

- for each real capability agent $agt_i \in \ddot{A}$, a payment selection function:

$$\pi_i: \Theta_1 \times \dots \times \Theta_N \to \mathbb{R}$$

- for the virtual capability agent, a quality selection function:

$$\phi: \Theta_1 \times \dots \times \Theta_N \to \mathbb{R}$$

In Sandholm's automated mechanism design, there are two types of constraint on designers: an *IR* constraint and an incentive compatibility *(IC)* constraint. *IR* constraint says that the utility of each agent has to be at least as great as the agent's fallback utility. *IC* constraint states that the agent should never have an incentive to misreport its type. These constraints are used in requirements-driven automated mechanism design. The differentiation is that the virtual agent and the real agent have different utility functions, and so the computation problem should satisfy an integrated utility function.

With this setting, we can define the computational problem of the requirements-driven mechanism design as an optimization problem:

We are given the setting of a requirements-driven automated mechanism design, an *IR* notion, and an *IC* notion. We are asked whether a deterministic mechanism exists that satisfies both the *IR* and *IC* notions and maximizes the integrated objective function.

10.2.5 CAPABILITY AGGREGATION: BENEVOLENT OBJECTIVE FUNCTION

A coalition denotes a way to realize a capability demanded by a virtual agent. Normally, a capability may have more than one stable coalition. The multiplicity comes from two aspects: (1) for a capability demanded by a virtual agent, there may exist more than one capability realization pattern; (2) for a capability realization pattern, more than one coalition may exist because of the different preferences of the real agents.

As mentioned earlier, both the virtual agent and the real agent are self-interested. That is, the virtual agent has its own preferences in choosing the effective real agents, whereas the real agents make their own decisions upon joining a particular coalition. Normally, the virtual agent prefers real agents that can provide a better quality of capability realization, whereas each real agent will prefer to join a coalition in which it can obtain higher payment. Whether a coalition can be the capability realization body depends on the preferences of the virtual agent and the real agents. Two criteria need to be defined to evaluate the feasibility of a coalition. Let:

$$Coal = \langle VirtAgt, RAgtS \rangle$$

be a coalition. For real agent $ragt \in RAgt$, the payment it can be offered when it joins in the coalition is:

$$P(VirtAgt, RAgtS) = \sum_{i=1}^{n} \omega_i \phi$$

in which (1) ϕ is the maximum payment that VirtAgt can offer, and (2) ω_i is the weight of the ith subcapability that $RAgt$ can realize. On the contrary, the virtual agent cares about the quality of the capability realization. Assume that we take m quality items into account and use a unique quality evaluation interval $[0, M]$, $M \in \mathbb{R}$. The quality of the realization of the capability cap by a real agent $RAgt$ is:

$$Q(RAgt, cap) = \sum_{i=1}^{m} \rho_i \kappa_i$$

in which $\kappa_i \in [0, M]$ is the evaluation value of the ith quality item by $RAgt$. ρ_i ($\sum_{i=1}^{m} \rho_i = 1$) is the weight of the ith quality item of $RAgt$. To evaluate the quality of a coalition, the virtual agent computes the weighted sum of qualities that every subcapability has and chooses the coalition that has better quality.

Hence, let $Coal = \langle VirtAgt, RAgtS \rangle$ be a coalition and $CapS$ be a set of capabilities in a possible capability realization pattern of $Cap(VirtAgt)$. Let p_i be the weight of ith capability $cap_i \in CapS$. Then $Coal$ is feasible and stable if:

- $CapS - \cup_{i=1}^{n} Cap(RAgt_i) = \phi$;
- $\forall j,\ CapS - \left(\cup_{i=1}^{n} Cap(RAgt_i) \right) \setminus Cap(RAgt_j) \neq \phi$;
- $\sum_{j=1}^{m} p_j \max_i Q(RAgt_i, cap_j)$ has the largest value among all coalitions

Here, the first constraint means that the coalition has the ability to realize the required capability. The second constraint means that no real agents are surplus (any surplus agents will shrink other agents' benefits). The third constraint means that the coalition can realize the required capability with the best quality. Under the three constraints, the surplus real agents are eliminated and the rest are capable of realizing the desired capability with the best quality.

10.3 CAPABILITY ASSIGNMENT PROBLEM (TANG AND JIN, 2010)

It is not straightforward to obtain a coalition of the best quality. According to the previous discussion, it is in fact a task assignment problem (Shehory and Kraus, 2005). Some algorithms have been devised to solve this problem. However, in terms of the setting of the requirements-driven capability aggregation, both the virtual agent and the real agents are autonomous and self-interested. The solution cannot be sorted out by maximizing only to the assigner's benefit, but should maximize the agents' total welfare under the condition that everyone is satisfied.

10.3.1 PROBLEM DEFINITION

The question is how to assign elementary capabilities to the real agents of a coalition so that the assignment can satisfy all real agents' reservation payoffs, and therefore each real agent can also get more than in other coalitions. Here, we consider "better" to be the real agent's total welfare, i.e., the degree of satisfaction that will be defined subsequently.

On the other hand, like real agents, the virtual agent has also its reservation payoff, which can be defined as the minimum expectant quality of realized capabilities. As usual, any virtual agent is concerned with a set of quality evaluation items, such as the response time, the throughput, the latency, the load balance, and so on. A quality evaluation function is introduced to compute the quality of the agent agt fulfilling capability cap. If there are n quality items that are on a unique evaluation interval $[0, M]$, $M \in \mathbb{R}$, the function is:

$$Q(agt, cap) = \sum_{i=1}^{n} \omega_i \sigma_i$$

in which $\sigma_i \in [0, M]$ is the evaluation value for the ith quality item and ω_i ($\sum \lim_{i=1,n} \omega_i = 1$) is the weight for the ith quality item of the virtual agent.

Let $Coalition = \{agt_1, agt_2, ..., agt_n\}$ be a stable coalition and $Cap = \{cap_1, cap_2, ..., cap_m\}$ be a set of elementary capabilities that the coalition needs to realize. $p_i \left(\sum \lim_{i=1,m} p_i = 1, \ 1 \leq i \leq m \right)$ is the weight of cap_i. agt_i is capable of realizing cap_j and the quality is $Q(agt_i, cap_j)$. Suppose $AgtCap_i \subset Cap$ is the set of elementary capabilities that agt_i is capable of realizing and $AssCap_i \subset AgtCap_i$ is the set of capabilities that are assigned to agt_i. An assignment S is an n-dimensional vector:

$$(AssCap_1, AssCap_2, ..., AssCap_n)$$

requiring $\{AssCap_1, AssCap_2, ..., AssCap_n\}$ to be a set-partitioning of Cap.

Given that $\overline{Q}$ is the reservation payment of the request agent and $\overline{P_l}$ ($1 \leq i \leq n$), the reservation payoff of each real capability agent, it is desirable to find an assignment S^* that satisfies:

- $\frac{Q(S^*)}{Q(C)} + \sum_{i+1}^{n} \frac{P_i(S^*)}{P_i(C)} = \max_S \left(\frac{Q(S)}{Q(C)} + \sum_{i=1}^{n} \frac{P_i(S)}{P_i(C)} \right)$

- $Q(S^*) \geq \overline{Q}, \quad P_i(S^*) \geq \overline{P_l}, \quad i = 1, 2, \ldots, n$

  in which:

- $Q(S) = \sum_{i=1}^{n} \sum_{j \in T_i} p_j Q(agt_i, \, cap_j)[0, \, M]$

  is the quality of assignment S

- $P_i(S) = \frac{\sum_{j \in T_i} p_j Q(agt_i, \, cap_j)}{Q(S)} P(S)$

  is the payment of cap_i in assignment S

- $P(S) = f(Q(S))$

  is the payment function that the virtual agent is willing to pay for S

- $Q(C) = \sum_{j=1}^{m} p_j \max_i Q(agt_i, \, cap_j)$

  is the virtual agent's ideal assignment

- $P_i(C) = \frac{\sum_{j \in W_i} p_j Q(agt_i, \, cap_j)}{Q(S)} P(S)$

  is agt_i's maximum payment in S
  Let C be an effective coalition, S an assignment. Then,

$$SDR(C, S) = \frac{Q(S)}{Q(C)}$$

is the degree of satisfaction of the virtual agent:

$$SDA_i(C, S) = \frac{P_i(S)}{P_i(C)}$$

is the degree of satisfaction of real agent agt_i

$$SD(C, S) = SDR(C, S) + \sum_{i=1}^{n} SDA_i(C, S)$$

is the total degree of satisfaction of the coalition. The assignment problem is to find an assignment that maximizes the total degree of satisfaction and satisfies the respective reservation payoffs. The feasible coalition will be chosen collaboratively by the real agents and the virtual agent.

However, the complexity of the assignment problem is nondeterministic polynomial time (NP)-complete. The illustrative proof could be: Consider a special case, i.e., let $n = 2$:

$$Cap(agt_1) = \{cap_1, \ cap_3, \ cap_4, ..., \ cap_m\}$$

$$Cap(agt_2) = \{cap_2, \ cap_3, \ cap_4, ..., \ cap_m\}$$

and

$$Q(agt_1, cap_j) = Q(agt_2, cap_j)$$

Here, $(j = 3,4,...,m)$. For any assignment S:

$$Q(S) = p_1 Q(agt_1, cap_1) + p_2 Q(agt_2, cap_2) + \sum_{j=3}^{m} p_j Q(cap_j)$$

is constant. Let:

$$\overline{P}_1 = \left(p_1 Q(agt_1, cap_1) + \frac{1}{2} \sum_{j=3}^{m} p_j Q(cap_j) \right) \frac{f(Q(S))}{Q(S)}$$

$$\overline{P}_2 = \left(p_1 Q(agt_2, cap_2) + \frac{1}{2} \sum_{j=3}^{m} p_j Q(cap_j) \right) \frac{f(Q(S))}{Q(S)}$$

We are finding an assignment S^* such that $P_i(S^*) \geq \overline{P}_l$. Notice that:

$$P_1(S^*) + P_2(S^*) = \overline{P}_1 + \overline{P}_2 = f(Q(S))$$

This is equivalent to the partition problem which is an NP-complete problem.

10.3.2 NORMATIVE SYSTEMS

Norms like obligations, permissions, and prohibitions have been proposed in multi-agent systems to deal with coordination issues of those systems, to model legal issues in electronic institutions and electronic commerce, to model multiagent organizations, and so on (Agotnes, et al., 2007). A normative multiagent system is a system together with normative systems in which, on the one hand, agents can decide whether to follow explicitly represented norms, and on the other, the normative systems specify how and to what extent the agents can modify the norms.

Because the requirements-driven capability aggregation is treated as a multi-agent system and normative systems have been considered to be a highly influential approach to coordination in the area of multiagent systems, we take the advantage of technologies in multiagent systems. Also, some other technologies are helpful to model the assignment problem, such as Kripke structures and Computation Tree Logic (CTL) (Emerson, 1991).

Let $Coal = \{agt_1, agt_2, ..., agt_n\}$ be an effective coalition and $CapS(req) = \{cap_1, cap_2, ..., cap_m\}$ be the set of elementary capabilities of the virtual agent. Then, an assignment S is an n-dimensional vector:

$$S = \{\chi_1, \chi_2, ..., \chi_n\}$$

Here, $\{\chi_1, \chi_2, ..., \chi_n\}$ is a partition of $CapS(req)$ and indicates that the capability in χ_i is assigned to agent agt_i. The Kripke structure of the assignment problem is defined as a 6-tuple:

$$\langle S, S^0, R, A, \alpha, V \rangle$$

where:

- S is a finite, nonempty assignment set
- $S^0 = \{\chi_1^0, \chi_2^0, ..., \chi_n^0\} \in S$ is an initial assignment. The assignments in S^0 satisfy:

$$\forall cap \in \chi_i^0, \quad Q(agt_i, \ cap) \geq Q(agt_j, cap) \quad i = 1, 2, ..., n, \quad j \neq i$$

- $R \subseteq S \times S$ is a total binary relation on S, which is called the transition relation between assignments
- $A = \{agt_1, agt_2, ..., agt_n\}$ is a set of agents
- $\alpha : R \to A$ labels each transition in R with an agent, i.e., $r \to agt$ ($r \in R$, $agt \in A$) indicates that agent agt causes the transition between assignments
- $V : S \to \mathbb{R}^n$ represents the set of payoffs of all real agents in a certain assignment, i.e., $S \to (p_1, p_2, ..., p_n)$, ($p_i \in \mathbb{R}, i = 1, 2, ..., n$), means that agent agt_i's payoff is p_i in assignment S

A normative system is a special multiagent system in which agents need to follow a set of constraints on the behaviors of agents in the system. That is, a normative system distinguishes between the legal state transitions and illegal state transitions. Agents are not allowed to make changes along illegal transitions. Different normative systems may differ as to whether a transition is legal.

For the Kripke structure of an assignment problem, state transitions are changes of assignment. Thus, any assignment change can be legal or illegal. Let $\eta \subseteq R$ be the set of illegal transitions. Therefore, $R \setminus \eta$ is the set of legal transitions. Hence, let:

$$K = \langle S, S^0, R, A, \alpha, V \rangle$$

be the Kripke structure of the assignment. Then the effect of the normative system η on K is to eliminate from it all transitions that are forbidden according to η and lead to the Kripke structure:

$$K' = \langle S, S^0, R \setminus \eta, A, \alpha', V \rangle$$

in which

$$\alpha' = \begin{cases} \alpha(S, S') & \text{if } (S, S') \in R \setminus \eta \\ \text{undefined} & \text{otherwise} \end{cases}$$

Call (K, η) a normative system over K. K' is the Kripke structure obtained from K by deleting transitions forbidden in η.

Next, we use CTL to express the objectives of the normative system. The semantics of CTL are given with respect to the satisfaction relation "$\vDash$", which holds between pairs of the form (K, s), where K is a Kripke structure and s is a state in K, and formulas of the language. The satisfaction relation is defined as follows:

- $(K, s) \vDash T$
- $(K, s) \vDash p$ if $p \in V(s)$ (where $p \in \mathbb{R}^n$)
- $(K, s) \vDash \neg \varphi$ if not $(K, s) \vDash \varphi$
- $(K, s) \vDash \varphi \vee \psi$ if $(K, s) \vDash \varphi$ or $(K, s) \vDash \psi$
- $(K, s) \vDash A(O\varphi)$ if on all paths, φ is true next
- $(K, s) \vDash E(O\varphi)$ if on some paths, φ is true next
- $(K, s) \vDash A(\varphi \, \mathcal{U} \, \psi)$ if on some paths, φ until ψ
- $(K, s) \vDash E(\varphi \, \mathcal{U} \, \psi)$ if on some paths, φ until ψ

Notice that transitions change the assignments. When a current assignment satisfies the expectations of all agents, the agents will not propose making further changes. This assignment is desired by all agents and becomes the agreement of the coalition. Let S_1^i, S_2^i, ..., S_k^i be acceptable to agent agt_i; thus:

$$\varphi_i = \left[S_1^i\right] \vee \left[S_2^i\right] \vee \ldots \vee \left[S_k^i\right]$$

is the objective of agt_i, in which $[S]$ is the state of the system with assignment S. Hence, the system's objective is:

$$\Phi = \varphi_1 \wedge \varphi_2 \wedge \ldots \wedge \varphi_n$$

It corresponds to a set of assignments in which each assignment is acceptable to all agents agt_i $(1 \leq i \leq n)$.

By providing a suitable normative system, the assignment problem can be solved. This builds the bridge from the requirements-driven agent aggregation with the available work on normative systems, games, mechanisms, etc. With this works, some interesting issues such as robustness or applying power indices can be introduced. The next section will provide a normative system for the assignment problem in a negotiation-based manner.

10.3.3 NEGOTIATION-BASED TASK ASSIGNMENT

This section presents a negotiation framework in which real agents and virtual agents negotiate to change the state of the system. The main issue is the state transition in the Kripke structure, i.e., a state transition, is viewed as a proposal by an agent. In the process of negotiation, one agent transits the state to another; another agent can accept or refuse it. If the proposal is accepted, the state transition happens; otherwise, the first agent proposes a new proposal for transiting the state to a new one. This process is showed as a Unified Modeling Language sequence diagram in Fig. 10.4.

In Fig. 10.4, the virtual capability agent first chooses a state to make a proposal, meaning that it wants the assignment of that state. It is the initial state of the Kripke structure, i.e., every elementary capability is assigned to the real agent that has the best quality to realize the capability. This is reasonable because any virtual agent wants to get the best capability. Then the real agents evaluate the state to see whether it is satisfiable. If a real agent accepts the state, it will do nothing; otherwise, it will transit the state. The decision regarding being "accepted" or "refused" is made based on the reservation payoff. States that satisfy the real agent's reservation payoff will be accepted but others will be refused.

After that, the real agents that refuse the proposed state should negotiate with others and then modify the states. They trigger transitions that are included in R. Any real agent *agt* will not negotiate with real agents that are assigned capabilities

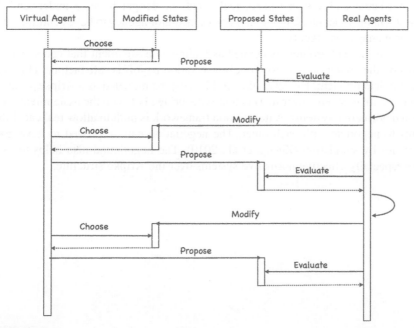

FIGURE 10.4

Process of negotiation (Tang and Jin, 2010).

that are not included in its capable set Cap_i. They may work out several states that have already satisfied some of the agents but not all. Then the virtual agent chooses one state that best satisfies itself (with the greatest total quality); after that, the virtual agent proposes it to the real agents. This proposed state starts the new round of negotiations.

Three possible situations will terminate the negotiations:

- If all real agents accept the virtual agent's proposal in some round, the negotiation ends with success.
- If the real agents cannot make a valid transition when it negotiates with others, the negotiation ends in failure.
- If the virtual agent cannot make a choice in modified states, i.e., all modified states worked out by the real agents cannot satisfy the virtual agent's reservation payoff, the negotiation ends in failure.

10.4 SUMMARY

In requirement-driven capability aggregation, real agents actively search for virtual capability and then match themselves with elementary capabilities in the requests. In this mechanism, on the one hand, real agents no longer have to understand the request. On the other hand, it does not need a mediator agency to have central control over or manage real agents.

The assignment problem is defined as finding an assignment that can satisfy all agents on the condition that everyone's reservation payoff is satisfactory. This is an NP-complete problem. However, this problem can be modeled as a Kripke structure with normative systems over it. This builds the bridge between the assignment problem and normative systems. A negotiation framework is built to allow real capability agents to negotiate with each other. The negotiation can be proved to have good properties by simulation (Zheng, et al., 2010). The negotiation also helps to exert more especially effective normative systems over the Kripke structure.

Part Three References

T. Agotnes, W. Hoek, M. Wooldridge, Normative system games, in: Proceedings of the 6th International Joint Conference on Autonomous Agents and Multi-Agent Systems (AAMAS-2007), 2007, p. 129.

R. Alur, S. Kannan, M. Yannakakis, Communicating hierarchical state machines, in: Automata, Languages and Programming (ICALP'99), 1999, pp. 169–178.

J.L. Austin, How to Do Thing with Words, Oxford University Press, 1976.

D. Berardi, D. Calvanese, G. De Giacomo, M. Lenzerini, M. Mecella, Automatic composition of e-services that export their behavior, ICSOC 2003 (2003) 43–58.

X. Chen, Z. Jin, Capturing requirements from expected interactions between software and its interactive environment: an ontology based approach, International Journal of Software Engineering and Knowledge Engineering 26 (1) (2016) 15–39.

E.A. Emerson, Temporal and Modal Logic, MIT Press, 1991.

J.G. Hall, L. Rapanotti, M. Jackson, Problem oriented software engineering: solving the package router control problem, IEEE Transactions on Software Engineering 34 (2) (2008) 226–241.

Z. Maamar, S.K. Mostefaoui, H. Yahyanoui, Toward an agent-based and context-oriented approach for web services composition, IEEE Transactions on Knowledge and Data Engineering 17 (5) (2005) 686–697.

M. Jackson, Problem Frames: Analyzing and Structuring Software Development Problems, Addison-Wesley, 2001.

Z. Jin, X. Chen, D. Zowghi, Performing projection in problem frames using scenarios, in: Proceedings of the 16th Asia-Pacific Software Engineering Conference (APSEC2009), 2009, pp. 249–256.

S. Kraus, O. Shehory, G. Taase, Coalition formation with uncertain heterogeneous information, in: Proceedings of the 2nd International Joint Conference on Autonomous Agents and Multiagent Systems (AAMAS2003), 2003, pp. 1–8.

A. van Lamsweerde, Requirements Engineering: From System Goals to UML Models to Software Specification, John Wiley, 2009.

M. Papazoglou, P. Traverso, D. Dustdar, F. Leymann, Service-oriented computing: State of the Art and Research Challenges, IEEE Computer 40 (11) (2007) 38–45.

C. Peltz, Web services orchestration and choreography, IEEE Computer 36 (10) (2003) 46–52.

T. Sandholm, Automated Mechanism Design: A New Application Area for Search Algorithms, in: Proceedings of the International Conference on Principles and Practice of Constraint Programming (CP'03), 2003, pp. 19–36.

Z. Shen, J. Su, Web service discovery based on behavior signatures, in: IEEE International Conference on Services Computing (SCC005), 2005, pp. 279–286.

O. Shehory, S. Kraus, Methods for task allocation via agent coalition formation, Artificial Intelligence 101 (1–2) (2005) 165–200.

A. Sutcliffe, Scenario-based requirements engineering, in: Proceedings of the 11th IEEE International Requirements Engineering Conference (RE'03), 2003, pp. 320–329.

K. Sycara, S. Widoff, M. Klusch, J. Lu, LARKS: dynamic matchmaking among heterogeneous software agents in cyberspace, Autonomous Agents and Multi-Agent Systems 5 (2002) 173–203.

J. Tang, Z. Jin, Assignment problem in requirements driven agent collaboration and its implementation, in: Proceedings of the 9th International Conference on Autonomous Agents and Multi-Agent Systems (AAMAS2010), 2010, pp. 839−846.

P. Wang, Z. Jin, Web service composition: an approach using effect-based reasoning, in: Proceedings of 2nd International Workshop on Engineering Service Oriented Applications: Design and Composition (WESOA 2006), ICSOC Workshops 2006, Lecture Notes in Computer Science 4652, 2006, pp. 62−73.

P. Wang, Z. Jin, L. Liu, G. Cai, Building towards capability specifications of web services based on an environment ontology, IEEE Transactions on Knowledge and Data Engineering 20 (4) (2008) 547−561.

P. Wang, Z. Jin, H. Liu, Capability description and discovery of internetware entity, Science in China 53 (4) (2010) 685−703.

L. Zheng, J. Tang, Z. Jin, An agent based framework for internetware computing, International Journal of Software and Informatics 4 (3) (2010) 401−418.

Environment-Related Nonfunctionalities

4

Some nonfunctional concerns are mainly derived from the properties of the environmental entities, e.g., dependability, adaptivity, security, safety. The environment modeling-based approach is helpful for an analysis of these nonfunctionalities because environment models characterize these properties. This part discusses some environment-related nonfunctionalities and presents approaches to eliciting, modeling, and specifying those nonfunctionalities.

This part includes three chapters, i.e., Chapters 11–13. Chapter 11 discusses system dependability. We assume that the dependability issue is derived from the characteristics of the system's interactive environment, including external entities or other systems that will interact with the system. Dependability is an issue because failing to deal appropriately with these external entities may cause negative effects or even disasters. This makes the system undependable.

Next, Chapter 11 introduces an approach to using the environment model as the background to identifying dependability concerns and integrating countermeasures to the threat. Chapter 11 also proposes modeling the dependability requirements as threat controllers. This leads to fine-grained function points to guarantee the system's dependability.

Adaptivity is another important feature in modern software systems, e.g., cyber-physical systems, mobile applications. Like dependability, adaptivity depends on the interactive environment of the system. The system needs to adapt its own behavior, mainly because of the changing environment. Chapter 12 clarifies the relationships among the three most important elements in requirements engineering: the requirements goal model, the interactive environment model, and the system configuration model. It proposes modeling the adaptation logic separately from the application logic. A view-based rule language is advised and defined to specify the adaptation logic. This simplifies the construction of the system model and facilitates the evolution of the model at runtime.

Nonfunctional concerns are not easy to elicit and analyze. Inspired by the Problem Frame approach (Jackson, 2001), Chapter 13 defines a set of nonfunctional requirement patterns in a problem-oriented way. These patterns can be used to capture the nonfunctional aspects and introduce appropriate nonfunctional requirements into the system's functional model. Afterward, extended capabilities corresponding to the original function capabilities will be obtained. During the capability extension, some new environment entities may be further identified or designed. These concerns about patterns can help to derive specifications for the extended capabilities.

The System Dependability Problem

11

CHAPTER OUTLINE

Software systems are being increasingly applied to critical industry sections such as finance, aviation, and power plants. When developing software systems, developers generally discuss what the systems should do to make customers' lives easier. That is, they consider the positive features. However, in those areas, customers need the systems to do good things but also avoid doing bad things, e.g., especially avoid the side effects of the system's behaviors that may cause disasters. That leads to thinking about dependability.

Environment Modeling-Based Requirements Engineering for Software Intensive Systems
https://doi.org/10.1016/B978-0-12-801954-2.00011-X

The International Federation for Information Processing Working Group 10.4 (IFIP WG 4.0) defines dependability as the trustworthiness of a computing system that allows reliance to be justifiably placed in the services it delivers.[1] The term "dependability" becomes an integrating concept that encompasses a set of quality attributes that leads to some qualitative or quantitative overall measures of the system (Avizienis et al., 2004): (1) availability: readiness for correct service; (2) reliability: continuity of correct service; (3) safety: the absence of catastrophic consequences to the system's interactive environment; (4) confidentiality: the absence of unauthorized disclosure of information; (5) integrity: the absence of improper system alternations; and (6) maintainability: the ability to undergo modifications and repairs.

An examination of dependability-critical systems shows that dependability relies heavily on complex interdependencies that exist between the system and its interactive environment. The characteristics of environment entities lead directly to many critical problems. For example, valuable assets need to be kept safe to avoid loss (reliability concern), sensitive data cannot be exposed (privacy concern), the system needs to resist attack from hostile actors when delivering critical services (security concern), the system cannot hurt users in the process of delivering services (safety concern), etc. Failing to do these may result in negative effects or disasters.

Identification, elicitation, and modeling of dependability requirements are inherently difficult. First, the dependability requirements of such systems are heavily affected by regulations and organizational policies; interactions among software, hardware, people, physical devices, and spaces, and so on. It is difficult to understand the properties of a multifaceted environment. This prevents dependability concerns from being precisely defined. Second, because of the openness and dynamics of the interactive environment, the system may encounter various threats during operation, which can include active defects, malicious attacks, human operational errors, or noisy networks. These may all cause risks that may violate the system's dependability. How to identify these threats and define suitable countermeasures to avoid potential risks becomes the key issue.

Environment modeling—based requirements engineering provides a direct way to identify these critical problems because of its explicit descriptions of the environment entities and their attributes. The environment model can serve as a guide to identifying threats. Furthermore, countermeasures that can be used to deal with threats can be precisely integrated into interactions referring to the threats. In addition, inspired by cybernetics, dependability requirements can be understood as different ways to control the threat; i.e., the system should be able to monitor threats and decide on countermeasures that are able to deal with them. This chapter introduces a cybernetics-based approach to eliciting and modeling dependability requirements.

---

[1] www.dependability.org.

11.1 **BACKGROUND AND PRINCIPLES**
11.1.1 **BACKGROUND**

Although there is no overall consensus on the exact definition of dependability, many agree that **dependability** is the capacity to provide services that can defensibly be trusted. As shown in previous chapters, a system is assigned to do something to fulfill some business goals. What are the goals are and how to fulfill them are described in the functional capability specification. An environment-based approach assumes that these functional services are delivered by the system via its interactive behavior, by sharing phenomena with the environment entities. Because on an Internet platform a software-intensive system is operational in an open sociotechnical environment, it interacts with its environment, which consists of hardware, software, humans, devices, and the physical world with its natural phenomena. The system boundary, which consists of phenomena shared with its environment entities, is the common boundary between the system and its environment.

In this sense, we can say that **a system is dependable** if it can be depended upon, or trusted or relied upon, to perform a particular task. That is, dependable services are delivered when the services implement the system's functional capabilities and fulfill the system's goals without causing negative effects. **Dependability requirements** are those that can make a system more dependable if they have been realized. Dependability requirements include capabilities that can prevent the system from producing negative effects.

11.1.2 **STATE OF ART**

Functional requirements are driven by business goals, while dependability requirements are driven by various potential threats or deviations in the system. Much research in this area tends to address dependability requirements in a top-down fashion by focusing on different dependability attributes separately (e.g., security, reliability, safety): for example, to apply a risk analysis approach to address dependability by dealing with the different attributes of dependability. Because there is no consensus regarding what the attributes of dependability are, and because different attributes are usually interrelated, it is not easy to determine what attributes of dependability need to be considered.

Furthermore, dependability is an integrated and synthetic property at the system level. Any individual attribute cannot represent system dependability. It is necessary to model dependability requirements through unified terminology regardless of the attributes of dependability.

11.1.2.1 *Unified Model of Dependability*

Essentially any rigorous approach based on available models and classification will help to extract the requirements for dependability. One such example of a practical framework built on the concept of the issue of dependability is the Unified Model of Dependability (UMD) (Basili et al., 2004). The UMD focuses on dependability issues, i.e., the undependable behaviors of the system. The conceptual model of the UMD framework is given in Fig. 11.1. Important concepts include issue, scope, event, measure, and reaction. The UMD framework permits stakeholders to express their requirements by specifying what they see as the actual dependability **issue** (failure and/or hazard) or class of issues that should not affect the system or a specific service (**scope**). An issue can be the result of an external **event**. For an issue, stakeholders may also specify tolerable manifestations (**measure**) and the desired corresponding system **reaction**.

In terms of the conceptual framework, UMD elicits the dependable requirements:

- by identifying the potential scope of functional requirements that may ask for dependability
- by eliciting and modeling the dependability requirements:
  - within the current scope, identifying the potential issues of the system
  - identifying the event that may cause the issues
  - deciding measurements to detect the issues
  - choosing the desired system reactions

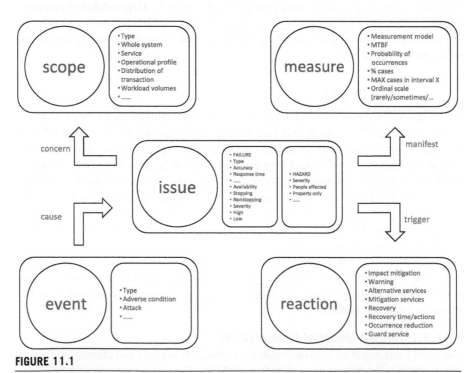

FIGURE 11.1

Unified model of dependability concepts and relationships. *MAX*, maximum; *MTBF*, mean time between failures (Basili et al., 2004).

UMD is able to provide help to elicit dependability requirements according to three aspects: (1) it establishes a common framework to discuss the dependability attributes; (2) it defines attributes related to dependability needs and elicits measurable parameters; and (3) it helps stakeholders to better understand their dependability needs.

11.1.3 PRINCIPLES OF IDENTIFYING DEPENDABILITY REQUIREMENTS

Capabilities derived from business logic, which impose desired or positive effects onto environments, are functional requirements, whereas the dependability requirements are capabilities that can avoid negative effects in the process of delivering services. Different from functional capabilities, dependability capabilities are not independent but need to be integrated or interweaved with the functional capabilities. They are in fact designed to enhance the system's functional capabilities so that the system can avoid negative effects to the environment and the system when delivering the services (Jackson, 2009). This is termed threat control. To clarify the description, we term the latter **control capabilities**. This means that we distinguish two kinds of capabilities when eliciting requirements: Business capabilities are decided by business functional requirements and control capabilities are decided by dependability requirements. Table 11.1 presents the differences between these kinds of capabilities.

The environment modeling approach includes important ideas and initial principles including:

- **Dependability is an emergent property, not a separate feature.**
  Dependability is an emergent property of a system. Mechanisms to make a system more dependable need to be built in as a critical part of the design from the beginning. Building in dependability requires making explicit trade-offs when determining system specifications to provide a cost-effective system solution, because mechanisms that enable dependability are costly. Thus, dependability requirements engineering needs to be integrated into business functional requirements engineering.

Table 11.1 Business Capability and Control Capability

Business Capabilities	Control Capabilities
To realize functional requirements	To realize dependability requirements
To impose positive or desired effects directly onto the environment	To prevent the system from receiving external attacks or imposing undesired effects onto the interactive environment
To be directly decided by business goals	To be decided by a risk assessment of the potential negative effect that may be imposed onto the system or the interactive environment

- **Environment entity characteristics reveal risks that need to be avoided.**
  Dependability requirements may not be directly implied by the need for business
  to avoid risks in the process of running the system. There is no explicit source of
  dependability requirements. The dependability requirements are implied by the
  threats that may result in **risks**. However, often the assumptions of the system
  may indicate what threats there are to the system. These assumptions can be
  about the environment entities as well as the system: for example, users do not
  always have bad intentions, the devices will always work well, there are no
  external interruptions, the system will not fail, etc. They normally become
  threats to the system when the assumptions are false. Threats may also exist
  because of some characteristics of the environment entities, e.g., some sensitive
  data cannot be exposed, some valuable entities may be stolen, some entities may
  be sensitive to shared phenomena, and improper effects may cause a disaster.
  These threats become critical problems and the system needs to be able to
  control them. Then the ability to know when they happen and to decide how to
  deal with them becomes the dependability requirement.
- **Dependability is a good enough property. Making it perfect is not possible or
  necessary.**
  On the one hand, the consequence of dependability requirements is cost. Even
  worse, customers sometimes think that the consequence of such capabilities is
  waste when risks have not yet happened. Elicitation of such requirements needs
  explicit argumentation. On the other hand, like functional requirements,
  dependability requirements can also experience the risk of scope creep.
  Sometimes developers think that additional threats or included countermeasures
  need further controls. In this case, the scope to be controlled will spread. A
  combination of dependability know-how and experience with the subject matter
  to prioritize dependability requirements is needed to strike the right balance
  between cost and value.

11.2 CYBERNETICS AND MODEL OF DEPENDABLE SYSTEMS

Identification, elicitation, and modeling of dependability requirements are inherently
difficult. First, dependability requirements do not explicitly come from business logic
but are heavily affected by interactions between a theoretical system and people, physical devices and spaces, regulations, organizational policies, etc. It is difficult to understand all of the multifaceted environment properties to enable the precise
prevention of dependability problems. Second, because of the openness of the environments, the systems may encounter various unpredictable threats during operation
that can be activated by defects, malicious attacks, human operational error, or noisy
networks. These may result in risks that will violate the system's dependability.

Control theory (Goodwin et al., 2001) deals with influencing the behavior of
dynamical systems. Although a major application of control theory involves control

system engineering, which deals with the design of process control systems for industry, other applications range far beyond this. This section presents the basic principles for modeling a dependable system as a control system. This will provide a framework for eliciting and modeling the dependability requirements.

11.2.1 CYBERNETICS AND CONTROL LOOPS

Cybernetics (Wiener, 1948), control theory, is a transdisciplinary branch of engineering and computational mathematics. It deals with the behavior of dynamical systems with inputs and how their behavior is modified by feedback. This term was defined by Norbert Wiener in 1948 as "the scientific study of control and communication in the animal and the machine" (Wiener, 1948). Nowadays, the term is often used loosely to imply the "control of any system using technology."

The objective of control theory is to control a system so that the system's output follows a desired control signal, called the reference. To do this, a (normally feedback) controller is designed that determines what output needs to be monitored, how to compare it with the reference, which system behaviors need to be adjusted, and how to adjust them. The difference between actual and desired output, called the error signal, is applied as feedback to the system input, to bring the actual output closer to the reference.

A control system is composed of two components: the controlled object and the controller. The controlled object is what is given, which is the component implementing the business functional capabilities. The controller is what is designed, based on the model of the controlled object. In the presence of various disturbances to the controlled object, the system's goal is to maintain some specified properties of the controlled object's output at, or sufficiently close to, the reference input (also called the set point). To achieve the system's goal, the controller needs to activate some actions to affect the controlled object through the manipulated variables (i.e., the input of the controlled object). These actions are the controls adopted by the controller.

Generally, there are three types of basic control systems, as shown in Fig. 11.2A–C. An open loop control system (Fig. 11.2A) imposes no controls on the controlled object even if it is disturbed by events from its interactive environment. A feedforward control system (Fig. 11.2B) detects an external disturbance and imposes some controls on the controlled object to reduce the impact of the disturbance. A feedback control system (Fig. 11.2C) detects the output of the controlled object and imposes controls on the object to reduce deviation in the output, but it does not take care of the external disturbance. In open loop and feedforward control systems, the control action from the controller is independent of the output of the controlled object, whereas in the feedback control system, control action from the controller depends on the output of the controlled object.

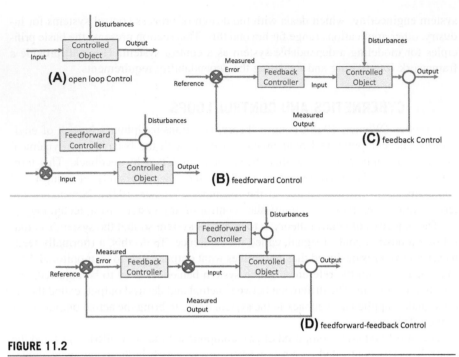

FIGURE 11.2

Three types of control systems and the feedforward/feedback control system.

The feedforward control and feedback control can be combined, as shown in Fig. 11.2D, in which the feedforward controller monitors disturbances from the interactive environment and controls the controlled object so that it can take measures to compensate for and eliminate the impact of the external disturbance. In the meantime, the feedback controller measures the output, compares it with the reference, and adjusts the controlled object's behavior.

11.2.2 MODEL OF DEPENDABLE SYSTEMS

Functional requirements engineering starts from an understanding of the business goals that need to be achieved and a determination of the services that the system needs to deliver to achieve the goals. However, in many cases a system that can satisfy the functional requirements is not always dependable, especially in the presence of various potential external (malicious or benign) threats or internal faults, as discussed earlier.

To make the system more dependable, we need to address how the system can be dependable in the presence of potential threats or system deviations, which may lead to risks. Apart from the business functional requirements, the development of a dependable system necessitates identifying and modeling dependability requirements to deal with potential threats and/or reduce risks. Therefore, identifying potential risks is the first step.

The environment modeling-based approach models both dependability and functional requirements in a unified terminology and provides an integrated view. Cybernetics inspires the essential idea of the approach, i.e., to treat a dependable system as a feedforward-feedback control system, as shown in Fig. 11.3. In such a system, the core system that delivers the required services is the object to be controlled. Two kinds of controllers (the feedforward controllers and the feedback controllers) react to potential threats. The feedforward controllers implement a set of controls for those identified threats. The feedback controllers, which supplement the feedforward controllers in case some threats are unidentified, implement a set of controls for possible system behavior deviations that uncover the unidentified threats. The system ensures its dependability in the presence of various threats via these two kinds of controllers.

This method separates the requirements elicitation of dependable systems into two subtasks. The functional requirements elicitation describes the required services from the users' perspective. The dependability requirements elicitation describes the required controls from the perspectives of potential threats and deviations in the system's behavior.

Chapter 7 presents the capability profile to determine the functional requirements, whereas the cybernetics-inspired dependable system extends the capability profile by introducing the control profile. The feedforward and feedback control indicates two kinds of control profiles (namely, the feedforward control profile and the feedback control profile) to model the dependability requirements. This extension

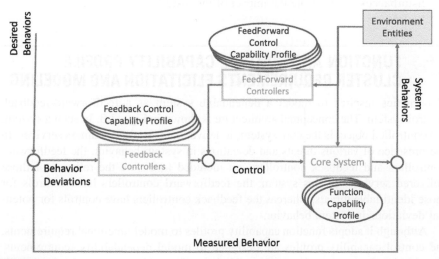

FIGURE 11.3

Dependable system: feedforward-feedback control model.

results in the "function and control capability profile cluster (FC-CPC)." The relationships between the function profile and the control profile show which critical factors have been measured and taken into account in the system behavior.

The main points are summarized as follows:

- **Integration view**: This is an integrated view of the functional requirements and dependability requirements. It facilitates engineers' specifications of the dependability requirements as well as why they are required. Especially important, in addition to the dependability requirements for those identifiable threats, it considers supplementing the dependability requirements for unidentifiable threats based on the cybernetics feedback principle.
- **Separation of concerns**: The feedforward controller monitors potential disturbances at runtime; once disturbances are detected, it takes uses predefined anticipatory controls to preempt the disturbances directly. The feedback controller monitors the measured output at runtime and evaluates the controlled variable against the reference input and computes the difference between them. Once the difference occurs, the controller adjusts the manipulated variables, according to the size of the difference, to affect the controlled object regardless of the disturbances.
- **Complementarity**: The feedforward principle and feedback principle are complementary. The feedforward principle requires knowledge of what the disturbances are and how to monitor them. The feedback principle complements the feedforward principle. It disregards the disturbances. On the other hand, the feedback controls lag behind the effects of the disturbances. The control lag may cause serious damage in some situations. In this case, the feedforward principle is complements the feedback principle to monitor some identifiable disturbances and mitigate the impact of the disturbances.

11.3 FUNCTION AND CONTROL CAPABILITY PROFILE CLUSTER REQUIREMENTS ELICITATION AND MODELING

Cybernetics inspires to model a dependable system as a feedforward-feedback control system. The conceptual architecture is shown in Fig. 11.3. In such a system, the controlled object is the core system; it delivers the required business services. In the presence of various threats and deviations in system behavior, the feedforward controllers and feedback controllers are included to ensure the reliance of those delivered services. In this system, the feedforward controllers have controls for those identifiable threats, whereas the feedback controllers have controls for potential deviations in system behavior.

Although it adopts function capability profiles to model functional requirements, the control capability profiles are designed to model dependability requirements. Two kinds of control profiles are provided: feedforward control profiles and feedback control profiles. The feedforward control profiles determine the controls for the threats. The feedback control profiles determine the controls for deviations in the system's behavior. In this way, the FC-CPC model provides a unified framework to express both functional requirements and dependability requirements.

11.3.1 FUNCTION AND CONTROL CAPABILITY PROFILE CLUSTER METAMODEL

Fig. 11.4 presents the conceptual framework for the FC-CPC metamodel, in which we include several new concept categories such as the threat, deviations in the system's behavior, and the control profile, and relationships among concepts. We explain these new concepts and relationships as follows:

- **control profile**: A control profile describes a sequence of actions that the system adopts to ensure dependability. The actions form the control that will act on a function profile or another control profile to *control* it.
  - **feedforward control profile**: A feedforward control profile describes the controls to *detect* and *counter* an identifiable threat. Because most threats identified at the requirements analysis stage are external, the threats that will be countered by feedforward control profiles are usually external ones that will be detected based on current phenomena.

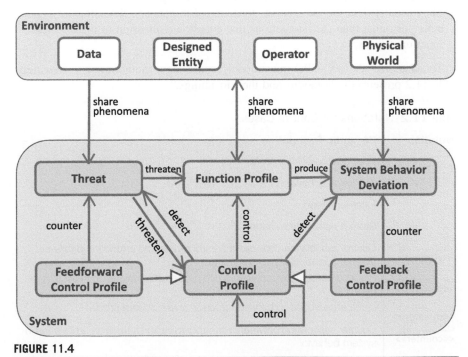

FIGURE 11.4

Function and control capability profile cluster metamodel.

- **feedback control profile**: A feedback control profile describes controls that *detect* and *counter* an identifiable deviation in system behavior. The feedback controls normally predict potential external failure based on currently detected phenomena.
- **threat**: Here, threats refer to the shared phenomena that will ***threaten*** function profiles or control profiles to cause some undesirable effects. The threats can be like misuses of the system (Hope, et al., 2004), for example, operators' errors or malicious attacks. They are phenomena that may hurt the system.
- **system behavior deviation**: System behavior deviations refer to potential shared phenomena that indicate that the system's behavior deviates from the desired path. It can be ***produced*** by a function profile. Deviations in the system's behavior can be, for example, a delay or unavailability of provided services, inaccuracy of produced values, or potential damage to external entities. They are phenomena that may hurt the environment.

Compared with function capability profiles, control profiles have the following specific features:

- They determine system behaviors from the perspective of external threats or deviations in system behavior instead of business functional goals. If external threats or deviations in system behavior do not occur, the capability described by the corresponding control profiles will not be triggered.
- They usually describe the controls for external threats and deviations in system behavior rather than the interactions that enable a realization of the business functional goals.

To visualize the FC-CPC metamodel, some new notations are invented. Table 11.2 presents the notations and their meanings.

Table 11.2 Notations for Control Cases

Notation	Semantic Description
	Feedforward control profile
	Feedback control profile
(T)	External threat
(D)	System behavior deviation
→ <<control>>	Control association between a control profile and a function profile or another control profile
→ <<produce>>	Produce association between a use profile and a deviation in system behavior
→ <<threaten>>	Threaten association between a threat and a control profile
→ <<counter>>	Counter association between a control profile and a threat or a deviation in system behavior
→ <<detect>>	Detect association between a control profile and a threat or a deviation in system behavior

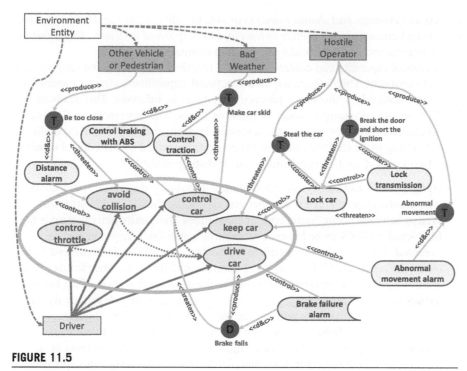

FIGURE 11.5

An example: partial function and control capability profile cluster model. *ABS*, automatic braking system; *d&c*, detect and counter.

We use a sample embedded system for a car (from (Alexander, 2003)) as an example to explain these notations. Fig. 11.5 shows a fragment of the system model described by following the FC-CPC metamodel.

In Fig. 11.5, there are five functional profiles surrounded by a green circle. They are the functional capabilities, i.e., drive car, control car, avoid collision, control throttle, and keep car. These are designed to satisfying the normal operator's needs directly. Four environment entities are driver, other vehicle or pedestrian, bad weather (these are natural phenomena), and hostile operator. Driver is a normal operator.

In the process of normal operations, some undesirable environmental entities may hinder these normal capabilities. For example, a hostile operator may want to steal the car, another vehicle may be too close to the car, and bad weather may make the car skid. These are threats to the safety of the car system. Apart from the environment entities, the system itself may produce threats. For example, brake failure may occur if a brake pad is worn. These threats to the system may result in negative/undesirable effects to the system or the environment.

Control capabilities are designed to deal with these threats. For example, *lock car* detects and counters *hostile operators steal the car* to help *keep car. Control traction* detects and counters *bad weather makes car skid* to help *control car*. *Distance alarm* detects and counters *other vehicle is too close* to help *avoid collision*. *Brake failure alarm* detects and counters *brake fails* to help *control car*.

A control capability can control not only a functional capability but also another control capability. This is because, like functional capabilities, control capabilities may be threatened by threats or produce deviations in behavior. This leads to the FC-CPC model becoming a model of multiple levels. The innermost level contains the functional capabilities whereas the outermost levels contain the control capabilities.

According to the characteristics of the controls described by the control capabilities, two kinds of control capabilities can be distinguished:

- **static control capability**: A static control capability describes static controls whose activations disregard whether corresponding threats or deviations in system behavior occur. Static control capabilities are usually activated once the functional capabilities or lower-lever control capabilities they control are executed. For example, the feedforward control capabilities *lock car* and *lock transmission* in Fig. 12.5 are the static control capabilities. In other words, these control capabilities are always activated without online detection of the threats.
- **dynamic control capability**: A dynamic control capability describes dynamic controls whose activations will depend on what corresponding threats or deviations in system behavior occur. In practice, dynamic controls are usually equipped with monitors to detect at runtime the corresponding threats or deviations in system behavior. For example, the feedforward control capabilities *control traction* and *distance alarm*, and the feedback control capability *brake failure alarm* in Fig. 11.5 are dynamic control capabilities.

Similarly, with functional capabilities, control capabilities need to have important information to implement the controls. Any feedforward control capability specification needs to describe the event that can indicate a particular threat and the countermeasure that can deal with that threat. Any feedback control capability specification needs to describe the event that can indicate a particular deviation in system behavior and a countermeasure for dealing with that deviation.

An event normally means an occurrence, something that happens or is regarded as happening. Here, we focus on the detectable event that implies a threat to the system or a deviation in system behavior that may lead to loss or disaster.

- An action event is an action, occurrence, or change for some environment entity or the system. The event happens when the action or the occurrence happens, for example:
  - a state transition of a causal entity
  - a state sinking of a causal entity
  - a command/message interaction from an autonomous entity
- A function event is an assertion about the entity's attribute and the attribute values. The event happens when the assertion becomes true.
- A composite event is a combination of events.

For example, threat *denial of service attack* may be implied by the request amount in a period. System behavior deviation *service response delay* may be implied because the average service response time is above a threshold.

The template of the control capability specification is:

Controller Capability: name of the controller
Controlling Capability: name of the controlled profile
Threat/System behavior deviation:
    Description: narrative description
    Event: detectable factors and condition which indicate the event
Counters:
    Alternative:
        Name: name of counter
        Precondition: condition of counter
        Action: a sequence of actions
    Alternative:

        ......

---

in which each control capability can have a *precondition* and a *postcondition*. The precondition is a condition that should be true before the control capability is executed. The postcondition is a condition that should be true after the control capability is executed. Each alternative, which contains a sequence of actions, defines a countermeasure and is equipped with preconditions. For example, for system behavior deviation *service response delay*, the alternatives can be *increase the computing resource* and *response delay alarm*. For the alternative *response delay alarm*, we can define its precondition as being that available computing resources are exhausted; i.e., only when available computing resources are exhausted can control *response delay alarm* be activated.

11.3.2 ELICITATION OF DEPENDABILITY REQUIREMENTS

Control capabilities have shown us how to model dependability requirements. However, how to elicit dependability requirements systematically is still in question. This section presents an iterative process to guide the elicitation of dependability requirements.

A hazard and operability study (HAZOP) (Kletz, 2006) is a structured and systematic examination of a complex planned or existing process or operation to identify and evaluate problems that may represent risks to personnel or equipment. The intention of performing a HAZOP is to review the design and identify design and engineering issues that may not have been found. It conducts a structured process to identify the possible deviations systematically from normal or intended behaviors.

Along with the deviations and the causes and effects of those deviations, appropriate suggestions are identified.

The main feature of a HAZOP is to apply a series of guide words (shown in Table 11.3) to prompt the brainstorming of possible deviations. In detail, during a HAZOP analysis, for each component to be analyzed, analysts first identify important attributes of the component and then apply the guide words to the attributes to derive possible deviations related to the component. For example, for a chemical plant, when considering a reacting furnace of the plant, the guide word *more* can be applied to the *temperature* of the reacting furnace. Then, a possible deviation, *the temperature of reacting furnace is high*, is derived. Essentially, such deviations are the heuristics, which motivate the analysts to consider potential flaws in the design, and the corresponding required improvements.

The proposed HAZOP-based control capability identification is an iterative process (Fig. 11.6). This process takes the set of the function capabilities of the system as the input. For each function capability, this process executes four activities:

1. HAZOP-based control requirements identification (Liu, et al., 2014): This activity takes the function capabilities or identified control capabilities as the analysis object, and conducts the HAZOP process. For each function capability or identified control capability, it will produce the possible threats and deviations in system behavior, if there is any.
2. risk assessment: In this activity, the analysts assess the risk of each threat and deviation in system behavior identified in previous activity.
3. control capability determination: In the third activity, according to the degrees of risk of the identified threats and deviations in system behavior, the analysts decide whether to adopt some controls and/or what kind of controls are needed.
4. control capabilities specification: In this activity, the analysts determine the control capability in terms of the predefined templates to document the determined controls and related information.

Table 11.3 Hazard and Operability Study Generic Guide Words

Guideword	Meaning
No/not	Complete negation of the intention
More/less	Quantitative increase or decrease
As well as	Besides the expectation, something extra
Part of	The intention is not completed
Reverse	The logical opposite of the intention
Other than	Complete substitution
Early/late	Refers to the time attribute
Before/after	Forward or backward in order

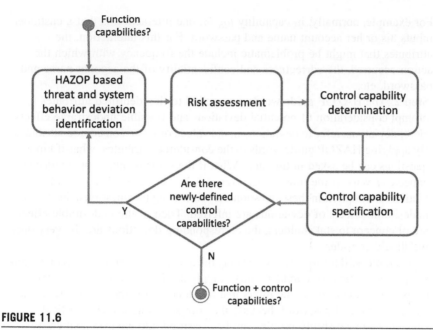

FIGURE 11.6

The hazard and operability study based iterative process for control capability elicitation.
HAZOP, hazard and operability study.

Any newly identified control capability may also be threatened by some other threats and may also produce deviations in behavior; thus, the process of these four activities needs to be iterated. The output of the iterative process is a set of control capabilities, each of which is associated with a function capability, which means that the function capability will be controlled by the control capability in case there is threat or deviation in behavior.

11.3.2.1 *Hazard and Operability Study—Based Threat and System Behavior Deviation Identification*

To identify the potential threats and deviations in system behavior, we take the sequence of interactions in a business capability profile (or a control capability profile) in Chapter 7 as that to be analyzed by HAZOP. Specially, we treat each interaction in the sequence as a component of the sequence. For each interaction, we conduct the following three steps by following HAZOP:

Step 1: The important attributes of the interaction are brainstormed. Attributes to be considered represent the different quality aspects of the action. They can be the attributes of the interaction itself (e.g., the time the action occurred, the frequency with which the action occurred), or the attributes of the environment entities involved in the interaction (e.g., the capability of the interaction's initiator, the accuracy of the values involved in the interaction).

For example, normally, in capability *log in*, one interaction is that a customer inputs his or her account name and password. For this interaction, the attributes that might be problematic include the frequency with which the action occurred, the correctness and confidentiality of the account name and password, etc.

Step 2: The HAZOP guide words are applied to the identified attributes to prompt consideration of potential deviations and possible undesirable effects. Here, deviations refer to deviations in the values of those considered attributes. By applying HAZOP guide words to the considered attributes, what-if kinds of questions can be asked in this step: What if the value is bigger or smaller than expected? What if the time of occurrence is late or early? The possible deviations are implicit in these questions. By following the questions, the possible undesirable effects of deviations are inferred. Then, if the undesirable effects are of concern to stakeholders, the corresponding deviations are the very ones we should consider.

For example, still for *log in*, when asking the question "What if the account name and password have *no confidentiality*" (applying the guide word *no* to the attribute *confidentiality*), one infers that the deviation is the disclosure of the account name and password, because the corresponding effect is critical.

The actions in capability profiles can be classified into environment entity-initiated actions and system-initiated actions. Environment entity-initiated actions represent the actor's behavior, while the system-initiated actions reflect the system behavior. The deviations derived from the system-initiated actions represent the system behavior deviations.

Step 3: Given those inferred deviations, the possible threats to cause them are identified. The common threats and their sources are shown in Table 11.4. One point to be emphasized is that, for one inferred deviation in system behavior, if the threats leading to it are determined, the deviation in system behavior does not need to be considered. Otherwise, the deviation in system behavior needs to be considered.

11.3.2.2 Risk Assessment

This activity assesses the risks of identified threats and deviations in system behavior. The risks are produced by multiplying the ratings assigned to the likelihood of threats or deviations in system behavior, and the ratings assigned to the severity of the undesirable effects they cause. To assess the likelihood and severity properly, the participation of domain experts may be needed. For simplicity, the values of the likelihood and severity can adopt a relative scale such as the three-level relative scale: high, medium, and low. Analysts with the help of domain experts can determine the ratings of the likelihood and severity based on certain criteria, such as those shown in Tables 11.5 and 11.6. Finally, the values of the risk are determined according to reference tables of risk values, such as the one shown in Table 11.7.

Table 11.4 Common Sources of Risk and Threats

Threats/ Deviations	Risk Source	Risk Description	Threats/Deviations Example
Threats	Autonomous entity: illegal attacker	Person who launches some threats to harm the system or access confidential information	Malicious logic threats (e.g., Trojan horses, viruses, worms), or unauthorized intrusion
	Autonomous entity: legal user	Person who directly interacts with the system	Operation errors, such as omission and commission
	Causal entity: external interactive system/device	External system or physical device with which current system interacts to fulfill some capabilities	Deviations in behavior of external interactive system or device
	Autonomous entity: natural phenomena	Natural phenomena that will cause some damage to the system: for example, fire, bad weather, power failure	Damage that such natural phenomena cause to system
System behavior deviation	System: state deviation	Capability failure	Traffic control failures lead to train collision
	System: value deviation	Output value accuracy	Computerized medical radiation therapy machine: computer selects wrong energy
	System: event deviation	Exceptional event	Computerized medical radiation therapy machine: computer selects wrong mode

Table 11.5 Description of Levels of Likelihood

Level of Likelihood	Description
High	This indicates that all factors contributing to the threats or deviations in system behavior exist. For example, attackers have not only the motivations but also the capabilities to launch threats.
Medium	This indicates that some factors exist that contribute to threats or deviations in system behavior exist. For example, the attackers have motivations but may not possess sufficient capabilities to launch threats.
Low	This indicates that some key factors contributing to threats or deviations in system behavior currently do not exist. For example, the attackers do not have a motive.

Table 11.6 Description of Levels of Severity

Severity Level	Description
High	This indicates that the undesirable effect is not acceptable. Such an undesirable effect can be, for example, injury to a human or the disclosure of confidential information.
Medium	This indicates that the undesirable effect is not acceptable but can be tolerated under some conditions. Such an undesirable effect can be, for example, the loss of money or harm to reputation.
Low	This indicates that the undesirable effect (e.g., waste of time) can be ignored.

Table 11.7 Reference Table of Risk Values

Likelihood/Severity	High	Medium	Low
High	High	Medium	Low
Medium	Medium	Medium	Low
Low	Low	Low	Low

11.3.2.3 *Control Capability Determination*

This activity determines the appropriate controls the systems need to adopt to counter threats and deviations in system behavior. According to the risk of threat and deviations in system behavior, analysts first need to decide whether to adopt some controls for them.

As low as reasonably practicable (ALARP)[2] is a term used in the regulation and management of safety-critical and safety-involved systems. The ALARP principle is that the residual risk should be reduced as far as reasonably practicable.

According to the ALARP principle, risks are classified into three levels: acceptable, unacceptable, and those in between. Acceptable risks refer to those that are low and do not need to be controlled. In contrast, unacceptable risks refer to risks that are high and have to be controlled. Risks in between are considered ALARP. For those risks, if the costs of the required controls are disproportionate to the reduction in risk that would be achieved, they can be tolerated. According to this principle, the potential costs of the candidate controls can be taken into account. If they cost so much that the benefits they bring are disproportionate to their costs, it is reasonable to tolerate the corresponding threats or deviations in system behavior.

11.3.2.4 *Control Capability Specification*

This activity defines the control profiles by including control cases to document the controls that are determined and other related information. In one iteration, once the

---

[2]http://www.hse.gov.uk/risk/expert.htm.

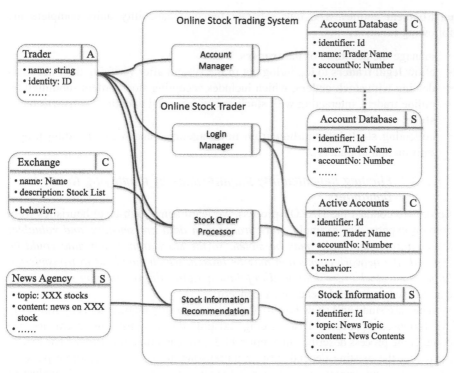

FIGURE 11.7

Capability specification of online stock trading system.

controls have been determined for identified threats and deviations in system behavior, analysts define corresponding control profiles. According to some predefined templates, the defined control profiles will document all information including the threat or system behavior deviation model, and the required controls. The new defined control profiles will be analyzed in the next iteration. If there are no control cases defined in one iteration, the iterations will stop.

11.3.3 CASE STUDY: ONLINE STOCK TRADING SYSTEM

This section presents the case study of an online stock trading system to illustrate the process of eliciting dependability requirements.

> *The online stock trading system is developed for institutional investors. It has the role of an electronic broker. A simplified capability diagram is illustrated in Fig. 11.7, which shows that it ignores the interaction between the function capability units and the environment entities.*

As shown in Fig. 11.7, the system has four separate function capability units (one composite capability units), four internal environment entities and three external environment entities. The four separate function capability units complete the following functions:

- manage the **accounts** of the **trader**s
- allow **legal traders** to log in/log out of the system after verifying their accounts
- dealing with **stock orders**, which includes accepting stock orders submitted by online traders, interacting with **stock exchanges**, and updating **transaction states** of orders
- collecting **stock information** from **news agencies** and recommending proper information to traders

11.3.3.1 Eliciting Dependability Requirements by Identifying Needs for Controllers

Before we conduct the HAZOP process, we learn some high-level heuristics from domain experts. For example, *stock transaction data are sensitive and valuable; the identity of the trader may be stolen, so the stock transaction data could be exposed; the network connection may be broken, which may lead to transmission failure;* and *stock order data need to follow certain rules or common sense.* These can be used as initial dependability concern.

The case study will show how to derive dependability requirements by following the proposed approach. Disregarding existing dependability requirements, we conduct the process described in Section 11.3.2 for each function profile. The results show that the existing dependability requirements are covered and some possible new threats and deviations in system behavior are also identified. The analyst of the developing team feels that the proposed approach can make the developing team more confident in deriving the dependability requirements, and that explicitly associating the dependability requirements with the functional requirements can make the dependability requirements more understandable.

Fig 11.8 gives the capability profile diagram. Table 11.8 presents textual descriptions of two scenarios: *submit an order* and *log in*.

As examples of the result, Fig. 11.9 shows the business/control profile diagram we have derived when considering business capability profiles: *submit an order* and *log in*. The text description of controllers *encrypt order* and *decrease order process time* can also be seen in Table 11.9.

As shown in Fig. 11.8, three controllers, *encrypt order*, *enable alternative connection*, and *decrease order process time*, have been defined for function *submit an order*. Two feedforward controllers, *encrypt order* and *enable alternative connection*, counter the threats *data interception* and *exchange connection failure*, respectively. Feedback control scenario *decrease order process time* counters the deviation in system behavior, *submission delay*.

When analyzing the action, *the trader clicks the submission button to send the order to the system*, we identify threat *data interception* by considering the order's confidentiality. In reality, *data interception* can be achieved by sniffers. If the orders are intercepted, this may cause great loss to stock investors. Thus, the risk of this

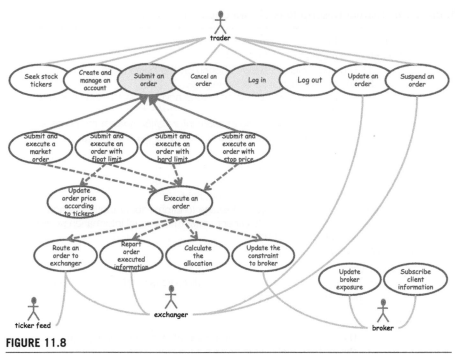

FIGURE 11.8

Diagram of capability profile interrelationship of online stock trading system.

threat is high. Thus, control of *encrypt order* is required here. Details of the corresponding controller are shown in Fig. 11.8. This feedforward controller is obviously a static controller. Threat *exchange connection failure* and deviation in system behavior *submission delay* are identified when going through the interaction *the system routes the order to the exchange where there are stock lists for trading*. Threat *exchange connection failure* is identified when the availability of the exchange is considered. Because timely trading is important for a stock order but the connection to exchange may fail for some reasons, the corresponding controller *enable alternative connection* is thus defined for this threat. The deviation in system behavior, *submission delay*, is identified when the process time of the action is considered. The reason for considering this deviation is that the system may delay submitting the order to the exchange for some reason. For this deviation, the corresponding controller *decrease order process time* has been defined to determine two alternative controls, the details of which can be seen in Table 11.9. Obviously, this feedback controller is a dynamic controller.

For function *log in*, two controllers, *encrypt account* and *limit the number of password attempts*, have been defined for the threats *data interception* and *password cracking*. When going through the action, *the trader enters the account name and password, and clicks the submit button*, threat *data interception* is identified by

Table 11.8 Textual Descriptions of Two Capability Profiles

Capability Profile: Log In

Main interaction flow:
1. The trader clicks the log-in button on the home page.
2. The system displays the log-in page.
3. The trader enters the account name and password, and clicks the submit button.
4. The system validates the account information against the persistent account data and returns the customer to the home page.

Post conditions:
- The trader has logged in the system.

Alternative flows:
4a. The account information is not right:
4a1. The system displays a message to inform about the failure and prompts the trader to either reenter the account information or click the create account button.

Capability profile: submit an order

Preconditions:
- The exchange in which the order will route is connected and can accept instructions from the system.
- The trader has logged in.

Main interaction flow:
1. The trader clicks the submit order button on the home page.
2. The system displays the order submission page.
3. The trader sets the basic information of the order: the stock symbol, the size, the type of the order in the remote flag field, the price, and the type of the transaction (buy or sell).
4. The trader clicks the submit button to send the order to the system.
5. The system checks whether the order is legal.
6. The system routes the order to the exchange where there are stock lists for trading.
7. The system sends a submission success message to the trader.

Post conditions:
- The system has received an order from the trader.
- The system waits for the trading result of the order.

Alternative flows:
5a. The order is not legal.
5a1. The system asks the trader to reset the information of the order.
7a. The order's submission fails.
7a1. The system returns the failure information to the trader.

considering the confidentiality of the account name and password. For this threat, controller *encrypt account* is defined to determine the required encryption controls. Obviously, both controller *encrypt account* and *encrypt order* describe the encryption controls. However, we argue that they are two different controllers. This is because they are located in different contexts, for different purposes, and also represent different dependability requirements. Threat *password cracking* is identified

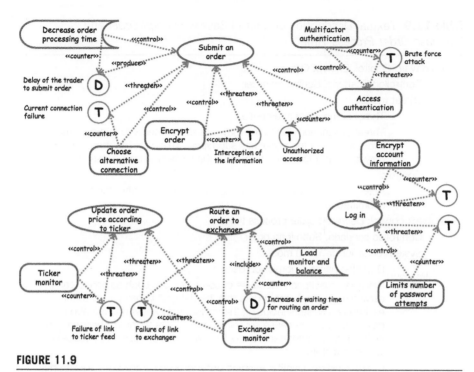

FIGURE 11.9

Interrelationships of function profiles, controllers, and threats.

when considering the times the action occurred: *the system displays a message to inform the failure and prompts the trader to either re-enter the account information or click the create account button.* This threat is common in practice and its risk is high. Therefore, the controller *limit the number of password attempts* is defined in the end for this threat.

11.4 SUMMARY

By modeling a dependable software system as a feedforward-feedback control system, this chapter proposes a FC-CPC model. In this model, the function capability profiles are adopted to represent functional requirements and the control capability profiles are designed to describe dependability requirements. The FC-CPC model provides an integrated view at a highly abstract level while it to separates the problems. To elicit dependability requirements systematically, a HAZOP-based iterative process has also been designed.

Through the case study, we observe that the success of the proposed bottom-up approach depends on the sufficient knowledge of analysts about the application

Table 11.9 Textual Description of Control Cases: *Encrypt Order* and *Decrease Order Process Time*

Feedforward Control: Encrypt Order
    Controlled Scenario: Submit an order
    Threat model:
        Threat name: Data interception
        Threat description: Someone may use some agents to intercept the order information that the trader has submitted. This way, the malicious person may fake the information to destroy the system or cause loss to the trader.
    Controls:
        Actions: 1: The system needs to encrypt the order after the trader has submitted it.
Feedback control: Decrease order process time
    Controlled scenario: Submit an order
    System behavior deviation model:
        Deviation name: Submission delay
        Deviation description: Because of some reason, such as an increase in service requests, some orders may be delayed in being sent to the exchange. Investors including the traders may know nothing about the delay. However, because submitting the orders to the exchange needs to be timely and is important for stock trading, this deviation may cause serious loss to investors.
        Characteristics quantity: Average order process time in one trading day
        Acceptable interval: [0−0.8 s]
        Event: Average order process time >0.8 s
    Controls:
        Alternative 1: Increase computing resource
        Precondition: There are idle servers that can be allocated
        Actions: 1. The system allocates more servers to deal with orders accepted from traders.
        Alternative 2: Submission delay alarm
        Precondition: There are no allocatable servers.
        Actions: 1. The system activates the submission delay alarm to report that the submission delay has occurred and the allocatable resources are exhausted.

domain. Only with sufficient knowledge can analysts identify as many potential threats as possible. In the future, we will attempt to investigate how to structure domain knowledge related to dependability requirements to support dependability requirements elicitation.

The System Dynamic Adaptability Concern

CHAPTER OUTLINE

Human society increasingly depends on software-intensive systems, as is evidenced by the many systems deployed in banks, airports, companies, etc., and by daily applications operating in distributed and mobile devices such as phones and personal digital assistants. In such systems, the software interacts intensively with other software, systems, devices, and sensors, and with people. There are increasingly beneficial and inspired application areas that include cyber-physical systems, mobile computing, ambient intelligence, and ubiquitous computing. One significant feature of such systems is that the software needs to control and adapt the system's behaviors continuously according to the interaction or execution environments as well as the users' goals or needs, which may change frequently and dynamically (Cheng et al., 2009a). This means that change is a critical feature to be dealt with for modern software applications because they are subject to uncertain interactive and execution environments. Therefore, runtime changes cannot be ignored during development process. Software adaptability is becoming ever more important (Yang et al., 2014).

It is widely recognized that a self-adaptive system is one that is able to reconfigure itself autonomously or adjust its behavior at runtime in response to its perception

Environment Modeling-Based Requirements Engineering for Software Intensive Systems
https://doi.org/10.1016/B978-0-12-801954-2.00012-1

of the environment and the system itself while fulfilling its specified goals. The development of such a system requires modeling the capability that deals with business function concerns as well as the capability that deals with adaptation concerns. From the perspective of requirements engineering, the former relates to fulfilling business needs by implementing business logic and the latter relates to satisfying adaptation needs by realizing the behavior adjustment or system reconfiguration. The task of a modeling system adaptation is to capture and define the adaptation logic, i.e., how to fulfill the adaptation needs.

Based on the environment modeling-based requirements engineering, this chapter presents an approach to capturing and modeling system self-adaptability. This approach explicitly uses the requirements goal model (R), the environment model (E), and the system configuration model (S). With the perspective that the adaptation is to pursue the conformance, i.e., $E, S \vdash R$, of the three kinds, it allows S to be reconfigured at runtime given that both R and E may change. The adaptation logic is represented by the conformance relationships among the three elements at a coarse-grained level and by a system configuration binding adjustment at a fine-grained level. Furthermore, a view-based rule language, *vRule*, is advised and defined to specify the adaptation logic. The main features include: (1) the requirements goal settings, the environment elements, and the system configurations have been explicitly and separately identified and specified; and (2) a view-based rule language is invented that allows modeling of the adaptation logic on two levels, one for significant changes (that may lead to a big adjustment) and the other for insignificant changes (that ask only for system fine-tuning). In this way, concerns about system adaptability can be well-separated. This helps the model construction of such systems and the constructed models can support the evolution of the system model at runtime.

12.1 DYNAMIC ADAPTATION MECHANISMS

The traditional way to realize system adaptation is to use *built-in* adaptation, e.g., programming an adaptable application that interweaves the adaptation logic with the application logic. For example, the system may predefine several application logics, e.g., ones implemented by application codes, and each may include constraints on the environment or on user behaviors. Violation of the current constraints triggers the adaptation by following the prespecified way to change the application logic. Then the system adapts its behaviors by migrating to another application logic. In this way, it allows the system to adapt its behavior when environment conditions change.

However, in many other cases, because of the uncertainty of the dynamic environment and the changeable user goals, determinedly interweaving the adaptation logic and the application logic at the design time might not be possible because it is difficult to foresee the dynamic changes. Dynamic adaptation (Morin et al., 2009) is becoming an important feature for such systems. Dynamically adaptive systems are assumed to be capable of managing themselves according to the goals that must be satisfied at runtime in response to changes in the environment and in themselves. Some proposed dynamic adaptive systems are able to operate in highly dynamic sociotechnical ecosystems in which requirements, models, and contexts change at runtime, such as autonomous cars and home robotic systems (Cheng et al., 2009a). In such systems, not only the system's behaviors but also the adaptation logic may change at runtime.

Obviously, the development of dynamically adaptive systems involves more than developing those systems without taking care of dynamic adaptation. More effective techniques are needed to help developers order their thoughts. Again, "separation of concerns" is used here as a fundamental principle to control complexity. Explicit separation between the application and adaptation logic becomes necessary for the development of dynamically adaptive systems to allow the updating of dynamic adaptation logic at runtime (Tamura et al., 2013). This means that the adaptation logic should be modeled and specified separately so that it can be created and changed independently even after the system has been deployed.

There are several dynamic adaptation mechanisms in the literature. Each has its own particular concern and modeling approach. This section briefly presents some of the representative approaches.

12.1.1 RULE-BASED DYNAMIC ADAPTATION

The rule-based approach is feasible for the purpose of determining which actions should be performed to react to monitored interaction or execution environment changes (Lanese et al., 2010). It has the advantages of elegance and readability of each individual rule, the efficiency of plan process, and the ease of rule modification. It provides a mechanism to program dynamic adaptable systems, in which simple adaptation rules are used to specify the adaptation logic of the particular action that should be performed, to react to detected environmental changes.

Event condition action (ECA) is widely adopted by rule-based adaptation mechanisms. Such a rule traditionally consists of three parts:

- event part: specifies the precondition that triggers the invocation of the rule
- condition part: specifies the logical test. Its satisfaction means that the action needs to be carried out
- action part: specifies the actions to be carried out

which is understood as: when event $< event >$ becomes true, if condition $< condition >$ is satisfied, then take action $< action >$, i.e., $< event >$ serves as the trigger and is normally fired as a result of some monitoring operations, $< condition >$ serves as a guard that can be satisfied or evaluated to true and $< action >$ contains an operation sequence to perform in response to the trigger.

The mechanism of rule-based dynamic adaptation is obvious. Fig. 12.1 gives the framework. A simple example has been included along with the components. This application is adaptable by deploying different numbers (from 1 to 10) of servers, and it needs to adapt to react to the response time. When the response time is longer

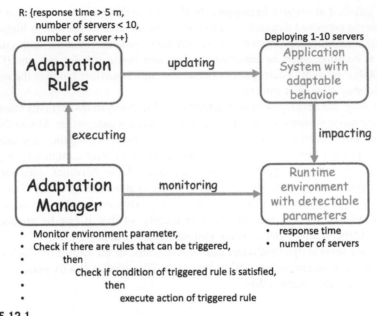

R: {response time > 5 m,
number of servers < 10,
number of server ++}

Deploying 1-10 servers

Adaptation Rules — updating → Application System with adaptable behavior

executing

impacting

Adaptation Manager — monitoring → Runtime environment with detectable parameters

- Monitor environment parameter,
- Check if there are rules that can be triggered,
- then
- Check if condition of triggered rule is satisfied,
- then
- execute action of triggered rule

- response time
- number of servers

FIGURE 12.1

Rule-based adaptation mechanism.

than a thread, the system needs to take appropriate action, e.g., increasing the number of servers if there are any available.

Dynamic adaptation asks for the system to make online decisions about how to enable system adaptation not only to react to environmental changes but also to satisfy the user's goal. That means that the system should take into account at least four aspects when performing online decision making: (1) monitored environment parameters, (2) conditions about the monitored environment parameters, (3) actions that need to be taken if the adaptation is required, and (4) the user's goal that needs to be satisfied. The last point is important for dynamically adaptive systems. Ignoring this point may result in the degradation of satisfaction of the user's goal. For example, the strategy of selecting adaptation rules is expected to rely on the system's goal.

However, ECA rules are predesigned and lack associations with users' goals. Such an adaptation mechanism is thus unable to support the online evaluation of satisfaction of users' goals. The performance will be degraded when users' goals change. For such an example, a user becomes concerned more with energy consumption than response time. Rather than include one more server, he or she might prefer to extend the response time or limit the number of online users for saving the energy.

Other recognized drawbacks of the rule-based mechanism are recognized as potential violations of the trustworthiness of dynamically adaptive systems, e.g., possible runtime conflicts, because any individual rule in a rule-based mechanism is global and it is not easy to deal with efficient conflict resolution for the whole rule base.

12.1.2 GOAL-ORIENTED ADAPTATION MECHANISM

A goal-oriented approach is popular in the requirements engineering community. Many existing efforts in modeling-system adaptability are along the lines of the goal-oriented approach (Cheng et al., 2009b). Representative work on modeling-system adaptivity focuses on explicitly factoring uncertainty into the requirements analysis process. In a concrete manner, in the iterative process for requirements elaboration, top-level goals are decomposed and a conceptual domain model to identify important physical elements of the system and their relationships is then built. Any uncertainties identified during the process result in adaptation factors. A representative example is the requirements description language, Regular Language description for Extensible Markup Language (RELAX) (Whittle et al., 2009).

RELAX is a structured natural language for describing requirements in goal-orientation style. Its purpose is to support the explicit expression of uncertainty in requirements. The basic idea is that the system may wish to relax noncritical requirements temporarily in an emergency situation to ensure the satisfaction of critical requirements. By designing a set of operators, RELAX enables requirements engineers to identify requirements explicitly that should never change (invariants), as well as requirements that a system could temporarily relax under certain conditions by supporting uncertainty.

RELAX defines a set of operators to enable requirements engineers to identify requirements explicitly, including modal, temporal, and ordinal operators. The contribution of RELAX is in the operators that support uncertainty by using the phrase "as possible" to relax the constraints, e.g., "as early (late) as possible," "as close as possible to [frequency]," "as close as possible to [quantity]," "as many (few) as possible," etc.

Another important part of RELAX is that it indicates what *uncertainty factors* warrant a relaxation of these requirements, thereby requiring adaptive behavior. This information is specified using the MON (monitor), ENV (environment), REL (relationship), and DEP (dependency) keywords, in which the ENV section defines a set of observable environment parameters; the MON section defines a set of monitors that can be used by the system to perceive the environment; the REL section defines the relationship between the environment parameters and monitors; and the DEP section identifies the dependencies between the (relaxed and invariant) requirements. The following is an example of RELAX requirements representations, which shows the meaning of each slot of the RELAX requirements representation frame (Whittle et al., 2009):

R1: The synchronization process SHALL be initiated AS EARLY AS POSSIBLE AFTER Alice enters the room and AS CLOSE AS POSSIBLE TO 30 min intervals thereafter.

ENV: location of Alice

synchronization interval

MON: motion sensors

network sensors

REL: motion sensors provide location of Alice

network sensors provide synchronization interval

Other examples of extended goal orientation include "*adaptive requirements*" (Qureshi and Perini, 2009) and "*awareness requirements*" (Souza et al., 2011) frameworks. The former captures requirements in goal models and links them to an ontological representation of the environmental context, to capture alternatives together with their monitoring specifications and evaluation criteria. The latter is a kind of metaspecification of other requirements in a goal model, which captures the uncertainty of the success and failure of other goals. In addition, the system always chooses the configuration with a higher goal satisfaction.

The principle of goal orientation is used only to capture and model system adaptivity. Generally, the work views system adaptivity as an optimization problem. Adaptivity modeling reduces dynamic adaptation as an optimization process and leaves the system the task of reasoning on the actions required to achieve high-level goals. The intuition is that the purpose of system adaptivity is to keep satisfying goals in a dynamically changing situation, to be capable of dealing with uncertainty, and to keep making optimal adaptation decisions even when unforeseen conditions occur.

12.1.3 CONTROL LOOP–BASED SYSTEM MODEL

Another line of current attempts comes from "autonomic computing," which was first coined by IBM in 2001 (Kephart and Chess, 2003). The company envisioned that computing systems should be able to manage duties independently relating to maintenance and optimization. The properties of self-management are:

- self-configuration: A system is told what to accomplish, not how to do it
- self-optimization: Resources are used in an optimal manner
- self-healing: Fault tolerance is an important aspect of the system
- self-protection: Protection on two fronts, malicious users and unknowing users

Here, the core mechanism is the autonomic control loop which includes Monitor, Analyze, Plan, Execute, Knowledge (MAPE-K). Fig. 12.2 shows the MAPE-K reference architecture. Essentially, the Monitor is in charge of collecting detailed environment data and aggregating, correlating, and filtering these details until it determines a symptom that needs to be analyzed. Sensors, probes, gauges, and so on feed information to a Monitor. The system then proceeds to analyze the data and reasoning on the symptoms provided by Monitor. When the Analyzer determines, the system proceeds to invoke the Plan function to create a procedure of actions that is used to enact a desired adaptation. Finally, the Executor changes the system's behavior using effectors based on the action recommended by the Plan.

There is a great amount of effort to develop self-adaptive systems using the MAPE-K framework. However, from the viewpoint of requirements engineering, there are still many challenges. Among others, the most difficult challenge is that there is a lack of tools that can help developers acquire and represent high-level specifications, e.g., goals, constraints, or utility functions, and more importantly, that can map the high-level specification onto lower-level actions.

Furthermore, all autonomic function units of a system need to upgrade or evolve themselves from time to time, to deal with unforeseen situations. This requires being able to update the adaptation logic (Knowledge), build modifiable runtime models, and map the updated models onto the reconfigurable application function units of the system.

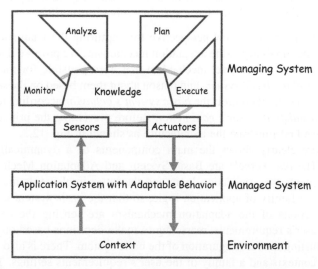

FIGURE 12.2

Monitor, Analyze, Plan, Execute, Knowledge model for self-adaptive systems.

From IBM White Paper, An architectural blueprint for autonomic computing, 2005.

12.2 MODELING DYNAMIC ADAPTATION CAPABILITY

Going back to the environment modeling-based approach, the main task of system capability modeling is to derive the system specification in terms of the system environment models and system goal models. As we can see from Figs. 12.1 and 12.2, a common unit in both architectures is the application system with adaptable behavior. This is, in fact, the system implementing the business logic. We call it the basic or core system. For a dynamic adaptive system, apart from the capabilities of its basic system, the functions, e.g., sensing, deciding, planning, reconfiguring, etc., are within the scope of the adaptation capability.

However, different from other capabilities, the dynamic adaptation capability has three special concerns:

1. It relies on an adaptation mechanism, which implements the adaptation logic. The adaptation mechanism is responsible for dynamically adapting the basic system, which implements the particular application logic.
2. The adaptation mechanism needs to be aware of changes in the interactive environment as well as changes to users' goals, so that it can make a decision about whether the system needs to adapt and decide how to adapt the basic system's behavior, according to the adaptation logic, to better satisfy users' goals.
3. To allow the adaptation logic to be easily updated, it is better for adaptation logic to be explicitly defined separately. In this way, the adaptation logic can also evolve at runtime even if the basic system evolves at runtime.

This section proposes a new perspective for capturing the adaptation logic; it then explores the capability of the adaptation mechanism. We propose that the adaptation mechanism is a metalevel mechanism that is responsible for managing the *runtime models of the basic system*, and reason about them based on the *sensed environment state*, and that it controls the *basic system's behavior* according to the *adaptation logic* to *satisfy the user's goal better*. Before presenting the principles of the perspective, we first illustrate the architecture as shown in Fig. 12.3.

This picture clearly shows the main components of a dynamically adaptive mechanism. The two kernels are Basic System and Adaptation Mechanism. The former implements the application logic and the latter implements the adaptation logic. There is a family of application logic, so that the basic system is adaptable. The main functions of the adaptation mechanism are sensing the environment, knowing the user's requirements, reasoning to make decisions based on adaptation logic, and actuating the reconfiguration of the basic system. There is also a family of environment contexts and a family of the user's requirements settings. The former represents how many distinguishable situations the basic system can work in, and the latter captures users' different desires when they use the basic system.

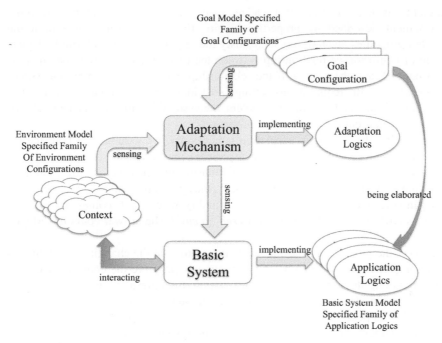

FIGURE 12.3

Architecture of the dynamically adaptive systems.

In the following subsections, we will explain the main principles of this architecture.

12.2.1 CONFORMANCE AMONG *REQ*, *ENV*, AND *SPEC* AS DYNAMIC ADAPTATION LOGIC

As we mentioned before, because it is different from application logic, dynamic adaptation logic is somehow a kind of metalevel requirements. It takes the objective-level capabilities, i.e., functions implementing business logic, as the basis and decides and controls the scheduling and execution of the application logic according to the context of the environment and the requirements setting.

The following analytical structure that relates the system specification to its goal requirements and the environment (or surroundings) of the system is well-recognized:

$$env, \; spec \vdash req$$

which means that if a system that realizes *spec* is installed in and interacts with the environment described by properties in *env*, the environment will exhibit the required properties given in *req*, i.e., satisfy the requirements. This formula depicts a kind of conformance relationship between the requirements setting, the environment context, and the system. If the relationship holds, we say the system (*spec*) is competent to the requirements setting (*req*) in an environmental context (*env*). For a normal system development problem, the system specification is the final artifact of the requirements engineering process.

However, when dynamic adaptation is necessary, we assume that both the requirements setting and the environment context may change from time to time. When some changes happen, does the relationship that held before still hold after the changes? In a concrete manner, at time t_1, the system realizing *spec* is competent to *req* in *env*. During the period between t_1 and t_2, when *req* becomes *req′* and *env* becomes *env′*, is *spec* still competent to *req′* in *env′*? The answer could be "Maybe not."

Hence, the purpose of dynamic adaptation is to face the changing requirements setting and environment context and continuously preserve the conformance relationship among the current requirements setting, the current environment context, and the system. This requires the system to be adapted accordingly, as smoothly and quickly as possible at runtime, when violation of the conformance is detected. All three elements have to reside in the runtime system.

Fig. 12.4 uses a sequence diagram to show the behavior of the three elements with changes to the relationship at runtime. The three actions annotated in the

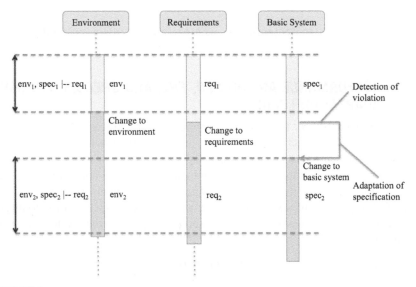

FIGURE 12.4

Adaptation along the time and tasks of the adaptation mechanism.

lifeline of the system are the tasks of adapting the basic system, whereas the changes to the environment context and requirements setting are out of the system's control.

If we use the terminology of the Problem Frame approach (Jackson, 2001), the task of developing a dynamic adaptive system can be stated as:

> *There is a basic system whose solution is to be controlled, in accordance with the environment context, as well as the requirements setting, and the problem is to build a system that will detect the changes in both the environment context and the requirements setting, to decide a suitable solution for its behavior and impose the control accordingly.*

To simplify the explanation, in this chapter we use feature models to represent the families of requirements settings, environment contexts, and basic system configurations. Furthermore, to unify the representation, we use feature models to represent the functionality of the dynamic adaptation mechanism. Then, recalling the feature models and the family of feature models, we let:

$$\{env_1, env_2, \ldots, env_l\} \subseteq \Lambda(Efm)$$

$$\{req_1, req_2, \ldots, req_m\} \subseteq \Lambda(GFm)$$

$$\{spec_1, spec_2, \ldots, spec_n\} \subseteq \Lambda(Sfm)$$

The conformance relationship among *Efm*, *Gfm*, and *Sfm* can be instantiated as a set of associations:

$$env_i, spec_k \vdash req_j$$

such as that given env_i and req_j, when the system that realizes $spec_k$ is deployed in env_i, we have their collaboration, which can meet req_j ($1 \leq i \leq l$, $1 \leq j \leq m$, and $1 \leq k \leq n$). That means $spec_k$ is a solution that is fitted to the problem in env_i with req_j. That can read as:

if IN $< env_i >$ WITHDESIRE $< req_j >$ then DEPLOY $< spec_k >$

With such a conformance relationship as the adaptation logic, the high-level features of the adaptation mechanism may contain (1) detecting and deciding the current environment context env_i; (2) detect (potential) requirements setting req_j's violation; and (3) reconfigure and deploy basic system $spec_k$.

12.2.2 STRUCTURING THE ENVIRONMENT

In many cases, we do not need to detect all environment features to decide whether to change. Some important features can deliver a hint that implies the necessity of the dynamic adaptation. We include another factor, situation *Situ*, to capture such a kind of hint. Each significant situation *Situ* consists of a subset of environment features. For any situation *Situ* there is at least one $efc \in \Lambda(Efm)$ such as $Situ \subseteq efc$. Hence, situation *Situ* in fact groups environment configurations into an environment configuration class.

Situation is meaningful in decision making about the adaptation. For example, *"everybody is sleeping"* is a situation that represents *"everybody has been in bed."* When in this situation, the system, e.g., the heating/cooling system, normally switches to *"sleeping mode"* without taking into account other environmental features.

In fact, *situation* is a concept to which philosophers and logicians have paid much attention. The earlier formal notion of *situation* was introduced as a way to give a more realistic formal semantic to speech acts than was previously available. In contrast to a *"world,"* which determines the value of every proposition, a situation corresponds to the limited parts of the reality we perceive, reason about, and live in. With limited information, a situation can provide answers to some but not all questions about the world. The advantage of including *situation* is that the sensing cost is decreased, because normally only parts of the environmental parameters need to be detected to decide a situation. This is important when the number of environmental entities is large. The other advantage is fit to human recognition; i.e., in many cases, to identify a situation often some feature constraints are mandatory and need to be met strictly, but others do not need as much care.

Correspondingly, a similar concept, *"behavior pattern"* (*Patn* in brief), can also be named as a partially assigned basic system configuration. It assigns only part of the system's features but allows others to be, i.e., for any *patn*∈ *Patn*, there is a valid system configuration *sfm* such as *patn*⊆*sfm*.

Then, to enable a dynamic decision about system adaptation, three categories of conformance relationship can be identified:

- **situation** → **goal setting**:
  The first is a relation between situation *situ* and goal configuration *gfm*. It is for capturing phenomena that users have for different desires in different situations.
- **goal setting: situation** → **behavior pattern**:
  The second is a relation between situation *situ* and behavior patterns *patn* for a given goal setting *gfm*; i.e., when in a particular goal setting, the basic system behaves in different patterns when situated in different situations.
- **goal setting: environment features** → **basic system features**:
  The third is fine-grained conformance compared with the second one. This is conformance between individual environment features (compared with situation, it is a group of environment features) and individual basic system features (compared with behavior pattern, it is a group of basic system features).

The sequence diagrams shown in Fig. 12.5 specify interactions between the components related to an adaptation mechanism. The important idea is to maintain the system configuration (that can be realized as the runtime system) that synchronizes with the environment configuration and the goal configuration by following the conformance relationships. The environment configuration is updated when changes are perceived in the interactive context of the runtime system. The goal configuration is updated because the user changes his or her preference, or he or she prescribes

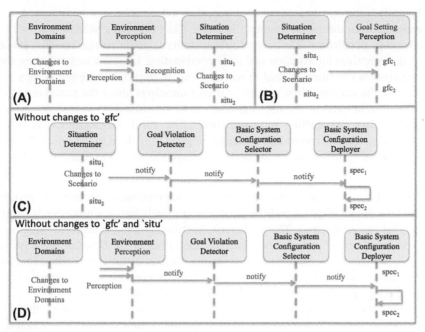

FIGURE 12.5

Sequence diagrams for specifying components related to adaptation mechanism for implementing conformation-based adaptation logic: (A) situation awareness; (B) goal adaptation; (C) coarse-grained adaptation of basic system; and (D) fine-grained adaptation of basic system.

updating the goal preference when the software is in a certain situation. Then the configuration of the basic system may need to be reconfigured accordingly.

12.2.3 CAPABILITY MODEL FOR ADAPTATION MECHANISM

To develop the adaptation mechanism, we need to decide its capability requirements. The adaptation mechanism needs to possess three aspects of capability:

Capability One: Situation Awareness: A formal definition of term "*situation awareness*" is given in Endley and Jones (2012). It says that situation awareness is "the perception of the elements in the environment within a volume of time and space, the comprehension of their meaning, and the projection of their status in the near future." This obviously implies three subcapabilities:

- **environment perception**: The first subcapability is about the perception of environment entities, i.e., collecting necessary information. What information needs to be perceived (and how to perceive it) is among the concerns in this layer. It is important to ensure that necessary information can be obtained to estimate what the environment will behave like in the very near future.

- **situation prediction**: The second subcapability is about comprehending pieces of the perceived information and their combination, i.e., how to synthesize the perceived information to lead to meanings about the environment and then suggest the situation. It is needed to derive meanings about the perceived information in terms of the user's goals.
- **goal-setting perception or prediction**: The third subcapability is about perceiving the goal requirement changes or predicting them in the future. This is to alert the system to make the necessary response or to be proactive in the meantime.

Normally, conducting the perception—comprehension—projection process should take the users' goals and the priority of the goals into account (this is known as the goal-driven process). The goals serve as the guideline for what information is perceived and how to perceive and interpret the information. Besides, there is also the converse case in which when information that is completely independent of the currently concerned goal occurs to a significant degree, the system needs to reprioritize the goals (this is known as the data-driven process).

Capability Two: Decision Making: After predicting the status in the near future, decisions should be made regarding whether changes need to be made and how to change to match the estimated future status of the environment. Achieving this implies two subcapabilities:

- **goal violation detection**: The adaptation mechanism should know the current goal setting so that it can determine online whether the goal settings have been satisfied to a certain degree. If the satisfactory degree of the goal setting is lower than a certain thread, the goal setting is violated. This is the capability of obtaining the satisfactory degree of the system's goals.
- **basic system configuration selection**: If the adaptation mechanism decides to make a change, it should know the basic system variations to allow the change. This is the capability of inferring and selecting the optimal variation to match the current or future status of the environment and/or goal setting.

Capability Three: Performance of Actions: After the new configuration of the basic system has been generated, it needs to be deployed by activating the selected components. The effect of the activation is to enable the controllable environment entities to make transitions and finally stay in the states designated in the configuration. Then the users' goal setting can be satisfied as expected. This implies the following subcapability:

- **basic system redeployment**: After the adaptation mechanism selects an optimal basic system configuration for responding to the coming status of the environment and/or goal settings, the adaptation mechanism should switch the basic

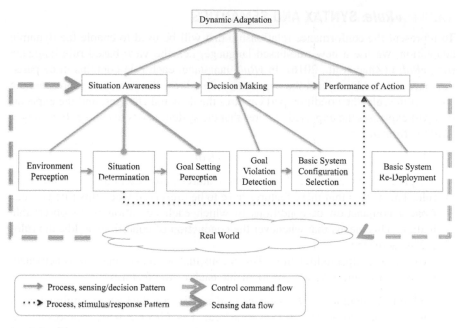

FIGURE 12.6

Metalevel feature model of adaptation mechanism and the control/data flows at runtime.

system from the current configuration to the selected one and redeploy the new configuration. This switching process should be as smooth as possible.

Based on this analysis, the metalevel model of the adaptation mechanism accommodates the three modeling elements, i.e., the environment model, the goal model, and the basic system model. The components of the mechanism and the relations among these components are shown in Fig. 12.6.

Of course, if the feature model is of the metalevel, the concrete capabilities should be identified when modeling a particular application by answering questions such as: What environment parameters need to be perceived? Which situations are significant? How will the goal violation be detected? How will the basic system migrate? These are based on the adaptation logic that the application needs.

12.3 EXPRESSION OF CONFORMANCE-BASED DYNAMICAL ADAPTATION

This section presents a rule-based language to represent the conformance-based dynamic adaptation. We show how to identify the necessary capabilities for realizing the required dynamic adaptation. Some criteria are given to evaluate the rule-based specification.

12.3.1 *vRule*: SYNTAX AND SEMANTICS

To represent the conformance relationship that will be used to enable the dynamic adaptation, we use a new rule-based language, i.e., the view-based rule language (i.e., *vRule*) (Zhao et al., 2016). In *vRule* language, each rule contains three parts: the view, the condition, and the expectation, in which, the view part represents the guard of the rule, the condition part captures the detected changes, and the expectation part expresses the expected features that the system needs to enable. Formally, a *vRule* is formed as:

$$v \vdash Con \Rightarrow Exp$$

- *v*: a predefined view, a set of observable features to represent the invariant of the rule. This means that these features have to be preserved when this rule is used
- *Con*: a conjunction of conditions in which each condition is an observable feature. This means that whenever the conduction of conditions holds, the rule can be activated
- *Exp*: a set of expected features. This means that whenever the rule is activated, the system should take actions to enable each of the features

With this formulation, a *vRule* can be read as: Given *v*, the feature combination of *Con* asks for the features in *Exp*. Or we can read it as: Given *v*, when features in *Con* are detected to be bound, the features in *Exp* need to be enabled (bound). The formal structure of *vRule* is defined as follows:

View-based rule	*vRule*	$::= v \vdash Con \Rightarrow Exp$	
View	*v*	$::= Con$	
Conditions	*Con*	$::= V_1^n con$	
Condition	*con*	$::= fb$	
Expectations	*Exp*	$::= U_1^m exp$	
Expectation	*exp*	$::= fb$	
Feature-binding	*fb*	$::= null$	No binding
		$\vert feature$	Logic value-binding
		$\vert (feature, value)$	Enum value-binding
		$\vert (feature, < type, cond >)$	Requirement value-binding

Using *vRule* as the specification language to express adaptation logics has advantages because *vRule* has some checkable correctable properties. Let Γ be a set of finite *vRules* that specifies the adaptation logic. The correctable properties include:

- (invariant of rule). A *vRule*: $v \vdash Con \Rightarrow Exp$ is invariant if the observable features of *v* are preserved after adaptation. That is, let (f, val) be a feature in *v*. For each (f', val') that can be an effect on an environment domain imposed by a basic system feature in *Exp*, if $f = f'$, then $val' = val$.

- (rule stability). Let *r* be a correct view-based rule, *sfc* a basic system configuration, and *r*(*sfc*) be the executing rule *r* on *sfc* resulting in a new basic system configuration. We have $r(r(sfc)) = r(sfc)$. We call rule *r* a stable rule.
- (order independence). Let r_i, r_j be two different *vRules*, and *sfc* a basic system configuration. Rules r_i and r_j are said to be order-independent if the execution result of r_i followed by r_j on *sfc* is the same as r_j followed by r_i. If two rules are order-independent, their effects on a configuration is either not overlapped or the same.
- (confluence). A set of *vRules* Γ is confluent if the execution result of all rules in Γ is always the same regardless how they are applied.
- (well-behavedness). Let r_i and r_j be two rules in Γ, $i \neq j$. If the following two conditions are satisfied: (1) each rule *r* is stable; (2) rules in Γ are order-independent, then Γ is confluent and stable.

12.3.2 CONFORMANCE RELATIONSHIPS BY *vRules*

According to the previous discussion, the conformance relationship for capturing the dynamic adaptation logic can be expressed as the following three categories of *vRules*:

- rule for "*if situation, then goal setting*":

$$\text{true} \vdash\, < Situ > \,\Rightarrow\, < req >$$

representing that the users may have different goal settings *Req* in different situations *Situ*, i.e., the users' goal setting may change at runtime when the system is in different situations. This is a **Type I** rule.

From now on, we will use "*smart home*," i.e., the new generation of "*home automation*," which may adapt its behavior to respond to changes, as a dynamically adaptive home automation. When "*nobody is home*" (the situation), the "*security*" needs to be at "*the highest level*" and the "*energy consuming*" needs to be "*as less as possible*," whereas we do not care about the performance and the comfort. This can be expressed as the rule:

$$\begin{pmatrix} \text{true} \vdash nodbodyHome \Rightarrow (security, < \$hard, securityDegree = 5 >), \\ (energy, < \$soft, \min(Consumption) > \end{pmatrix}$$

- rule for "*goal setting: if situation, then behavior pattern of basic system*":

$$< Req > \,\vdash\, < Situ > \,\Rightarrow\, < Patn >$$

representing the stimulus—response pattern (i.e., the shortcut pattern) under a certain goal setting. This means that situation *Situ* asks for system behavior pattern *Patn* with a certain goal-setting *Req*.

This is a **Type II** rule.

For example, in "*smart home*" applications, the users are used to choosing "*comfortness*" as the main concern (this is a certain goal setting). When "*everybody goes to sleep*" (this is a situation), users normally expect that the system can maintain the "*sleeping mode*" (this is the behavior pattern). This can be expressed as the rule:

$$\left(\begin{array}{c} (comfortness, < \$soft, \max(ComforDegree) >) \\ \vdash everybodyInSleeping \Rightarrow SleepingMode \end{array} \right)$$

- rule for "*goal setting: if fine environment features, then fine basic system features*":

$$< Req > \vdash < EnvFs > \Rightarrow < SpecFs >$$

representing that a set of environment features *EnvFs* asks for a set of system features *SpecFs* given a particular goal setting *Req* in particular situation *Situ*. It is for capturing the sensing or decision-making pattern under certain goal settings and in certain situations.

We call it a **Type III** rule.

For example, in the "*smart home*" application, when users choose "*comfortness*" as the main concern, users normally expect to "*set the air conditioner as heating mode*" (the basic system feature) when it is "*snowy*" (the environment feature). This can be expressed as the rule:

$$\left(\begin{array}{c} (comfortness, < \$soft, \max(ComfortDegree) >) \\ \vdash weather.snowy \Rightarrow airConditioner.heating \end{array} \right)$$

12.3.3 FUNCTION IDENTIFICATION ACCORDING TO *vRules*-BASED ADAPTATION LOGIC

With the set of user-defined *vRules*, we can identify the operational level features of the adaptation mechanism. In terms of a metalevel capability model, the elaborative capabilities can be derived step by step, as:

- situation awareness:
  This feature may have all of the sensing features as its subfeatures:
  - environment perception:
    These are the features that will enable the following sensing functions. They are also for answering how many sensors we need in the application, based on the adaptation logic. The sensors can be hard devices such as those in sensor networks or soft sensors realized by software. They are the same in

the sense that they can obtain the value or state of an environment domain. In a concrete manner, we have:

- For any r: $true \vdash < Situ > \Rightarrow < Req >$ of Type I, each environment feature in $< Situ >$ needs a functional feature in the adaptation mechanism to perceive its current value or state
- For any r: $< Req > \vdash < Situ > \Rightarrow < Patn >$ of Type II, each environment feature in $< Situ >$ needs a functional feature in the adaptation mechanism to perceive its current value or state
- For any r: $< Req >, < Situ > \vdash < EnvFs > \Rightarrow < SpecFs >$ of Type III, each feature in $< EnvFs >$ needs a functional feature in the adaptation mechanism to perceive its current value or state

Aggregating these features results in a set of environment perception features. These features are the subfeatures of "*environment perception*" in the adaptation mechanism.

- goal-setting perception

  For any r of Types II and III, each goal feature in $< Req >$ needs a sensor (often a soft sensor) in the adaptation mechanism to perceive the goal setting, e.g., the condition, the optimization objective, etc. These goal sensors are aggregated to form the subfeatures of "*goal-setting perception*" in the adaptation mechanism. For many applications, users want to choose the goal setting at runtime. In this case, the goal sensors may have an interface with users to allow them to set the goal setting at runtime.

- situation determination:

  For any r of Types I, II, and III, each situation needs a decider in the adaptation mechanism to decide the basic system to be situated in a particular situation when perceiving changes to the environment features. All of the situation deciders lead to the set of subfeatures of "*situation determination*" in the adaptation mechanism.

- decision making:

  We assume for a dynamically adaptive system S that:

  At any time point t, with the goal setting req_t and situation $situ_t$, when S runs according to specification $spec_t$, we have $env_t, spec_t \vdash req_t$. Here, env_t is an extension of $situ_t$.

  Then at time point t', the detected environment features lead to situation $situ_{t'}$. It is necessary to decide whether the basic system needs to change the behavior to preserve the invariant $Env, Spec \vdash Req$. To do this, the following two subfeatures can be defined:

  - goal-violation detection: This feature asks for realization by the adaptation mechanism for the following functions:
    - If $situ_t = situ_{t'}$, but $env_t \neq env_{t'}$. Check whether this is true:

    $$env_{t'}, spec_t \vdash req_t$$

If the relationship has been violated, select *ActRule* as the set of all Type III *vRules* that can be activated by $env_{t'}$ and send out a notification about the violation with *ActRule*. (This is a fine-grained change.)

- If $situ_t \neq situ_{t'}$, select *ActRule* as the set of all Type I *vRules* that can be activated by $situ_{t'}$. In terms of *ActRule*, select a goal setting $req_{t'}$ (otherwise, $req_{t'} = req_t$). (This is a goal change.)

Check whether this is true:

$$env_{t'}, spec_t \vdash req_{t'}$$

If this relationship has been violated, select *ActRule* as the set of all Type II *vRules* that can be activated by $req_{t'}$ and $situ_{t'}$, and send out a notification about the violation with *ActRule*. (This is a coarse-grained change.)

- Basic system configuration selection:

When receiving the violation notification, if $ActRule \neq \varnothing$, finds a system configuration $spec_{t'}$ such that:

$$env_{t'}, spec_{t'} \vdash req_{t'}$$

holds in the case of the best satisfaction (in terms of the optimization objectives associated with goals in $req_{t'}$) with the system features in *Exp* parts of the *vRules* in *ActRule* as the feature constraints.

When there is more than one configuration that can be suitable here, the best should be selected according to the degree to which it satisfies the goal, as well as the smoothness of switching from the current configuration to the new one. Finally, the profile of this configuration needs to be generated for redeployment.

- Basic system redeployment:

Redeploying the basic system from the old configuration that implements $spec_t$ to the new configuration that implements $spec_{t'}$. This includes all of the activities that make the system available for use in the setting of realizing $spec_{t'}$ according to the generated profile. Detailed activities about the deployment are out of the scope of this chapter.

We use the "*home automation*" system as an example to show the relationship between the basic system and the dynamic adaptive system. Fig. 12.7 gives a fragment of the feature model of a "*home automation*" system. It is a basic system. When it is enhanced to be dynamically adaptive, it is necessary to embed it into an adaptation mechanism.

Fig. 12.8 shows a fragment of the feature model of "*Smart Home.*" It extends the feature model of the "*Home Automation*" in Fig. 12.7 by including the features for "*adaptation mechanism*" as well as all the sub-features related to this specific application. These sub-features are identified under the guidance of the adaptation logics specified by *vRule* based on the smart home environment feature model (Fig. 6.2) and the goal feature model (Fig. 6.4).

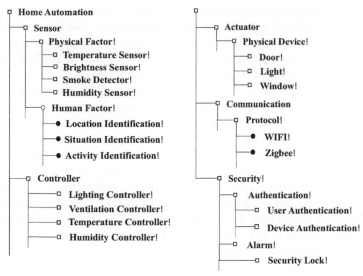

FIGURE 12.7

Home automation feature model.

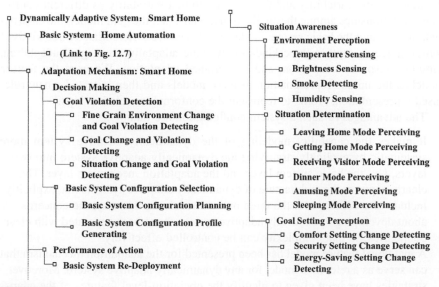

FIGURE 12.8

Feature model of a smart home including "*home automation*" as a basic system and adaptation mechanism.

After constructing the feature model of the adaptation mechanism, we may need to evaluate it and include a set of criteria for this purpose. The basic criteria may include correct sensor interpretation, correct adaptation initiation, correct adaptation planning, consistent interaction between adaptation logic and application logic, consistent adaptation execution, and correct actuator actions.

In addition, in terms of the three feature models, i.e., the environment feature model, the goal feature model, and the basic system feature model, we can let $\#EFC$, $\#GFC$, and $\#SFC$ be the numbers of the environment feature configurations, the goal feature configurations, and the basic system feature configurations, respectively. Also, we can let $\#Efc$ be the number of the environment feature configuration such that $\#Gfc$ and $\#Sfc$ are the numbers of environment feature configurations, the goal configurations, and the basic system configurations implied by Γ. Three measurements can be defined to measure the coverage of the specification of the adaptation mechanism. For $vRules$-based specification Γ, the environment configuration coverage is $\frac{\#Efc}{\#EFC}$; the goal configuration coverage is $\frac{\#Gfc}{\#GFC}$; and the basic system configuration coverage is $\frac{\#Sfc}{\#SFC}$.

12.4 SUMMARY

This chapter analyzed the essence of dynamic adaptation capability from the perspective of requirements modeling. We showed that dynamic adaptation is a kind of metalevel capability that is about the variability in the concrete application. We modeled the variability and the response to that variability as different conformance relationships among the application models, i.e., the goal model, the environment model, and the basic system model. Moreover, we differentiated three kinds of conformance to capture three kinds of dynamic adaptation, i.e., goal adaptation, stimulus—response adaptation, and fine-grained adaptation. We used the feature model as the unique representation of these models and then invented a new rule-based representation, $vRule$, to represent the conformance relationships.

The advantages of such a system configuration are that:

- It makes the capability modeling of the dynamically adaptive system more systematic by explicitly stratifying the dynamically adaptive system into two layers, i.e., the basic system layer and the adaptation mechanism layer. This clearly captures the architecture of dynamically adaptive systems that explicitly include interactions with the three online models. In this way, the concerns about developing dynamically adaptive systems have been separated with clear boundaries, so that complexity can be controlled effectively.
- A metalevel feature model has been presented for the adaptation mechanism that can serve as a reference model for any dynamically adaptive system. Moreover, strategies have been given to identify the operation-level features of the adaptation mechanism. This serves as a guideline to feature identification.

• It is along the line of the rule-based approach but extends the ECA rules by assigning conformance-based semantics to the rule elements. It also adds a new part to the ECA rule: the view part, to represent invariance during adaptation, to address the issues about a lack of dynamic strategy adjustment when using the ECA rules. It uses a formal language, *vRule*, that is on the basis of bidirectional transformation. This implies the possibility that the *vRule* specification of dynamically adaptive systems may be an executable specification based on the BX engine.[1] This is an important feature to enable the simulation of the dynamically adaptive system before design and implementation.

There are other topics worth investigating:

• The requirements of dynamic adaptation might need to evolvable. The reason for requirements evolving could be that users want to strengthen, weaken, or change their requirements for dynamic adaptation when certain conditions apply at runtime. Such evolving requirements have an important role in the lifetime of a system, in that the users define possible changes to requirements, along with the conditions under which these changes apply.
• The capability measurement and comparison are important for a sound method. This includes defining criteria to measure and use the criteria to compare different capability specifications.
• The system can be enhanced by including online learning. It will allow the systems to learn the new adaptation strategies automatically from historical data. This is important for coping with unanticipated changes at runtime. The learning capabilities will have a role after the system is put into use and is enabled by some pattern recognition or data-mining algorithms.

---

[1]Z. Hu, A. SchŁurr, P. Stevens, J.F. Terwilliger, Dagstuhl seminar on bidirectional transformations (BX), SIGMOD Record 40 (1) (2011) 35—39.

Other Nonfunctionality Patterns

13

CHAPTER OUTLINE

Apart from dependability and adaptivity, there are some other environment-related nonfunctional requirements (NFRs). As with the two NFRs that were mentioned, people who deal with NFRs require knowledge. Pattern-based approaches have been popular for describing software development knowledge, e.g., the software design patterns.[1] Some effort has also been made to extend pattern-based approaches to provide knowledge about elaborating NFRs. This shows that the pattern-based approach is useful for refining NFRs.

This chapter defines some NFR patterns in a problem-oriented way. These patterns can be used to describe nonfunctional problems and introduce appropriate NFR extensions into the function models of a system. After that, extended capabilities corresponding to original function capabilities will be obtained. During the extension of capabilities, some new environment entities may be further identified or designed. These NFR pattern problems can derive the specification of extended capabilities. Some examples are used to show the feasibility of these NFR patterns.

---

[1]https://en.wikipedia.org/wiki/Software_design_pattern.

Environment Modeling-Based Requirements Engineering for Software Intensive Systems
https://doi.org/10.1016/B978-0-12-801954-2.00013-3

13.1 INTRODUCTION

In contrast to functional requirements, which usually dictate specific desired behaviors or functions, NFRs specifies criteria that can be used to validate the implementation of a system. More specifically, NFRs generally define how a system is supposed to be; they are usually organized through a "system shall be <requirement>," whereas functional requirements define what a system is supposed to do and are usually in the form of a "system shall do < requirement>".[2] NFRs place restrictions on the product being developed and the entire development process, and specify external constraints that the product must meet.

As software complexity grows and customers demand increasingly high-quality software, NFRs can no longer be considered of secondary importance. Some NFRs, such as security, privacy, and usability, are critical to the success of many software-intensive systems. For example, for a stock exchange system, reliability tends to be a top priority. An online game system needs to have good usability. Empirical reports indicate that the failure of many projects results from improperly dealing with NFRs. Typical cases of such studies include the TJ Maxx incident[3] and the paralysis of the ticket system at the Beijing Olympics in 2007. NFRs have a crucial role during system development. However, treatment of NFRs is difficult and are highly dependent on the experience of system analysts.

In general, a pattern is a discernible regularity in the world or in a man-made design. In software engineering, a pattern is characterized as a general reusable solution to a commonly occurring problem that arises within a specific context. It is normally a description or template of a problem and it describes a solution for how to solve the problem. The most important advantage is that any pattern is trying to frame the problem and its solution in a more readily accessible form.

There has been research in the area of NFR analysis. For example, based on the goal-oriented NFR framework, an NFR pattern approach (Supakkul et al., 2010) proposes using four kinds of NFR patterns to describe and reuse knowledge about NFRs: objective, problem, alternative, and selection patterns. These patterns are mainly used to elaborate the refinement of NFRs. The patterns can be specialized to create more specific patterns, composed to form larger patterns, and instantiated to obtain instance patterns.

There has also been much research into security requirements patterns. One such effort is the proposal (Lin et al., 2003; Hope et al., 2004) that introduced anti-requirements and invented abuse frames to analyze security problems. The notion of anti-requirements is seen to be the intention of a malicious user (i.e., the attacker). An abuse frame represents a security threat. There are three kinds of abuse frames: interception, modification, and denial of access. Each abuse frame presents a threat

---

[2]Wikipedia, http://en.wikipedia.org/wiki/Non-functional_requirement.
[3]J. Pereira, Breaking the code: How credit-card data went out wireless door, The Wall Street Journal, May 4, 2007.

that can violate a particular security goal and is associated with a set of abuse frame problems that need to be addressed for an attack to succeed. Of course, any abuse frame should be composed with the base problem frame, because it is supposed that an attack needs to exploit vulnerabilities in the machine of the base problem frame and violate its property of security.

Other research includes security frames (Hatebur and Heisel, 2005) to describe frequently used solutions to system security. Four security frames are built: accept authentication frame, submit authentication frame, secure data transmission frame, and distribute security information frame. These security frames decompose complex security problems into simpler ones so that they can be dealt with more easily. These four frames are examples of a more complete collection of security frames and establish a security frame catalogue.

Based on the environment-modeling based approach, this chapter extends an elaboration of problem-oriented approach to accommodate, in general, environment-related NFRs, e.g., reliability, safety, security, and confidentiality and so on. We attempt to treat NFR pattern problems explicitly as an important guide to gain more insight into NFR patterns.

13.1.1 PROBLEM-ORIENTED NONFUNCTIONAL REQUIREMENT PATTERNS

What are problem-oriented NFR patterns? They are a kind of pattern that can be used to extend a problem by describing nonfunctional problems and introducing appropriate NFRs. After elaborating on pattern-guided requirements, extended problems corresponding to the original problems will be obtained and some new environment entities may be created or identified during extension of the problem. In contrast to primary problems, extended problems contain requirements with nonfunctional characteristics. Then system analysts can derive the system specification of the extended problem according to problems of the NFR pattern. The derived specification can reveal both functional and nonfunctional aspects of the requirements in the extended problem.

Each problem-oriented NFR pattern describes a template of some problem type that is presented as an interaction diagram with NFRs, and gives some typical solution strategy (i.e., some design decision or architectural style). The problem description includes environment entity types, shared phenomena between system and environment entities, and a description of requirements. The requirements description is of nonfunctional characteristics. The extension combines the nonfunctional problem template with the base problem.

13.1.2 STRUCTURE OF A PROBLEM-ORIENTED NONFUNCTIONAL REQUIREMENT PATTERN

A detailed description of each problem-oriented NFR pattern is given in terms of its application background, problem, NFRs, application condition, extension strategy, and NFR pattern problems.

- **application background**: The application background briefly describes the problem to be solved in this problem-oriented NFR pattern.
- **problem**: Each problem-oriented NFR pattern focuses on a problem that describes interactions between the system and the environment entities to meet some functionalities. The problem description is an interaction diagram that contains the system, the environment entities, and the phenomena shared between them.
- **related NFRs**: Each problem-oriented NFR pattern focuses on one or more NFRs.
- **application condition**: Each problem-oriented NFR pattern focuses on different kinds of problems. The application condition is used to check whether an existing problem can be combined with the problem of this NFR pattern.
- **extension strategy**: Guidance can be provided on how to extend an existing interaction diagram with the problem of the problem-oriented NFR pattern.
- **NFR pattern concerns**: Each problem-oriented NFR pattern has a set of concerns that identify the descriptions to-be-made and how to fit them together in an adequate argument. System analysts must address these problems to derive a specification satisfying NFRs.

13.1.3 PROCESS OF USING A PROBLEM-ORIENTED NONFUNCTIONAL REQUIREMENT PATTERN

Assuming there is a problem, the process of using a problem-oriented NFR pattern is that:

- System analysts are asked whether the related NFRs of the NFR pattern are needed in the problem.
- System analysts are asked whether the application background of the NFR pattern applies to the problem.
- System analysts are asked whether the application condition of the NFR pattern is satisfied by the problem.
- If the answers to these three questions are all "yes," system analysts start to extend the problem with the guidance of the extension strategy of the NFR pattern. Then a new problem is obtained.
- System analysts address the NFR pattern concerns and derive a system specification to satisfy the NFRs in the new problem.

13.2 PROBLEM-ORIENTED NONFUNCTIONAL REQUIREMENT PATTERNS AND THEIR CONCERNS

It is not easy to address the concerns of NFRs. The guidelines are of practical importance to help system analysts obtain an implementable solution.

Some requirements engineering approaches provide guidance to identify potential nonfunctional aspects. Recalling the Problem Frames approach (Jackson, 2001), the world is structured into the machine domain and the problem domains. Problem domains are classified into three types, i.e., causal, biddable, and lexical. A biddable domain is usually people. It is impossible to compel a person to stop initiating an event. If a person is malicious, security issue should be taken into consideration during system analysis. If many people can initiate events simultaneously, the reliability of the system becomes an important aspect. A lexical domain is a physical representation of data. The data of a lexical domain may be confidential, which may place great emphasis on system analysis. If the amount of data is large, system analysts should focus on performing a search of the data. A causal domain is one whose properties include predictable causal associations among its causal phenomena. A causal domain is usually physical equipment. In this sense, safety and maintainability of the system are regarded as critical to the success of the project. These are all examples of nonfunctionalities. These nonfunctional aspects are directly related to the features of the Problem Frames approach and should be taken into consideration when describing NFRs.

The top-level environment ontology in Fig. 4.9 shows that there might be problems when the environment entities have certain characteristics. The remainder of this chapter introduces six problem-oriented NFR patterns: authorization, buffer, index, log, perception and reaction, and encryption and decryption. It also demonstrates how these patterns can be used to extend an existing problem to address nonfunctional issues.

13.2.1 AUTHORIZATION PATTERN

Fig. 13.1 shows the authorization pattern with an exemplar of capability analysis: a reliable editing system.

As shown in Fig. 13.1, the **application background** of an authorization pattern is thus: There is an autonomous entity that has an interface of shared phenomena with the system. The entity may have multiple instances that have different permissions to access the system. The **problem** is to reconstruct a system that is able to distinguish one individual from the others and grant different operational permissions accordingly. This is to build the capability of access control to enhance the security of the system. The **related NFR** of this pattern is reliability. Finally, the **solution** gives the extension strategy about how to extend the original problem to obtain the desired one.

The features of this problem can be illustrated using the following example. The system is an online editing system. There are operators, autonomous entities who can issue commands to edit the workpiece, which is a symbolic entity. Commands including *"download," "upload," "delete,"* and *"rename"* appear as phenomena shared with the system. The phenomena of *"delete," "insert,"* and *"update"* ask the editing system to change the values of the workpiece. The requirements

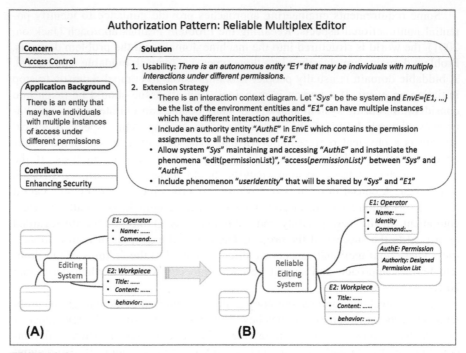

FIGURE 13.1

Authorization pattern and reliable editing system. (A) Original capability: plain editing system. (B) Enhanced capability: reliable editing system.

component is called correct editing; it stipulates what enables the effects of commands issued by operators on the workpiece.

The original **interaction diagram** is shown in Fig. 13.1A. Specifications are:

- Online editing system receives the operators' command.
- Online editing system causes events to change the workpiece accordingly.

The specifications do not consider how to keep the workpiece secure. This problem satisfies the application condition of the authorization pattern. When applying the authorization pattern in this problem, the interaction diagram is updated, as shown in Fig. 13.1B, by introducing an authorization entity to describe assigned permissions for different operators. Accordingly, shared phenomena between the system and this new entity are included.

The capability analysis process for the new problem is shown as a sequence of argumentations in the interaction diagram in Fig. 13.2; in this diagram, (1) stipulates which command is correct. However, the current operator may not be allowed to use this correct command. The system needs to obtain information about the operator's identity (2). Then the system searches the permission list (3) with the operator's identity (4). If the operation is allowed, the system causes corresponding events to

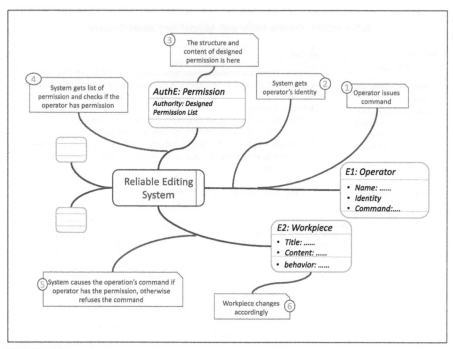

FIGURE 13.2

Capability analysis concern for authorization pattern.

update the workpiece accordingly; otherwise it refuses the command (5). After the permitted operation, the workpiece needs to be changed according to the operation (6). Then the new capability specification can be obtained:

- The editing system receives the operators' command.
- Based on the identity of the operation and the designed permission, the editing system decides whether the operation is allowed.
- If yes, the system causes the corresponding event to update the workpiece; otherwise it refuses it.

13.2.2 BUFFER PATTERN

Fig. 13.3 shows a buffer pattern with an example of capability analysis for a reliable editing system.

As shown in Fig. 13.3, the **application background** of the buffer pattern shows that there is an autonomous entity or a causal entity whose interaction speed does not exactly match the system's interaction speed. The **problem** is to reconstruct the system to keep the unprocessed interactions in a state of allowing the process of them in the right order later when the system is available. This is to enhance the reliability of the system. The **related NFR** of the buffer pattern is also reliability.

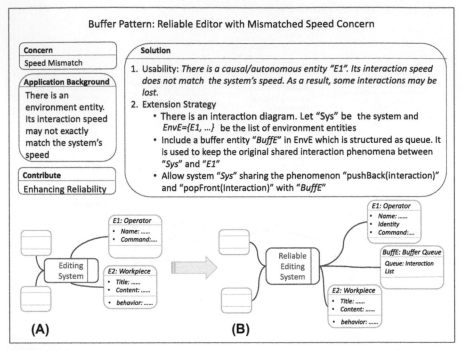

FIGURE 13.3

Buffer pattern and reliable editing system. (A) Original capability: plain editing system. (B) Enhanced capability: reliable editing system.

We also use the editor as an example to illustrate the features. Here the requirements are the same but the operator's interaction speed does not match the system's speed. Without losing generality, we assume that the former is faster than the latter. The original **interaction diagram** is shown in Fig. 13.3A. It does not consider the interaction speeds of the system and the operator. This issue is important. If the operator is too quick to submit requests to the system and the system cannot process them in a timely manner, some requests will be lost without responding. The reliability of the system must be improved. This problem satisfies the application condition of the buffer pattern. When applying the buffer pattern into this problem, the interaction diagram is updated, as shown in Fig. 13.3B, by introducing a buffer. There is a queue of requests and those unprocessed requests are placed into the queue. Accordingly, shared phenomena between the system and this new entity have been included.

The capability analysis process of the new problem is shown as a sequence of argumentations attached to the interaction diagram in Fig. 13.4, in which (1) stipulates that the request is correct. If the system is not available to respond to it, the system causes corresponding events, i.e., to push the interaction

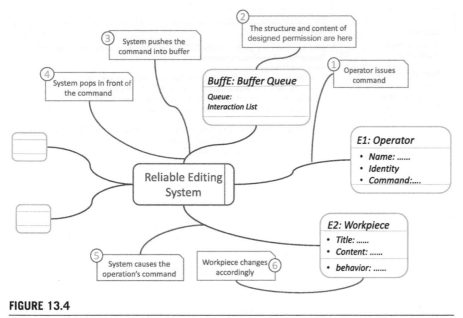

FIGURE 13.4

Capability analysis concerns of buffer pattern.

into the buffer (3). The buffer's structural properties (2) need to guarantee the request is saved correctly. When the system is ready for the next request, it obtains one request from the buffer (4). Then the system responds to the request and updates the workpiece accordingly (5). The domain properties (6) of the workpiece will guarantee the required effects (7). Then the new specification can be obtained:

- The editing system receives the operators' request.
- The editing system pushes the request into the buffer.
- The editing system pops in front of the next request.
- The editing system processes the request by triggering the event to update the workpiece accordingly.

We can see from the new specification that the system will keep the operator's request first, which needs less time than dealing with the request. Then the system obtains the request from the buffer again and deals with it when the system is available.

13.2.3 INDEX PATTERN

The third pattern is the index pattern. This is a pattern for enhancing performance. Its **application background** is that there is a symbolic entity that may contain a huge amount of information entries. The system needs to retrieve these entries frequently

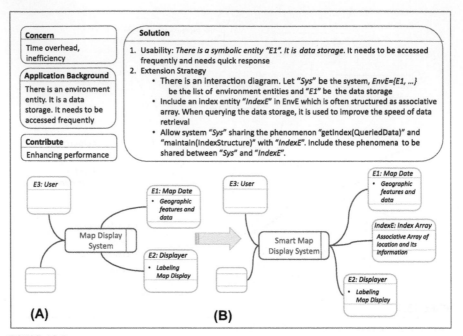

FIGURE 13.5

Index pattern and smart map. (A) Original capability: plain map. (B) Enhanced capability: smart map.

and must obtain the result quickly. The **problem** is to reconstruct the system by building an appropriate index to improve efficient retrieval. This is to enhance the efficiency of the system. The **related NFR** is efficiency.

Fig. 13.5 shows the index pattern with an example, the smart map. The strategy is to include a symbolic entity: the index entity. When applying the index pattern, there are two capability problems. One is for creating and maintaining the index entity and the other is using the index to speed data retrieval. Fig. 13.6 presents the two capability analysis problems.

The example shows how to extend the normal map into a smart map with a more efficient location display. A device is used to project the map of a city onto a screen to locate, for example, patients who have called emergency services. During the call, the user may change his or her location.

The original interaction diagram is give in Fig. 13.5A. The system is "Map Display System." It can access the phenomenon "*dataOfMap*" of the map data entity. The displayer is a casual domain. It shares an interface with the system, in which the system controls the event "*showPieceOfMap*." There is a user, who is a person and therefore an autonomous entity. The user issues requests such as "*refresh*," "*move*," "*zoomIn*," and "*zoomOut*," which are regarded as event phenomena at the interface between the system and the user.

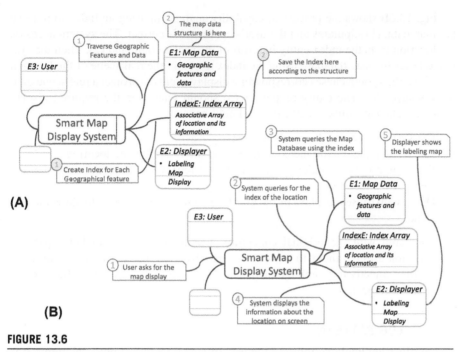

FIGURE 13.6

Two capability analysis concerns of the index pattern. (A) Maintaining index: create index correctly. (B) Using index: display the map efficiently.

The specifications of "Map Display System" are as follows:

- The system receives the user's request.
- The system traverses the map data entity and finds the location.
- The system causes the map display event to ask the displayer to show the real scene.

Because there is a huge amount of data entry in a map data entity, efficiency is low. The analysts decide to use an index pattern and include a new environment entity, the index entity. The extended interaction diagram is given in Fig. 13.5B. There are two kinds of capability problems. One is for analyzing capability referring to the index use. The other is for creating and maintaining the index entity.

Fig. 13.6A shows the process of creating and maintaining the index entity. The system traverses the map data (1A) and simultaneously creates the index entity (1B). The entity structure of the map data (2A) needs to be known by the system so that the system can obtain the information correctly. On the other hand, the structure of the index entity (2B) needs to ensure it is able to index the map data correctly. The capability specifications should be:

- The system traverses the geographic data of the map.
- The system creates an index for each geographical data entry.

Fig. 13.6B shows the process of capability analysis in using an index to retrieve the map data. (1) stipulates that the user's command is correct. The system accesses the location from the index entity in terms of the user's command (2). Then the system queries the map database using the index to obtain the real scene of the location (3). Next, the system causes corresponding display events to project a real scene onto the displayer (4). The entity properties (5) should guarantee the required display contents. The capability specifications should be:

- The system receives the user's request.
- The system queries the index entity to find the index for the location.
- The system uses the index of the location to retrieve the map data and the real scene of the location.
- The system causes displays of the events to be sent the displayer to show the real scene.

Compared with the original capability specification, the extended capability specification uses the index to retrieve the map data and real scene instead of using the location directly to search the map data. That greatly improves the efficiency of information retrieval.

13.2.4 LOG PATTERN

The **application background** of a log pattern is that there is a physical entity. It is causal and detectable. Its behavior is to be controlled regularly by the system. The **problem** is to reconstruct the system to record interactions between the system and this entity and the effect caused by the interaction. Collecting the historical interactions and their effects may help the system to learn to regulate the physical entity to obtain the behavior's trajectory. The **related NFR** is maintainability. When some failure happens, analysts can get help to locate the problem from the behavior's trajectory. Moreover, the behavior's trajectory of the physical entity can improve the system's control behavior by adapting the interaction between the system and the physical entity if the system is equipped with a self-adaptation capability.

Fig. 13.7 shows the log pattern with an example: an air-conditioner control. Fig. 13.7A presents the interaction diagram of the original problem. It develops a system that can:

- detect the air-conditioner's states and certain parameters collected by the air-conditioner, e.g., room temperature, indoor humidity, and so on
- control the air-conditioner, followed by some rules that can decide the system's command based on the detected parameters
- respond control command (including starting or stopping) of the operator. The system should follow the operator's command if it is there.

Next, the analysts want to make the air-conditioner smarter. For example, it knows the performance records and current user's preference so that it can diagnose when it is faulty or it can adapt control behavior according to the user's preference.

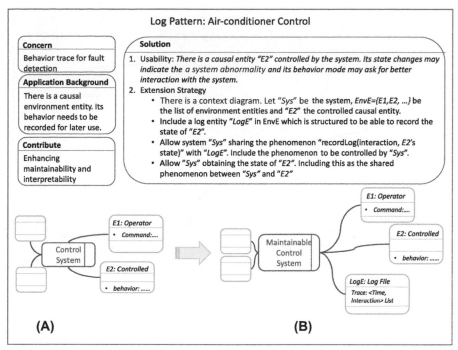

FIGURE 13.7

The log pattern and maintainable controller. (A) Original capability: control system. (B) Enhanced capability: maintainable control system

This is related to learning the behavior mode from historical data. The strategy is to include a symbolic entity: the log entity. The original problem is that the system needs to control the air-conditioner regularly. When applying the log pattern, the interactions between the system and the air-conditioner, and the effects of the interactions are recorded in the log entity. The log entity allows the system to retrieve information that has been recorded. This situation fits the application background of the log pattern. After the log pattern is used, a new interaction diagram can be obtained, as shown in Fig. 13.7B.

Fig. 13.8 gives the capability problem: (1) stipulates which command is correct. The system accepts and responds to the viable command but ignores the inviable ones (2). The system causes an event to control the air-conditioner (3) in terms of the operator's command or based on a predefined regulation. Here, the system needs to be able to resolve conflicts between the operator's command and the regulation-decided command, if any. The physical device's properties (4) will guarantee the required changes. The system causes an event to update the log entity to record the interaction and the effect (5). The log entity's properties (6) will guarantee required updating of the log entity.

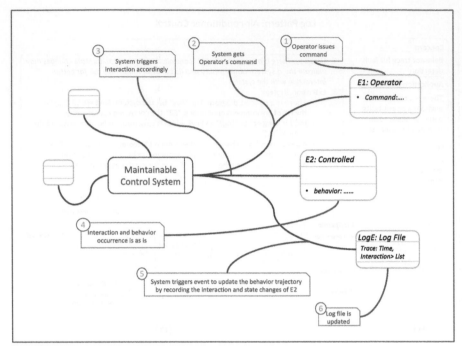

FIGURE 13.8

Capability analysis concerns of log pattern.

After that, the new specifications are obtained:

- The system receives the viable operator's command.
- The system causes an event to control the air-conditioner in terms of the operator's command or based on a predefined regulation.
- The system resolves conflicts between the operator's command and the regulation-decided command.
- The system causes an event to update the content of the log entity.

In the new specifications, the system keeps historical data about performance in the log entity so that it can decide about failure points along the behavior's trajectory. Thus, the maintainability of the system can be improved. It also allows to learn the operator's preference by using data mining techniques so that the system can become more suitable to the operator. In this sense, it is helpful to the system's adaptivity.

13.2.5 PERCEPTION AND REACTION PATTERN

As shown by its name, the **application background** of the perception and reaction pattern is that there is some environment entity whose behavior is to be controlled by the system. The **problem** is to reconstruct the system to monitor certain environment

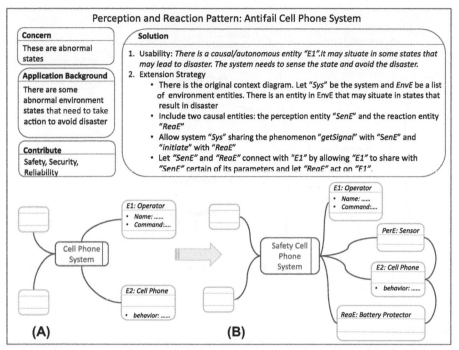

FIGURE 13.9

Perception and reaction pattern and safety cell phone system. (A) Original capability: cell phone system. (B) Enhanced capability: saety cell phone system.

states and take some action to enhance the safety, security, reliability, etc., of the system. The **related NFRs** of the perception and reaction pattern are safety, security, reliability, etc.

Fig. 13.9 shows the perception and reaction pattern and an example of a safety cell phone system developed using this pattern. The **application condition** of this pattern is that there is a physical causal entity in the interactive environment of the system. It can exist in a certain state or operating condition that may indicate or reveal the occurrence of some significant event that may cause a disaster. Fig. 13.9A shows an interaction diagram of a cell phone system. It functions normally just by following an operator's commands. Fig. 13.6B extends the normal cell phone system into a safety cell phone system. During the extension, two designed entities are included: one is a sensor and the other is a battery protector. Both the sensor and the battery protector are connected to the cell phone, i.e., they need to share phenomena with the cell phone. The sensor is in charge of sensing the significant state or operating condition of the cell phone continuously and sharing the sensed signal or parameters' values with the system; the battery protector will be initiated by the system when it needs to take action to protect the cell phone.

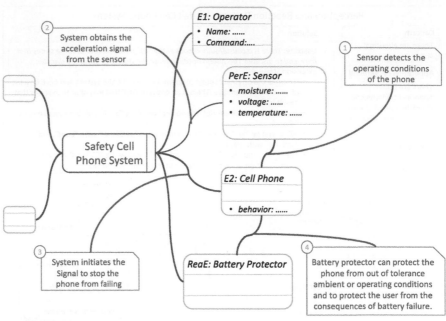

FIGURE 13.10

Capability analysis concerns of the perception and reaction pattern.

A capability analysis problem in the perception and reaction pattern is shown in Fig. 13.10. The entity properties (2) of the sensor ensure that the detected parameters' values are correct. The system obtains the parameters' values of the cell phone from the sensor (2). The system decides whether the cell phone is in an abnormal operating condition. If it is, the system causes corresponding events to control the battery protector (3). The entity properties (4) ensure that the battery protector takes the required actions to protect the phone and the user.

These interactions between the system and the sensor, and between the system and the battery protector, are new functionalities of the system:

- The system obtains the parameters' values from the sensor.
- The system decides whether the cell phone is in an abnormal operating condition.
- The system initiates the battery protector.

13.2.6 ENCRYPTION AND DECRYPTION PATTERN

The last pattern introduced is encryption and decryption. Its **application background** is that there is a symbolic entity that has an interface of shared phenomena with the system. The symbolic entity contains confidential data. The problem is to reconstruct the system to encrypt data of the symbolic entity to ensure the confidentiality of the contents of the data. The **related NFR** is confidentiality.

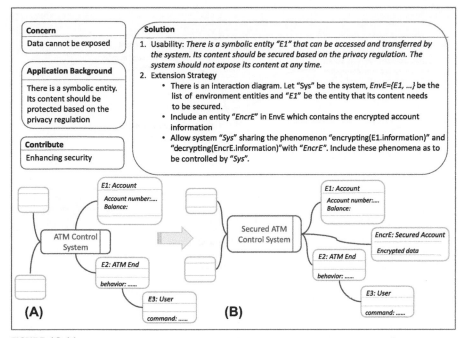

FIGURE 13.11

The encryption and decryption pattern and secured automatic teller machine (ATM) control system. (A) Original capability: ATM control system. (B) Enhanced capability: encrypted ATM control system.

Fig. 13.11 presents the interaction diagram for this pattern with an example.

The **application condition** of the encryption and decryption pattern is that there is a symbolic entity whose information cannot be exposed. There is an information accessing and transmission phenomenon shared by the system and the entity. The **problem** is to reconstruct the system so that the system can (1) encrypt the information when accessing and transmitting the information; and (2) decrypt the encrypted information when the information has been transmitted to its destination. The related NFRs are security and privacy.

Here is an example: A bank needs to construct an ATM-controlling system to access user's accounts from a remote database and show them on an ATM, as demonstrated in Fig. 13.11A. Each user's account includes user name, account balance, and trading records. The system is "ATM Control System," which will access the symbolic entity "Account" for phenomenon "accountInformation." Entity "ATM end" is causal. It shares an interface with the system, at which the system controls the events "showAccount" to control "ATM end." The specifications are:

- The system accesses information about the user's account from the account domain.

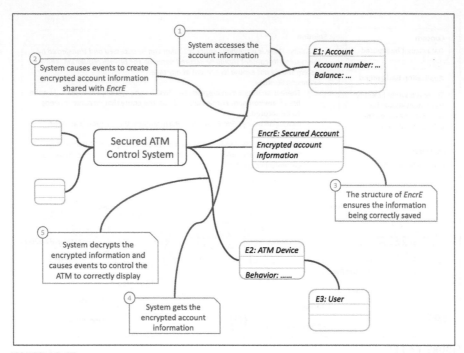

FIGURE 13.12

Capability analysis concerns of the encryption and decryption pattern. *ATM*, automatic teller machine.

- The system causes the events to control "ATM end" showing information about the user's account on the screen.

However, these specifications do not consider how to protect the privacy of the information. This interaction diagram satisfies the application conditions of the encryption and decryption pattern. After applying this pattern, a new interaction diagram can be obtained, as shown in Fig. 13.12.

The system accesses the information of entity "*Account*" (1). The system causes events to create encrypted data (2). Domain properties (3) of the encrypted data will ensure that the encrypted data are created correctly. The system accesses the encrypted account information from the entity "*Secured Account*" (4). The system causes events to decrypt the secured account information and control the ATM to display. The new specifications of the system could be:

- The system accesses the account information.
- The system causes events to create encrypted information.
- The system accesses the encrypted information.
- The system decrypts the encrypted information and causes the events to control the ATM to display.

In the new specifications, information about the user's accounts is encrypted before being transmitted and used. In this way, the confidentiality of the user's accounts are ensured.

13.3 A CASE STUDY

This section uses a case study to illustrate the whole idea. A fire rescue system is required for a city's fire rescue center. The goal of this rescue system is for each person who becomes trapped in the fire to be able to get into touch with the rescue system by using his or her cell phone and report his or her precise location, perhaps in a burning building. Firefighters can request information by connecting with the fire rescue system through a terminal device, which can provide firefighters with the scene of the building, the reported location of the trapped persons. Thus, the system must connect to a digital map database that is needed to store map information about all buildings in the city. The interaction diagram of the system is shown in Fig. 13.13.

There are four environment entities in the original interaction diagram: *Trapped Persons & Cell Phone*, *Terminal Device*, *Firemen*, and *Digital Map*. *Trapped Persons & Cell Phone* is autonomous. It shares with the *Fire Rescue System* that trapped persons can report their precise location in the fire. *Digital Map* is symbolic; it is used to store map information of the buildings in the city. It shares with the system that it can access information stored in it through the phenomenon of "*dataOfMap.*" *Terminal Device* is causal; it is used to connect the system and *Firemen*. At this interface, *Firemen* causes the events of "*requestForMap*" and "*requestForLocation*" to *Terminal Device*. *Terminal Device* shares these events with the system. The system controls the phenomena of "*showMap*" and "*showLocation*" to change the states of *Terminal Device*. The original interaction diagram is shown in Fig. 13.13A.

According to the strategies of using problem-oriented NFR patterns, we can extend the problem as follows:

- Step 1, the problem described earlier should take some NFRs into consideration.
  - The first is reliability. The reliability of the location-reporting function should be improved, which will provide the precise location of the trapped persons.
  - The second is safety, which means that the system must ensure the safety of the firefighters.
  - The third is the response time. The system must answer the firefighters' requests in the shortest time.

  Consequently, the buffer, index, and perception and reaction patterns are chosen to be applied to this problem.
- Step 2, the application backgrounds of these NFR patterns can match the description of this problem.
- Step 3, the application conditions of these NFR patterns can be satisfied by this problem.

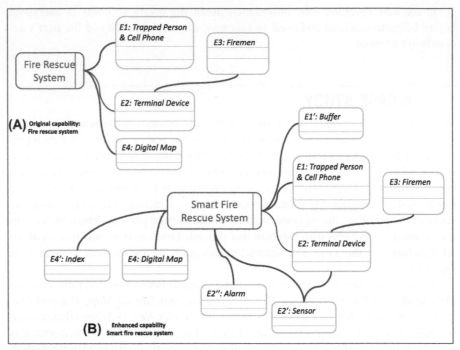

FIGURE 13.13

Fire rescue system and smart fire rescue system.

- Step 4, we extend the problem with the guidance of the extension strategies of these NFR patterns. An extended problem can be obtained. The extended interaction diagram is shown in Fig. 13.13B.
- Step 5, according to the concerns in these patterns, the new specifications are:
  - Specification 1: According to the concerns of the buffer pattern, we can get the machine specification showing the trapped persons' location:
    - The system receives the trapped person's location.
    - The system causes events to change the values of the buffer to save the trapped person's location.
    - The system accesses a trapped person's location from the buffer, which has the highest priority.
    - The system can receive all trapped persons' locations and save them into the buffer entity, which improves the reliability of the function about reporting the trapped person's location.
  - Specification 2. According to the concerns of the index pattern, we can get the system specification about showing map information:
    - The system receives the firefighters' request for a map picture.
    - The system searches the location of the picture from the index entity.

- The system obtains the data of this picture from the digital map.
- The system causes display events to show pictures.

The machine specification shortens the time to respond to the firefighters' request by improving the efficiency of map searching.

- Specification 3. According to the concerns of the perception and reaction pattern, we can get the machine specification about the alarm.
  - The system reads the temperature via a terminal device from the sensor.
  - If the temperature of the terminal device is too high, the system causes events turn on the alarm.

The alarm will be turned on when the temperature is high enough to be life-threatening, which protects the safety of the firefighters.

13.4 DISCUSSION

There are many efforts already to deal with the NFRs. Chung et al. (1999) presents a systematic way on the basis of the goal orientation. This chapter introduces six NFR patterns: authorization, buffer, index, log, perception and reaction, and encryption and decryption. These patterns correspond to the NFRs of security, reliability, efficiency, maintainability, safety, adaptivity, and confidentiality, respectively. These NFRs are often encountered in practice.

Of course, the six NFR patterns are far from being a complete set. However, they demonstrate how they can help system analysts extend an existing problem by adding NFRs and derive some solution strategies accordingly. It is a starting point for inventing many other NFR patterns. Thus, new NFR patterns can be defined from new architectural solutions to NFRs that are reusable by system analysts. The following are some tips or hints for designing and defining new NFR patterns:

- Any NFR pattern aims to satisfy some kind of NFRs.
- Any NFR pattern describes an entire problem in which mapping is built between a problem structure and its architectural solution.
- Any NFR pattern presents the process to extend an existing problem and the concerns to derive the system specification.

As shown in this chapter, the six NFR patterns describe problems whose environment entities are next to the system. How to find and develop the pattern in which the environment entities are a slightly farther from the system is more challenging. Answering this question will help to deal with the NFRs that refer to or constrain phenomena that are "deep in the physical world," that is, far from the system interface. We believe that some problem transformation techniques are needed to trace these NFRs.

Part Four References

I.F. Alexander, Misuse cases: use cases with hostile intent, IEEE Software 20 (1) (2003) 58–66.

A. Avizienis, J.-C. Laprie, B. Randell, C. Landwehr, Basic concepts and taxonomy of dependable and secure computing, IEEE Transactions on Dependable and Secure Computing 1 (1) (2004) 1–23.

L. Basili, P. Clements, S. Asgari, The unified model of dependability: putting dependability in context, IEEE Software 21 (3) (2004) 19–25.

B. Cheng, R. de Lemos, P. Inverardi, J. Magee, Software engineering for self-adaptive systems, in: Lecture Notes in Computer Science, vol. 5525, Springer-Verlag Berlin Heidelberg, 2009a.

B. Cheng, P. Sawyer, N. Bencomo, J. Whittle, A goal-based modeling approach to develop requirements of an adaptive system with environmental uncertainty, in: Proceedings of the 12th International Conference on Model Driven Engineering Languages and Systems (MoDELS'09), 2009, pp. 468–483.

L. Chung, B.A. Nixon, E. Yu, J. Mylopoulos, Non-functional Requirements in Software Engineering, Springer-Verlag Berlin Heidelberg, 1999.

M. Endsley, D. Jones, Designing for Situation Awareness: An Approach to User-Centered Design, CRC Press, Taylor & Francis Group, 2012.

G.C. Goodwin, S.F. Graebe, M.E. Salgado, Control System Design, Prentice Hall, 2001.

D. Hatebur, M. Heisel, Problem frames and architectures for security problems, in: Proceedings of 24th International Conference on Computer Safety, Reliability and Security (SAFECOMP 2005), 2005, pp. 390–404.

P. Hope, A.I. Anton, G. McGraw, Misuse and abuse cases: getting past the positive, IEEE Security and Privacy 2 (3) (2004) 90–92.

D. Jackson, A direct path to dependable software, Communication of ACM 52 (4) (2009) 78–88.

M. Jackson, Problem Frames: Analyzing and Structuring Software Development Problems, Addison-Wesley, 2001.

J. Kephart, D. Chess, The vision of autonomic computing, IEEE Computer 36 (1) (2003) 41–50.

T.A. Kletz, HAZOP and HAZAP: Identifying and Assessing Process Industry Hazards, Taylor & Francis, 2006.

I. Lanese, A. Bucchiarone, F. Montesi, A framework for rule-based dynamic adaptation, in: M. Wirsing, M. Hofmann, A. Rauschmayer (Eds.), TCG 2010: Lecture Notes on Computer Science, vol. 6084, Springer-Verlag Berlin Heidelberg, 2010, pp. 284–300.

L. Lin, B. Nuseibeh, D. Ince, M. Jackson, J. Moffett, Analyzing Security Threats and Vulnerabilities Using Abuse Frames, Technical Report No: 2003/10, The Open University, UK, 2003.

C. Liu, Y. Wang, W. Zhang, Z. Jin, Eliciting and modeling dependability requirements: a control-case based approach, Science China Information Science 57 (1) (2014) 1–15, https://doi.org/10.1007/s11432-013-4865-y.

B. Morin, O. Barais, J. Jezequel, F. Fleurey, A. Solberg, Models@run.time to support dynamic adaptation, IEEE Computer 42 (10) (2009) 44–51.

J. Overton, J.G. Hall, L. Rapanotti, Y. Yu, Towards a problem oriented engineering theory of pattern-oriented analysis and design, in: Proceedings of 33rd Annual IEEE International Computer Software and Applications Conference (COMPSAC2009), 2009, pp. 255–260.

N. Qureshi, A. Perini, Engineering adaptive requirements, in: Proceedings of the 2009 ICSE Workshop on Software Engineering for Adaptive and Self-managing Systems (SEAMS2009), 2009, pp. 126–131.

V. Souza, A. Lapouchnian, W. Robinson, J. Mylopoulos, Awareness requirements, in: Proceedings of the 2011 ICSE Symposium on Software Engineering for Adaptive and Self-managing Systems (SEAMS011), 2011, pp. 60–69.

S. Supakkul, L. Chung, T.T. Tun, J.C.S.P. Leite, An NFR pattern approach to dealing with NFRs, in: Proceedings of 18th IEEE International Requirements Engineering Conference (RE2010), 2010, pp. 179–188.

G. Tamura, N. Villegas, H. Muller, J.P. Sousa, B. Becker, et al., Towards practical runtime verification and validation of self-adaptive software systems, in: R. de Lemos, H. Giese, H. Muller, M. Shaw (Eds.), Software Engineering for Self-adaptive Systems II, Lecture Notes on Computer Science, vol. 7475, Springer-Verlag Berlin Heidelberg, 2013, pp. 108–132.

P. Vromant, D. Weyns, S. Malek, J. Andersson, On interacting control loops in self-adaptive systems, in: Proceedings of the 6th International Symposium on Software Engineering for Adaptive and Self-managing Systems (SEAMS2011), 2011, pp. 202–207.

N. Wiener, Cybernetics, or Control and Communication in the Animal and the Machine, MIT Press, 1948.

J. Whittle, P. Sawyer, N. Bancomo, B. Cheng, J. Bruel, RELAX: incorporating uncertainty into the specification of self-adaptive systems, in: Proceedings of the 17th IEEE International Requirements Engineering Conference (RE2009), 2009, pp. 95–103.

Z. Yang, Z. Li, Z. Jin, Y. Chen, A systematic literature review of requirements modeling and analysis for self-adaptive systems, in: Proceedings of 20th International Working Conference on Requirements Engineering: Foundation for Software Quality (REFSQ 2014), 2014, pp. 55–71.

T. Zhao, T. Zan, H. Zhao, Z. Hu, Z. Jin, A Novel Approach to Goal-Oriented Adaptation with View-Based Rules, Tech. Report GRACE-TR-2016-01, National Institute of Informatics, 2016.

Index

Printed and bound by CPI Group (UK) Ltd, Croydon, CR0 4YY

03/10/2024

01040327-0014